D0021304

The Korean War
in World History

The
Korean War
in
World History

EDITED BY WILLIAM STUECK

THE UNIVERSITY PRESS OF KENTUCKY

Publication of this volume was made possible in part by a grant
from the National Endowment for the Humanities.

Editorial and Sales Offices: The University Press of Kentucky
663 South Limestone Street, Lexington, Kentucky 40508-4008
www.kentuckypress.com

08 07 06 05 04   5 4 3 2 1

Library of Congress Cataloging-in-Publication Data

The Korean War in world history / edited by William Stueck.
    p. cm.
    Includes bibliographical references and index.
    ISBN 0-8131-2306-2 (Hardcover: alk. paper)
    1. Korean War, 1950-1953. 2. History, Modern—1945-1989.
3. World politics—1945-1989. I. Stueck, William Whitney, 1945-
DS918.K684 2004
951.904'2—dc22   2003024565

This book is printed on acid-free recycled paper meeting
the requirements of the American National Standard
for Permanence in Paper for Printed Library Materials.

∞ ✪

Manufactured in the United States of America.

[AAUP logo] Member of the Association of
American University Presses

Contents

Acknowledgments

The essays in this volume were initially presented as papers at a symposium on the Korean War at Texas A & M University. I wish to thank symposium organizer Bill Brands for asking me to edit them for publication. The contributors deserve special commendation for responding constructively and expeditiously to my suggestions for revision. CHEN Jian, Allan R. Millett, and Kathryn Weathersby offered valuable recommendations for revision of what became my introduction and conclusion. As outside readers, Xiaoming Zhang and an anonymous referee provided comments that made the entire manuscript better.

John F. Zeigler, the senior editor at the University Press of Kentucky when the manuscript was submitted, deserves special thanks for his enthusiastic response to the project, for expediting the review process, and for suggesting important changes to my own contribution. In my career as a publishing scholar, I have had extraordinarily good fortune with a number of editors, but none better than with him.

William Stueck

Introduction

WILLIAM STUECK

The Korean War had two faces. One grew out of the internal conditions of Korea extending back to the period of Japanese rule. The war was fought almost entirely within the confines of a small Asian country located far from Europe, the geographical focal point of great power competition. Whether in casualties suffered, property destroyed, or lives disrupted, Koreans endured the greatest burden of the war. In one sense, the fighting pitted Korean against Korean in a struggle to determine the balance of political power within the country.

Yet the conflict engaged Koreans with outsiders as well, and it had a huge impact on the international politics of the cold war. Eventually military personnel from twenty-one governments contributed to the fighting. At various times, especially during the months following China's intervention in October 1950, the combat in Korea threatened to extend well beyond the peninsula and even to directly engage the forces of the United States and the Soviet Union, which could have produced another global conflagration. Although the Korean War remained limited, it left in its wake a much-escalated arms race between the Western and Eastern blocs as well as greatly expanded opposing alliance networks. It also left Korea divided and in a state of tension that would outlast the cold war. The dynamics of that division remain and continue to threaten international peace and security in the twenty-first century.

This book presents synthetic essays on the latest thinking and research on the Korean War by a group of noted scholars. Each author focuses on the relationship of one country to the war. This introduction and the conclusion link the essays to the rich historiography of the event and draw upon them and my own earlier work to suggest both the war's place within the history of the twentieth century and some issues still beckoning historians to further research and analysis.[1] This book at once features the accomplishments of scholars over the last decade and challenges them and others to move into disputed or uncharted waters.

Origins of the War

Over the last thirty years, the origins of the Korean War have generated much attention and controversy in the United States. Prior to the 1970s, the scholarly literature tended to de-emphasize origins, as they seemed to be a cut-and-dried case of Communist aggression against the poorly prepared United States and South Korea.[2] Analysts devoted greater attention to the limited nature of the war, both because it contrasted with the two wars that preceded it, in which the United States had participated, and because the monumental controversy between President Harry S. Truman and General Douglas MacArthur, culminating in the latter's dismissal in April 1951, focused on that issue.[3] In the 1970s, however, the revisionism that had engulfed the field of cold war studies over the previous decade finally generated new thinking on Korea, and this development led not only to critiques of old positions but to the raising of questions heretofore largely ignored. U.S. involvement in Korea was often evaluated in the context of a larger attack on America's expanded involvement abroad, especially since World War II and particularly in the third world. This approach generated a reexamination of the U.S. decision of late June 1950 to intervene militarily to repulse North Korea's attack on South Korea as well as new interest in the initial American intervention on the peninsula in the aftermath of Japan's defeat. That interest, in turn, led to much greater attention to the internal history of Korea prior to June 1950. Bruce Cumings's publication in 1981 and 1990 of two massive volumes on origins brought revisionism, the local setting and doubts about the legitimacy of U.S. involvement to a high point. The appropriate weight of internal and external forces in causing the war remains hotly contested, but that Koreans played an active role is no longer in doubt.[4]

With the exception of Michael Schaller's piece on Japan, all of the essays herein deal extensively with the issue of origins and of the internal and external forces involved. Allan Millett devotes the majority of his essay to the Korean dimensions of the war's beginnings.[5] He views the peninsula as merely one of numerous areas of East Asia in which the collapse of Japan in 1945—following on the heels of its earlier victories against the West—set the stage for postcolonial revolution. The Koreans themselves, Millett asserts, were the main architects of the war from 1950 to 1953, and his analysis ranges from the political divisions that emerged among Korean nationalists during the forty-year Japanese occupation (1905–1945) to the lobbying employed in Moscow by North Korean leader Kim Il-sung from March 1949 through the spring of 1950 to garner Soviet support for a military assault across the 38th parallel.

Soviet premier Joseph Stalin's eventual support for Kim emerges clearly in Kathryn Weathersby's essay.[6] Weathersby devotes less than a third of her space to origins, focusing on the sixteen months prior to the 25 June 1950 North Korean attack. Her approach is historiographical, as she examines previous scholarly accounts on the Soviet role in light of the new evidence that emerged from the Russian archives during the 1990s. That evidence shows decisively that North Korea's conventional offensive was *not* in response to South Korean forays north of the 38th parallel, as revisionist accounts have suggested, but that the idea for the move originated with Kim Il-sung, who first approached Stalin on the matter in March 1949. Stalin demurred, although he did advise Kim to prepare to counterattack in the event an attack was initiated from the South. Despite Kim's initiative and persistence on the matter, he was in no position to launch the attack without Stalin's consent and assistance, as he was deeply reliant on the Soviet Union.

That consent showed no evidence of appearing until January 1950, and it was not until Kim's three-week visit to Moscow, beginning at the end of March, that Stalin gave a definite go-ahead for the attack. Even then, the green light was contingent on the approval of Mao Zedong, the head of the newly created People's Republic of China (PRC). As before, Stalin remained determined to avoid a direct clash with the United States over Korea. He now believed that American intervention in response to a North Korean attack was unlikely, but the Soviet leader made it clear that if the unlikely occurred Kim would have to look to Mao for help. For a variety of reasons, Mao was in a poor position to disagree, and his blessing followed in mid-May during Kim's visit to Beijing. To Weathersby, then, "the essential decision" for the attack was Stalin's.

Mao's part in origins was arguably less direct than Stalin's, but it was still necessary. As CHEN Jian points out in his essay, Korean Communists had for years enjoyed a close relationship with their Chinese compatriots.[7] During the 1930s, Kim Il-sung had joined the Chinese Communist Party (CCP) and later tens of thousands of ethnic Koreans joined Chinese Communist armies, first to fight the Japanese and then the Chinese Nationalists. Between 1946 and 1949, Chinese Communist forces frequently used North Korea as a secure base for their forces operating in Manchuria. As the CCP consolidated its position in the region during 1949, it returned tens of thousands of armed ethnic Korean soldiers to North Korea. Thousands more were returned in early 1950. The CCP's victory over the Nationalists on the mainland combined with Mao's conclusion of a military alliance with Stalin early in 1950 to constitute a major part of the latter's calculation in approving Kim's advocacy for an attack on South Korea.

Another factor in Stalin's calculations was the position of the United States, and Lloyd Gardner's essay provides a nuanced treatment of American policy.[8] Stalin believed that the United States would not intervene in the face of the North Korean attack, and the obvious question arises as to why Washington failed to give clear signals of its actual intentions. One answer, of course, is that Washington was uncertain of its intentions before the event. Gardner gives weight to this explanation by showing, first, that the United States possessed little interest in Korea prior to 1945 and, second, that a variety of factors prevented Korea from becoming a consistent focal point in Washington's calculations even after U.S. intervention there with the defeat of Japan. The location of the peninsula made it of some importance to both the defense and economic well-being of Japan and the direct contest between Soviet occupation forces in the North and American occupation forces in the South gave Korea symbolic significance in the evolving cold war struggle. But *important* and *significant* did not add up to *essential*. The demands elsewhere on U.S. resources, combined with the limited tolerance of the American public and Congress to commit those resources to foreign enterprises, left policy makers in a quandary as to how much effort to put into Korea.[9] Under the circumstances, the best Washington could manage was to convey ambiguity as to U.S. willingness to intervene militarily in the event North Korea, unexpectedly for the short term at least, launched an all-out attack. Ambiguity turned out to be an ineffective deterrent.

Yet, if U.S. intentions were not clear-cut in advance, either in Moscow or in Washington, when North Korea attacked there was little hesitation among American leaders as to what needed to be done. The Communist victory in China and the Soviet explosion of an atomic bomb had raised to new heights fears of the Soviet threat abroad, and the sharp attacks on the administration's Asian policy by Senator Joseph McCarthy and other Republican critics accentuated the risks of responding timidly to the attack. To President Harry S. Truman, the North Korean move reflected a new Soviet aggressiveness and a test of American will comparable to the challenge by Hitler to the European democracies during the 1930s. Secretary of State Dean Acheson saw an opportunity through strong action to consolidate the Western alliance and to unite Americans behind a major program of rearmament. So the war that had started with Koreans fighting Koreans quickly drew in the Americans. The North Korean move set off a process of escalation that rendered devastating human and material destruction to the peninsula, greatly escalated the military dimensions of the cold war, and solidified a division of Korea that survived by more than a decade the Soviet-American contest that was instrumental in its initial manifestation.

Together, the essays by Millett, Weathersby, CHEN, and Gardner demonstrate the complex domestic and international forces at work in the origins of the Korean War. Although Millett makes a strong case for Korean agency, Weathersby, CHEN, and Gardner show that the conflicts that existed among Koreans before Japan's defeat in 1945 were largely influenced by the decisions of the great powers. Millett himself shows that Korean independence groups prior to 1945 generally attempted to attach themselves to a foreign government or movement—the Nationalist Chinese, the Communist Chinese, the Communist Soviets, or the anit-Communist Americans—in order to further their cause, a clear reflection of their weakness. The obvious fact is that Koreans were saddled with foreign occupations in 1945 because they had contributed virtually nothing to their liberation from Japan. Indeed, more Koreans had served in the Japanese armed forces during World War II than had fought with the nations arrayed against them. Moreover, divisions among the Koreans who did actively resist Japan and their marginal contact with countrymen at home discouraged the United States and the Soviet Union from consulting the independence groups when deciding their course at war's end. Given the deep suspicions and ideological divergences that existed between those two powers, divisions among Koreans encouraged them to choose sides in a manner that could only serve to harden the separation of the two halves of the peninsula.

Course of the War

The war itself hardened separation still further. Millett's brief coverage of the 1950–1953 period focuses on the internal politics of North and South Korea. Millett argues that both Syngman Rhee and Kim Il-sung used the circumstances of war to strengthen their own holds on power, in relation to both their domestic competitors and their great power sponsors. As on origins, Millett refuses to take sides between the Republic of Korea (ROK) and the Democratic People's Republic of Korea (DPRK) leaders, viewing both as authoritarian and manipulative as well as solidly grounded with important elements of their populations. The ROK needed U.S. aid because Soviet assistance to the DPRK had given it decisive superiority over its enemy. Yet, if during the summer of 1950 the ROK army could not alone contend with North Korean forces, it could—and did—assist mightily with the American-led defense of the Pusan perimeter. In the last year of the war, ROK ground units controlled 70 percent of the line against the enemy.[10] That contribution gave Rhee considerable influence on U.S. policy, as is apparent in U.S.-ROK interaction in both a domestic political crisis during the spring and summer of 1952 and a controversy over the impending armistice in June and July 1953.

As for North Korea, Kim Il-sung moved during and immediately following the war to rid himself of potential opposition. Although large portions of the area above the 38th parallel were occupied by Chinese forces from late 1950 to 1958, Kim purged members of the Yenan (Chinese) faction of the Communist Party. He also suppressed a plot by the domestic faction to overthrow him and undermined key elements of the Soviet faction. With the Soviets and the Chinese both deeply involved in North Korea's fate, Kim could play them against each other to secure what he wanted in material aid and increase his independence from both patrons.

Weathersby's and CHEN's accounts, though, demonstrate the limits of Kim's influence with his patrons. Whether in the process leading to China's intervention in the fall of 1950, the decision to accept armistice talks and less than total victory in the spring of

1951, or the positions taken by the Communist side in those talks over the next two years, Stalin and Mao always behaved in accordance with a calculation of their own interests, and these interests often put them at odds with Kim. Stalin, for example, was willing to abandon North Korea to its fate in late 1950 if doing otherwise meant a direct military confrontation with the United States. In October Mao hesitated for more than two weeks to make the final decision to intervene while seeking to pin Stalin down on a high level of military support. During the following year, Soviet and Chinese leaders forced a reluctant Kim to accept a stalemate in Korea; later they combined to keep the war going when Kim had every reason to bring it to a halt. When it came to major issues of war and peace, Kim was an active but unquestionably junior partner in the threesome. Weathersby and CHEN highlight this fact and at the same time analyze the bilateral relationship between Moscow and Beijing. Although the authors diverge on degree, Stalin's seniority in the relationship clearly emerges.

On the anti-Communist side, the United States was the dominant player, despite the influence of South Korea and NATO allies. Gardner devotes little space in his essay to American policy or to alliance politics during the war, but he does reveal his dissent from much of the conventional wisdom on the U.S. course in Korea. Although he does not weigh in against the intervention to repulse the North Korean attack, as most revisionists do, he clearly objects to the way Truman and Acheson transformed the Korean enterprise into a global crusade. Containment in Korea may have been justified in June 1950, but later efforts to liberate North Korea, the massive military buildup in the West, and the creation of a global system of anti-communist alliances were not. Gardner also laments the role the war played in expanding the power of the presidency in the United States.[11] The collapse of the Soviet Union and the emergence of new documentation from the Communist side, in sum, have not persuaded all scholars that, despite occasional transgressions, the policies of American leaders during the Korean War, either at home or abroad, were for the best.[12]

Secondary Influences

Because the Korean War involved numerous actors beyond the principals discussed above, it is no surprise that much has been written about other participants in the conflict. The involvement of the United Kingdom, Canada, Australia, New Zealand, and Colombia all have been considered in major studies.[13] Yet one of the most important secondary powers in the war, Japan, did not send armed forces to participate in the fighting. Rather, it provided a critical logistical and supply base for United Nations (UN) efforts in Korea. The war also provided a needed stimulus to Japan's economy and a boost to momentum for a peace treaty that excluded the Soviet Union and China as well as creation of a Pacific security system that included Japanese armed forces. Michael Schaller's essay presents a concise yet broad-ranging assessment of the impact of the Korean War on Japan.[14]

We saw earlier in this introduction that concern about Japan influenced the U.S. reaction to the North Korean attack of June 1950, although the precise nature and weight of that influence remains contested. As Schaller points out, the war itself undeniably impacted Japan's economic development. On the eve of the conflict, Japan had sufficient capital and markets abroad to rebuild its industry from the devastating effects of World War II. The fighting in Korea created a need for huge quantities of war materiel and other supplies for the peninsula, and Japan was well-positioned geographically and in infrastructure to meet U.S. needs. Japan also benefited enormously from the increased demand for shipping, the rapidly expanding American military aid program for the struggle against communism in Southeast Asia, and U.S. technological and managerial assistance.

On the other hand, the entry of China into the war led to the virtual destruction, under U.S. pressure, of remaining Sino-Japanese trade. If Japan was to sustain its economic recovery over the long term, it would have to either move toward restoring its historic trade pattern with China, drastically increasing trade with an unstable Southeast Asia, or achieving a combination of the two. Elements of the U.S. State Department supported flexibility regarding Sino-Japanese commerce, but the attitudes of other agencies and important elements of Congress prevented a resolution of this problem during the Korean War.

The Korean War also impacted Japan in diplomatic and strategic areas. On the eve of the conflict, the U.S. State Department had been moving toward negotiations for a peace treaty with Japan, but, despite the support of General MacArthur, the Joint Chiefs of Staff dragged their feet. The outbreak of war in Korea pushed the process along, as it magnified the importance of integrating Japan into the Western alliance for the long haul. Only a combination of reestablishment of Japan's sovereignty and construction of a formal U.S.-Japanese security relationship to replace the occupation could achieve this purpose. The paths to Japanese peace and security treaties, ratified by the U.S. Senate in 1952, and to limited Japanese rearmament involved intense bargaining as well as domestic political pressures and discontent on both sides. Yet the outcome provided the foundation for a constructive relationship that survived the cold war by more than a decade.

Schaller does not ignore the negative side of developments either produced or magnified by the Korean War. If the war solidified the U.S. relationship with Japan, it also generated an American preoccupation with containing communism in Indochina and along the "Great Crescent" of East and Southeast Asia. The security treaties Washington negotiated during the war with the Philippines, Australia, and New Zealand were directly related to concerns in those nations over the settlement with Japan. The security treaty with Taiwan and the creation of the Southeast Asia Treaty Organization, both completed in the war's aftermath, grew from magnified concerns about Communist China, which in no small part were a result of its confrontation with the United States in Korea. These developments did not lead inevitably to the tragic U.S. commitment to a major war in Vietnam in the mid-1960s, but they certainly represented important segments in the road leading to that outcome.

The authors of the following essays all have written extensively on the Korean War. Together their specializations encompass the major diplomatic and strategic issues of that conflict. At the same time, the authors represent diverse perspectives and thus their points of view on specific events sometimes differ. We hope that the combination of up-to-date research, breadth of coverage, and range of arguments will both inform and engage readers, and perhaps stimulate them to delve further into the history of a pivotal event of the post–World War II era.

Notes

1. This introduction makes no effort to provide a comprehensive treatment of Korean War historiography. For the best recent effort along

these lines, see Allan R. Millett, "The Korean War: A 50-Year Critical Historiography," *The Journal of Strategic Studies* 24 (March 2001): 188–224.

2. The greatest exception to this de-emphasis on origins is the too often ignored Soon Sung Cho, *Korea in World Politics, 1940–1950* (Los Angeles: University of California Press, 1967), which still focuses on American unpreparedness and lack of commitment to Korea prior to June 1950.

3. I began studying the Korean War during 1968 in a graduate seminar on the Truman administration. When I approached the instructor about doing a research paper on the Korean War, his succinct response was, "Read David Rees and John Spanier." These were David Rees, *Korea: The Limited War* (New York: St. Martin's, 1964) and John W. Spanier, *The Truman-MacArthur Controversy and the Korean War* (Cambridge, Mass.: Harvard University Press, 1959) and, at the time, represented the two most prominent scholarly works on the war.

4. The first major scholarly revisionist account was Joyce Kolko and Gabriel Kolko, *The Limits of Power: The World and United States Foreign Policy, 1945–1954* (New York: Harper & Row, 1972), chaps. 10, 21, and 22. For my critique of a portion of that account, see William Stueck, "Cold War Revisionism and the Origins of the Korean Conflict: The Kolko Thesis," *Pacific Historical Review* 42 (November 1973): 537–60. For another major revisionist account from the 1970s, see Robert R. Simmons, *The Strained Alliance: Peking, Pyongyang, Moscow and the Politics of the Korean Civil War* (New York: Free Press, 1975). For my critique of a portion of that work, see William Stueck, "The Soviet Union and the Origins of the Korean War," *World Politics* 28 (July 1976): 622–35. The leading revisionist account prior to the 1970s was journalist I. F. Stone's *The Hidden History of the Korean War* (New York: Monthly Review Press, 1952).

Cumings's works are *The Origins of the Korean War*, vol. 1, *Liberation and the Emergence of Separate Regimes, 1945–1947*, and vol. 2, *The Roaring of the Cataract, 1947–1950* (Princeton, N.J.: Princeton University Press, 1981 and 1990). For other important work on the Korean context of the war's origins, see John Merrill, "Internal Warfare in Korea, 1948–1950: The Local Setting of the Korean War," in Bruce Cumings, ed., *Child of Conflict: The Korean-American Relationship, 1945–1953* (Seattle: University of Washington Press, 1984), 133–62; and John Merrill, *Korea: The Peninsular Origins of the War* (Newark: University of Delaware Press, 1989).

5. Millet, who is Mason Professor of Military History at Ohio State University, has written widely on the Korean War. In addition to his essay cited in the first note above, see his Allan R. Millet, "A Reader's Guide to the Korean War," *Journal of Military History* 61 (July 1997): 583–97; "The Forgotten Army in the Misunderstood War: The *Hanguk Gun* in the

Korean War, 1946–53," in Peter Dennis and Jeffrey Grey, eds., *The Korean War: A 50 Year Perspective* (Canberra: The Army History Unit, 2000), 1–26; "Korea, 1950–1953," in Benjamin Franklin Cooling, ed., *Close Air Support* (Washington, D.C.: Office of the Chief of Air Force History, 1990), 345–410. See also Xiaobing Li, Allan R. Millett, and Bin Yu, *Mao's Generals Remember Korea* (Lawrence: University Press of Kansas, 2001); and Korea Institute of Military History, *The Korean War*, 3 vols., Introduction by Allan R. Millett (Lincoln: University of Nebraska Press, 2000–2001).

6. Weathersby is an independent scholar whose publications on the Soviet Union and Korea include commentaries and translations in *The Bulletin of the Cold War International History Project*, vols. 3, 5, 6–7, and 11; and "Working Papers," nos. 8 and 30 of the Cold War International History Project (Washington, D.C.: Woodrow Wilson International Center for Scholars, 1993 and 2002 respectively). See also her "Stalin and the Decision for War in Korea," in David McCann and Barry S. Strauss, eds., *War and Democracy: A Comparative Study of the Korean War and the Peloponnesian War*, (Armonk: M.E. Sharpe, 2001), 85–103; "Making Foreign Policy Under Stalin: The Case of Korea," in Niels Erik Rosenfeldt, Brent Jensen, and Erik Kulavig, eds., *Mechanisms of Power in the Soviet Union* (New York: St. Martin's Press, 2000), 224–40; and "Stalin, Mao, and the End of the Korean War," in Odd Arne Westad, ed., *Brothers in Arms: The Rise and Fall of the Sino-Soviet Alliance* (Stanford, Calif.: Stanford University Press, 1998), 90–116.

7. CHEN is C. K. Yen Professor of Chinese-American Relations at the Miller Center of Public Affairs and Professor of History at the University of Virginia. His other work on the Korean War includes *China's Road to the Korean War* (New York: Columbia University Press, 1994) and *Mao's China and the Cold War* (Chapel Hill: University of North Carolina Press, 2001), chap. 4.

8. Gardner is Charles and Mary Beard Professor of History at Rutgers University, New Brunswick. His earlier work on the Korean War is *The Korean War* (New York: Quadrangle Books, 1972).

9. This argument is presented in greater depth in my *The Road to Confrontation: American Policy toward China and Korea, 1947–1950* (Chapel Hill: University of North Carolina Press, 1981), chaps. 3 and 5.

10. See Korean Institute of Military History, *The Korean War*, vol. 1, Introduction by Allan R. Millett (Lincoln: University of Nebraska Press, 2000), chaps. 2–4; John C. Oh, "The Forgotten ROK Soldiers of the Korean War," paper delivered at the conference "The Korean War: Forgotten No More," at Georgetown University, June 2000.

11. Two recent works on the domestic side of the Korean War have shown in some detail that, whatever the merits of the military buildup at home and the growth of presidential power, lively debates did continue in

the political arena over most issues and that the checks and balances system did place constraints both on defense spending and the president's authority. See Paul G. Pierpaoli Jr., *Truman and Korea: The Political Culture of the Early Cold War* (Columbia: University of Missouri Press, 1999); and Michael J. Hogan, *Harry S. Truman and the Origins of the National Security State, 1945–1954* (New York: Cambridge University Press, 1998). See also Aaron L. Friedberg, *In the Shadow of the Garrison State: America's Anti-Statism and Its Cold War Grand Strategy* (Princeton, N.J.: Princeton University Press, 2000), chaps. 4–6.

12. Prominently included in this category is Arnold Offner, *Another Such Victory: President Truman and the Cold War 1945–1953* (Stanford, Calif.: Stanford University Press, 2002), chaps. 13, 14, and 16.

13. On the United Kingdom, see Anthony Farrar-Hockley, *The British Part in the Korean War*, 2 vols. (London: HMSO, 1990 and 1995); and Callum MacDonald, *Britain and the Korean War* (Oxford, England: Basil Blackwell, 1990). On Canada, see David J. Bercuson, *Blood on the Hills: The Canadian Army in the Korean War* (Toronto: University of Toronto Press, 1999); and Denis Stairs, *The Diplomacy of Constraint: Canada, the Korean War, and the United States* (Toronto: University of Toronto Press, 1974). On Australia, see Robert O'Neill, *Australia in the Korean War 1950–53*, vol. 1 (Canberra: Australian War Memorial and Australian Government Publishing Service, 1981). On New Zealand, see Ian McGibbon, *New Zealand and the Korean War*, 2 vols. (Aukland: Oxford University Press, 1992 and 1996). On Colombia, see Bradley Lynn Coleman, "The Colombian-American Alliance: Colombia's Contribution to U.S.-Led Multilateral Military Efforts, 1938–1953" (Ph.D. diss., University of Georgia, 2001), chaps. 4 and 5.

14. Schaller is Regents' Professor of History at the University of Arizona. For his other work on the Korean War and Japan, see Michael Schaller, *Altered States: The United States and Japan since the Occupation* (New York: Oxford University Press, 1997), chaps. 2 and 3; and *Douglas MacArthur: The Far Eastern General* (New York: Oxford University Press, 1989), chaps. 11–14.

Chapter 1

The Korean People

Missing in Action in the Misunderstood War,
1945–1954

Allan R. Millett

In 1906 the Reverend George Trumbull Ladd, a graduate of Yale University and good citizen of New Haven, Connecticut, visited Japan for the third time. His host was Marquis Ito Hirobumi, the Resident-General of Japan for Korea, a protectorate since the Treaty of Portsmouth, which in September of the previous year had ended the Russo-Japanese war. Ito told Ladd that his only goal was to give "thirteen or fourteen millions of wretched people" good government and to protect "the Koreans against the evil influence and domination of foreign nations who cared only to exploit the country in their own selfish interests or to the injury of Japan."[1] Ito warned Ladd that the worst agitators were Christian Koreans, who used their faith to dupe gullible Americans into supporting the cause of Korean independence. The gullible Ladd agreed with Ito that Korea was most fortunate to have Japan assume the responsibility for its modernization and cultural enlightenment. No one cautioned Ladd that Dai Nippon—"a happy union of modern education and the spirit of Bushido"— might have limitations as a model for spiritual revitalization to western norms.[2]

Korean history is full of Reverend Ladds who seldom see the Koreans except as ingrates or victims. The view of the Korean War falls into the same pattern. To be sure, Koreans themselves encourage the cult of victimization because it reinforces their own self-perception as one of the most put-upon people in history. For example, they like to compare themselves with the Jews, the Polish, and the Irish as diaspora-driven survivors of colonizers and patronizers. Korean military historians claim that their nation has been invaded more than eight hundred times. When mere raids are subtracted, the number is less than one hundred. In modern times, Koreans claim to be winners of the victimization prize, but surely the Armenians, the European Jewry, and the Poles have a stronger claim as the targets of genocide. The Koreans, of course, have much justice in their assumption of victimization, but it contributes to the misunderstanding of the Korean War and its legacy for contemporary Korean politics.[3]

The Koreans view life as the province of *han*. *Han* is life's essence; the basic human condition. Unlike the unpredictable nature of *kismet* or God's Will, *han* is the certain fate of man to live in sorrow, anger, betrayal, poverty, disillusionment, helplessness, and death everlasting. *Han* is a cosmic law against which all struggle is futile. Confucianism gives social order to inevitable disaster; Buddhism teaches that disaster in life means nothing. Given the hold of *han* on the Korean mentality, it is no surprise that the grim versions of Christianity brought to Korea in the nineteenth century by Catholics, Presbyterians, and Methodists appeared joyous and hopeful by comparison. This was no small point in Korean politics when President Kim Dae-jung, a devout Christian, made reunification an issue of messianic religious faith and redemption, not a political and defense matter. A public opinion poll in August 2000 found that almost 90 percent of Koreans thought President Kim's "sunshine policy" perfectly reasonable.[4]

That policy combines with the fiftieth anniversary of the Korean War to provide a unique opportunity to raise American awareness of the roots of war and its continuing impact upon Korean culture and Korean-American relations. Although the United States, the Soviet Union, and the People's Republic of China (PRC) bear no small responsibility for Korea's physical destruction, the Koreans themselves are the principal authors of their catastrophe. That also means that they must find national liberation within themselves, not by condemning other nations or by seeking decisive assistance from anyone else.

The Two Revolutions

Korea's political *han* began with the resistance to the Japanese protectorate (1905), the annexation (1910), and the division of the resistance into two competing revolutionary movements. Korea's tragedy is that neither movement became dominant before 1945. Both lacked clear legitimacy for either the Korean people or the foreign powers that made Korean politics their business, namely China, the Soviet Union, Japan, and the United States. Moreover, both movements fell prey to the perils of expatriate nationalist movements: personalism, factionalism, betrayal, economic opportunism, and dependent relationships with foreign patrons. The only things the two movements had in common were the dedication to driving the Japanese from Korea and then creating a new, modern Korea upon the wreckage of the Yi Dynasty and the Japanese colonial political and economic system.[5]

The first modern Korean revolutionaries were the young men of Seoul who founded the Paejae Debating Society and Independence Club in 1896. They pressed King Kojong to reform his country on modern western lines. They opposed Chinese and Japanese influence on Korea's dying independence. Most of these revolutionaries' victories were symbolic, but powerful symbols: Independence Gate (*Tongnimun*) in Seoul, the Korean flag (*taegukki*), and a national anthem (*aegukka*). They urged that Kojong call himself Emperor to put himself on a par with the Chinese and Japanese heads-of-state. Kojong's conservative court agencies, with Japanese encouragement, destroyed the Independence Club in 1898 and imprisoned and tortured its leaders, who included a twenty-three-year-old firebrand named Yi Sung-man (Syngman Rhee). As the Japanese tightened their grip on Korea, an underground resistance movement formed around survivors of the Independence Club and their disciples. Their common bonds were a hatred of the Japanese ("the island savages"), an extreme attachment to Korean nationalism but *not* traditional culture; a faith in western concepts of progressive education and science; and a religious-spiritual revivalism, whether Christian, Buddhist, or the Korean hybrid *Chondogyo* or "Heavenly Way Teaching." Despite efficient, ruthless Japanese police work that drove nationalist leaders into jail or exile, a wide range of independence societies flourished either underground in Korea or Japan or openly in the United States and China. One such student association in Tokyo drafted a Korean Declaration of Independence in February 1919, which was redrafted in Seoul by a leading Korean literary figure and liberal, Choe Nam-son.[6]

The independence societies and religious groups in Seoul, moved by the January 1919 death of former Emperor Kojong, embraced the Declaration, and thirty-three notables—fifteen leaders of Chondogyo, sixteen Christians, and two Buddhists—signed the Declaration and then surrendered to the Japanese. Their passive resistance set off the March First Movement, a mass public protest that swept Korea's major cities as the *Samil-undong* (3.1 Event) or "Mansei Revolution." The Japanese police and army killed at least 7,500 people, wounded another 16,000, and arrested more than 20,000 Koreans during a three-month suppression campaign. The surviving leaders fled Korea for the comparative safety of China, Manchuria, and the United States. There they joined other Korean expatriate leaders, who had formed the Korean Provisional Government in Shanghai (April 1919) under the protection of the Chinese Nationalists. Syngman Rhee served briefly as president, but Kim Ku, a popular hero as an anti-Japanese terrorist since the 1890s, replaced Rhee in 1926 and built a revolutionary party and army modeled after the *Kuomintang*, aided by xenophobic authoritarians like Yi Pom-sok, his commander of the Korean Restoration Army (*Kwangbok*).

Except for seventeen unhappy months in China (1919–1920), Syngman Rhee remained in the United States where he had attended graduate school at Harvard and Princeton Universities. He established a home and power base in Hawaii, but often visited Washington to use his religious and educational connections to lobby for Korean independence. He moved to Washington in 1941. Rhee formed a small following of expatriate Korean intellectuals, usually Methodists or Presbyterians, and cultivated eastern and midwestern media moguls, corporate leaders, educators, philanthropists, religious leaders, and politicians. His coterie raised America's comfort level with Korea by dressing in conservative western fashion, speaking English, and using Christian names: John Chang, Louis Yim, Ben C. Limb, Hugh Cynn, and Henry Chung. Rhee even married a European, Francesca Donner, in 1934, an anti-fascist Austrian Jew who became her husband's principal political adviser.[7]

Not all the nationalist political leaders fled Korea, but to remain a nonviolent "justice fighter" (*uibyong*) required some

accommodation of the Japanese, a willingness to risk imprison-
ment, and the endurance to bear the burden of constant police sur-
veillance and job discrimination. Nevertheless, some nationalist
leaders survived: Cho Man-sik, Presbyterian elder and agricultural
reformer of Pyongyang, Korea's Gandhi; Cho Pyong-ok, Columbia
University Ph.D. (1925) and Yonhui College (Yonsei University)
faculty member; Chang Taek-sang, an Edinburgh University Ph.D.;
Kim Song-su, wealthy textile corporation founder and educational
philanthropist; and Yo Un-hyong, Christian socialist, athlete, school
teacher, journalist, and labor organizer. By dissimilation and clever
survivalism, these men and others kept the nationalist vision of a
free Korea alive into the 1940s.[8]

The rival Korean Marxists showed as much anti-Japanese ar-
dor and factionalism as the nationalists. They, too, depended on
external patrons in China for their survival, but the first Korean
Communist Party, in fact, organized as the Korean Section, Russian Communist Party, in Irkutsk, Siberia in January 1918. The
Russians encouraged these Koreans to fight against the Czarist
White Guards and the Japanese expeditionary force sent against
the Bolsheviks. Another socialist party formed in Shanghai around
Yi Tong-hwi, a former Korean imperial army officer and charismatic anti-Japanese Righteous Army leader. Yi Tong-hwi took his
Koryo Communist Party into a coalition with the Provisional Government and won the Comintern's recognition as the legitimate
Korean Communist Party in 1921, which meant money and support that was denied the rival Irkutsk faction. In 1922, the Russians despaired of ever bringing the Shanghai and Irkutsk factions
together and declared both parties defunct. Still, they brought Yi
Tong-hwi to Vladivostok to run a Far East Area Committee Korean Bureau as an anti-Japanese agency of the Russian Communist
Party.[9]

The Shanghai faction took on a new life as part of the Chinese
Communist Party and produced two aggressive leaders in Kim Tu-
bong, a political organizer, and Kim Mu-chong, a guerrilla leader
in the March First Movement. The latter, a trained artillery officer,
joined the Eighth Route Army and survived the Long March in a
unit lead by Peng Dehuai, future commander of the Chinese expeditionary force in Korea. The two Kims and other dedicated Korean revolutionaries formed the Yanan faction, which still
maintained ties to the Provisional Government through Yo Un-

hyong, and which participated with skill and conviction in the war against Japan after 1937.

The expatriate Korean Communists did not ignore their revolutionary duty to organize a Communist Party within Korea. Over and over again in the 1920s and 1930s the Shanghai-Yanan faction and the Irkutsk faction sent agents to Korea. Time after time Japanese police intelligence operatives, poor leadership, and ill-considered strikes and demonstrations decapitated the Korean Communist Party, which was formed in 1925 and had been destroyed four times by 1941. The career of Pak Hon-yong, twenty-one years old when he joined the Shanghai faction in 1921, had enough *han* for several lifetimes. Intelligent, attractive, articulate, honest, and courageous, Pak was the Korean Kirov, the noble revolutionary too good to escape his rivals. The Japanese imprisoned him in 1925–1929 and again in 1933–1939, and his torture and squalid isolation during the latter period so imbalanced him that the Japanese paroled him as mad and harmless. Pak was angry, not insane, and he organized another Korean Communist Party. With the Japanese police in hot pursuit, Pak fled to South Cholla province, a hotbed of radicalism and resistance. Finding anonymity as a brickyard laborer in 1941, Pak stayed in touch with underground organizers and vowed that he would return to Seoul someday to continue the revolution.[10]

In Manchuria, other Korean Communists found places in the Soviet party bureaucracy and armed forces, especially when it seemed likely that Russia and Japan would go to war in 1938–1939. Thousands of Koreans joined the Red Army. Others rose in the ranks of the Soviet-Asian Communist Party, the extractive-industrial bureaucracy, and the transportation system. The career of Nam Il (age thirty-two in 1945), the Korean People's Army's (KPA) chief delegate at Panmunjom, is illustrative. Born in Hamgyongbokdo, Nam Il fled the Japanese as far as Tashkent, Uzbekistan. There, he graduated from a teacher's college and then a military school. He finished World War II as a Red Army division staff officer. Koreans in the Russian service were Soviet citizens and dutiful functionaries. Some were even revolutionaries. More importantly, they were numerous, trained, and disciplined; nearly eighty Koreans held top civil and party positions in the Democratic People's Republic of Korea (1948–1950), and more than fifty were in the defense establishment. They became the "Soviet faction" in Korean Communist politics.[11]

Among all the Korean Communists spawned by the Irkutsk

faction and the World War II Soviet army and bureaucracy was a minor guerrilla leader who won only two notable, but small battle-field victories and led a raid on Pochonbo, a Korean town just across the Yalu River from Manchuria. Kim Song-ju, a middle-school dropout and student agitator, found a home in the North-east Anti-Japanese United Army (NEAJUA), a partisan force of Chinese and Korean Communists operating against the Japanese Kwantung Army and the Chinese-Korean Manchukuo Army. Japa-nese intelligence services estimated the partisans at 15,000. Kim Song-ju began his guerrilla career as a twenty-two-year-old com-mon soldier, but rose to command a partisan column of perhaps 300 to 500 fighters of the Sixth Division, Second Army, First Route Army, NEAJUA. Kim had flair and skills; he spoke good Chinese, won the loyalty of tough subordinates, married a revolutionary heroine, and commanded with intelligence and personal courage. He also adopted an imaginative *nom de guerre*, Kim Il-sung, a name favored by earlier Korean guerrilla chieftains. Kim's greatest skill was survival. When he and about forty comrades crossed into Sibe-ria just ahead of the Japanese in 1941, he was the senior surviving officer of the First Route Army.[12]

For four years Kim Il-sung worked to make himself useful to the Soviet army in the Maritime Province and Siberia, and he re-ceived a Red Army captain's commission for joining and command-ing a battalion of the 88th Special Reconnaissance Brigade, a force of Koreans and Chinese partisans formed around veterans of the NEAJUA. Kim and his fellow veterans, such as Kim Chaek and Choe Yong-gon, gave the Russians a dependable, well-trained, and *small* group of Korean paramilitary operatives designed to seek out anti-Japanese Korean partisans. It is unlikely that Kim's unit had a mission outside of Manchuria until August 1945. It certainly did not lead the Soviet expeditionary force into northern Korea. Kim started his new life as the Great Leader following his Russian patrons into a land he had not seen since his youth.

As the war in the Pacific dragged toward its doleful end in 1945, the Korean Nationalists and Communists intensified their planning for a hasty return to Korea and a political coup de main that would confound their rivals. Neither the expatriates nor the resident "inde-pendence fighters" attempted to form a coalition government-in-ex-ile; instead the major factions turned inward and closed ranks. The Yanan faction broke off from the Provisional Government in

Chungking; the Irkutsk faction and Soviet faction remained estranged, and neither paid attention to the Kapsan-partisan faction of Kim Il-sung. Syngman Rhee remained distant from Kim Ku and lobbied all his Washington contacts for support. He showed his Wilsonianism by sending observers to San Francisco for the founding of the United Nations. The reality, however, was that Korea's immediate future rested on the outcome of the Asia-Pacific war and how the Koreans would deal with their return to independence.

The Struggle for Korea, 1945–1948

The Japanese surrender on 14 August 1945 ended one big war and started many smaller wars throughout the wreckage of the Japanese empire. The Japanese had accomplished one of their grand goals only too well: they had broken forever the mystique of Euro-American colonialism throughout Asia. Whether one called colonialism *le mission civilatrice* or "the white man's burden," native nationalists would have none of it. Many of them, socialists of varying degrees of conviction, looked to the Soviet Union and to Chinese Communists for assistance and encouragement. Even before the Japanese Army, still spread out all over Asia and the Pacific in numbers approaching 2.5 million, could turn in its weapons and go home with a like number of Japanese colonizers, the liberated Asians drew new battle lines against each other and their European overlords. Civil strife with anti-colonial overtones broke out everywhere but Thailand from India to Manchuria.[13]

Although Koreans did not recognize the phenomenon or describe it in programmatic terms, in 1945 Korea entered the first phase of a classic People's War or revolutionary socialist insurrection. Certainly in those salad days in which Mao Zedong, Ho Chi Minh, Tito, and Fidel Castro had not yet replaced Adoph Hitler and Joseph Stalin as household words, few Americans recognized the shape of the wars to come, let alone believed that the United States would be involved in conflicts in such places as Vietnam. Nevertheless, the United States, the Soviet Union, China, and Japan all influenced the political course of Korea after 1945, but more as accomplices to suicide rather than as premeditated or unwitting murderers. All had different objectives—none of them long-range—that did not work well with the Koreans' strident demands for immediate, complete, and geographically whole independence. They did not appreciate the irreconcilable nature of the two Korean revolutionary movements.[14]

The Allied coalition of World War II had considered Korea's fate in an abstract way whenever Franklin Roosevelt, Winston Churchill, Joseph Stalin, and Chiang Kai-shek reorganized the Japanese empire. At the conferences at Cairo and Tehran, at Yalta, and finally at Potsdam, the Allies made abundantly clear that Japan would not retain the lands it had conquered by arms since 1895. Former European colonies would revert to their prior regimes and would have to deal with their own restless native peoples. Manchuria, Formosa, China, Sinkiang, and Korea posed different problems as the claimants were China, Russia, and Japan with the Japanese suddenly removed as the governing power but remaining the occupying power. Korea got a promise of independence in the Cairo Declaration (December 1, 1943) in "due course," a phrase that reflected Roosevelt's belief that the Koreans needed some changes in their underground-exile politics before becoming a peaceful democratic republic with an elected government. Roosevelt was correct about the Koreans, but if he assumed that the Chinese (Nationalists or Communists) and the Russians shared his mild interest in a free Korea, he was wrong.[15]

The Japanese surrender in 1945 created a vacuum and a prize that proved irresistible to the Russians and Korean revolutionaries. The vacuum was one of political power and governance, and the immediate prize was Japanese economic assets in Korea, estimated to be worth billions of *yen*. Seeking to recover its lost economic privileges in Manchuria—or at least some compensation—the Soviet Union first made an agreement with the Chinese Nationalists (the Treaty of Friendship and Alliance, 14 August 1945) that gave the Russians strategic and economic concessions throughout Manchuria in return for military assistance against the Japanese and a lack of assistance to the Chinese Communists. When the Soviets abandoned their neutrality treaty with Japan and launched their invasion of Manchuria and Korea on 9 August 1945, one of the missions of the three Soviet army groups (eighty divisions, 1.5 million men) was to seize industrial centers, mines, and transportation assets before the Japanese could destroy them. As they had already demonstrated in Eastern Europe and Germany, the Soviets had an answer to the reparations question: take as much as possible while their armies held the ground. Because Korea, like Manchuria, fell into the category of conquered Japanese territory, all the declarations of 1943–1945 notwithstanding, Colonel General Ivan M. Chistiakov's 25th Army, part of Marshal K. A. Meretskov's First Far Eastern Front of four armies, invaded Korea by land and sea with a long shopping list in its sheaf of orders. Its "forced reparations" would be easier if cooperative Koreans assisted in the division of Japanese property and the deportation of Japanese nationals, soldiers and civilians alike. Unlike the Manchurian phase of the offensive, the Russian occupation of northern Korea occurred largely after the Japanese surrender. By the end of August 1945, Russian soldiers had advanced as far as Kaesong, just south of the 38th parallel. The 25th Army's march of liberation left dead, raped, and robbed Japanese and Koreans behind (especially on the eastern coast) but it was comparatively mild when contrasted with the deaths in Manchuria, estimated in the 50,000 to 80,000 range.[16]

For four months the Russians indulged in a moveable industrial feast. They shipped factories, machine tools, coal and minerals, lumber (even telephone poles), and trade goods back to the Maritime Province. Soviet technicians took control of hydro-electric power plants, railroads, textile and cement factories, and oil refineries. The Soviets also took 2.7 million prisoners and internees, including Koreans, in Manchuria and Korea, and 340,000 to 370,000 of these human reparations incorporated into the Soviet-Asian workforce, where most of them died. One estimate, compiled by an American reparations investigating committee led by Ambassador Edwin W. Pauley, put the value of Russian extractions at nearly $1 billion and the value of destroyed property at $2 billion. The commission believed that most of the "liberated" industrial assets had come from Manchuria, not Korea. Since the Pauley Commission spent only six days in northern Korea in December 1946 and faced non-cooperation by Russians and hostile Koreans, its findings were hardly exhaustive. The testimony of refugees from northern Korea and a few courageous holdouts left a clear impression that the Soviets intended to add northern Korea to their restored economic zone in Manchuria.[17]

The first task of the Russo-Korean occupiers was to insure that no domestic revolutionary hero would challenge the returned expatriates. The Kapsan faction provided heroic leaders from the defunct NEAJUA, backed by the organizational and technical skills of the Soviet-Koreans. The Yanan faction joined the expatriate coalition after three months of Soviet stalling along the Yalu when it was faced with 4,000 well-armed followers of Kim Tu-bong and General Kim Mu-chong. Only after Kim Il-sung decided that the Yanan faction could share the fight against his internal foes did the Maoist Koreans reach Pyongyang and assume positions in a government that did not call itself a government. As in southern Korea, local notables formed People's Committees (*inmin wiwonhoe*) to replace the Japanese colonial officials and take custody of abandoned public and private Japanese property; the committees drew some legitimacy from a loose affiliation to a national committee of notables in Seoul headed by Yo Un-hyong. The expatriate Communists, however, could not tolerate political leadership that did not answer to General Chistiakov, the occupation commander, and his two assistants for political affairs and civil administration, Major General Nikolai Ledcbev and Major General Alexei A. Romaneko. Chistiakov appears to have been Kim Il-sung's personal champion. Certainly he used his wide discretionary powers and control of the security forces to push the Kapsan faction ahead.[18]

The first move of the Russian-expatriate Korean coalition was to centralize authority in one group, the People's Committee of Pyongyang, and then shift its powers to an executive agency, the Five-Province Administrative Bureau (October 1945), headed by the Chairman of the People's Committee of Pyongyang, the venerated scholar, liberation fighter, and Presbyterian elder, Cho Man-sik. Tired of Cho's protection of Christianity, civil liberties, and property rights and his opposition to any form of political tutelage, the Russians and expatriate Communists called together a People's Assembly in February 1946 and established a new executive agency, the Provisional People's Committee of North Korea, controlled by a coalition of expatriate Communists with Kim Il-sung and Kim Tu-bong the key leaders. Cho Man-sik went off to jail where he died in 1950. The only other local leader of consequence, a dedicated Communist and charismatic teacher named Hyon Chun-hyok, died on the streets of Pyongyang in a hail of bullets on 28 September 1945, shot by a defector to the Kapsan faction. When the students of Sinuiju mounted a protest strike in November, Kim took the lead in crushing the movement.[19]

The political struggle in southern Korea had much the same character as the Communist consolidation of power in Pyongyang:

an expatriate coalition with a foreign sponsor swept the field by 1948 and laid the foundation for a civil war. The political struggle began with a Japanese initiative: if a Korean political authority would take over the government from Governor-General Abe Nobuyuki, the Japanese would make their departure as peaceful as possible. Until the American army arrived—and General Abe received messages from Tokyo saying the Americans were coming—the Japanese army, the colonial police, and any Korean militia the interim authority might establish would prevent any anti-Japanese vendetta and property destruction. Abe found his man (a fourth choice) in the dapper, handsome, well-educated sportsman turned British-style socialist, Yo Un-hyong. On the promise that Abe would open the political prisons, surrender all his offices and authority, and control his troops, Yo formed in Seoul the Preparatory Committee for National Reconstruction from political activists who claimed some popular power base and who could show adequate anti-Japanese credentials.[20]

The sudden creation of the Preparatory Committee galvanized other groups into action, either to challenge Yo's proto-government or to join and reshape it. Although unwilling to govern, a coalition of prominent businessmen and landholders, led by Kim Song-su, Song Chin-u, and Kim Chun-yon, announced they would not support the Preparatory Committee, whose leading members were "beet" revolutionaries (red all the way through). Instead, the conservatives—on property ownership at least—looked for some alternative to the Preparatory Committee and waited for the Americans. The southern Korean Communists, on the other hand, flooded into Seoul, determined to form a mass party of working-class loyalists and to take control of the Preparatory Committee. One group claimed the title communist (*kongsandang*) on 15 August and became the Changan faction, named for its meeting place, the Changan Building.

On 16–17 August, Pak Hon-yong rallied a group of freed political prisoners and loyalists and declared the Seoul District, Korean Communist Party open for revolutionary business, which included the complete political and economic destruction of Japanese collaborators, land reform, the nationalization of industry, tax reform, debt forgiveness, and workers' and women's rights. Four days later Pak and his Seoul faction created the Korean Communist Party Reconstruction Committee, which ignored the Changan faction. During September and October 1945, Pak persuaded some of the Changan faction to defect, and largely due to his success in penetrating Yo Un-hyong's Korean People's Republic, a fusionist collection of notables formed on 6 September without Yo's initial approval. After a week of intense bargaining and reciprocated intimidation, the "government" of the People's Republic had names attached to positions.

The government of the People's Republic was a centrist coalition on paper but tilted slightly left since many of the right-center members remained in exile—most importantly President Syngman Rhee and Minister of Interior Kim Ku. Vice President Yo Un-hyong, Prime Minister Ho Hon, and Minister of Security Choe Yong-dal held the critical posts; the latter two officials were close associates of Pak Hon-yong's. Of the ten senior officials, only three were communists, and none of them were expatriates under Soviet influence. The only northerner placed on the cabinet was Cho Man-sik and the only member of the Korean Democratic Party, Kim Song-su. Six different political groups received seats, and none had a controlling plurality.

Pak Hon-yong, still embroiled in a factional dispute with the Changan faction, remained in the background as he and the Changans tried to determine which communists in Pyongyang were in power. The Changans seemed to have the best access to Pyongyang, sending two leaders north for consultations with the Russians; the Changan-faction newspaper *Hyongmyong sinmun* ["Revolutionary Daily"] praised both Syngman Rhee and "General Kim Il-sung" as the most worthy returned expatriates, "great leaders of the entire nation." Kim Il-sung's name was listed as a legislative representative of the People's Republic.[21] In the meantime, the U.S. Army landed at Inchon on 8 September and found that the situation definitely was not in hand. The arrival of the U.S. Army's XXIV Corps, three infantry divisions commanded by Lieutenant General John R. Hodge, USA, introduced a new element to southern Korean fratricidal politics over power and property. Hodge proved an uninspired proconsul and his staff a model of reluctant confusion. The problems Hodge faced as the commander of U.S. Armed Forces in Korea (USAFIK) and supervising authority for the U.S. Army Military Government in Korea (USAMGIK) stemmed from the uncertain policy of the American government toward Korean independence. Processing 103,000 Japanese soldiers and

320,000 Japanese expatriates back to the home islands—Hodge's mission—did not make the occupation easier. Sharing the chore of liquidating the Japanese presence in Korea with the Red Army complicated Hodge's task, as the War and State Departments worried constantly about how Korean affairs would affect the occupation of Japan and the restoration of the Chinese Nationalist government in northern China and Manchuria.[22]

Like many other aspects of American influence on Korean history, the primary concern in Washington was to move troops to Japan (an army corps and a marine amphibious corps) and to northern China (a second marine amphibious corps) in order to expedite the Japanese surrender and halt the incipient civil wars and postcolonial power struggles breaking out all over Asia.

The fear that the Soviet march of revenge and confiscation might take the Russians to Pusan influenced the United States' decision to offer the Russians on 15–16 August a zonal boundary at the 38th parallel, exactly like similar demarcation lines established for Germany, Austria, China, and French Indo-China. The XXIV Corps had the same priority on shipping as the III Amphibious Corps, which landed its lead elements in China on 30 September 1945, or the V Amphibious Corps, which landed on Kyushu on 22 September 1945.

The Supreme Allied Commander in the Pacific, General of the Army Douglas MacArthur, published his guidance, General Order No. 1 (7 September 1945), only after it had been well-staffed in Washington, coordinated with the Allies, and approved by President Harry S. Truman. The guidance was to dismantle the Japanese empire, preserve the peace in the occupied or liberated areas, restore civil liberties, and await further instructions on formation of a successor regime. For Korea the latter mission was especially vague since there was no dominant national claimant or returning colonial power; the Americans knew nothing about the Korean People's Republic (Seoul) and too much about the Provisional Government in Exile (China). General Hodge understood his repatriation mission and had detailed plans on how to send the Japanese home. His own Field Order 55 (1 September 1945) directed the American forces "to avoid friction, misunderstanding and undesirable incidents."[23] He had no notion of how to create a process that would bring about a legitimate government for all of Korea in the spirit of the Cairo Declaration, nor was that his mission.

For the first four months of the occupation, the USAMGIK enjoyed more Korean cooperation than it anticipated. To repatriate the Japanese, the Americans found it expedient to continue the colonial police force. Renamed the Korean National Police (KNP), the *Kyongchalchung* was stripped of its Japanese supervisors, reduced by 60 percent to 9,000 Koreans by purges and defections, and placed under the supervision of American line and military police officers. Rapid recruitment brought the KNP back up to 25,000 within six months. Many of the recruits were Korean veterans of the Japanese army or youthful toughs from the street gangs and paramilitary forces formed by every political faction. The KNP became a bastion of power for the nationalist revolutionaries of authoritarian bent and the darling of Korean property owners, at least those wealthy enough to escape the crudest sort of extortion. So pervasive was theft, robbery, property destruction, and racketeering that in December 1945, Hodge received permission to form a second force, the "police reserve" or Korean Constabulary, initially planned for 25,000 and trained as a mobile provincial force (nine regiments, one for each province) capable of quick reaction to mob violence or guerrilla attacks on KNP substations. Every political faction—including the communists—managed to get its loyalists into the Constabulary officer corps. The most apolitical and professional Constabulary officers, ironically, bore the onus of service in the Japanese and Manchukuo armies.[24]

Aided by a corporal's guard of expatriate American "old Korea hands," drawn largely from the Protestant missionary community, the USAMGIK and its civil affairs teams tried to sort out all the claims by Koreans that *their* group represented the true aspirations of the Korean people. Economic emergency—4,000 refugees a day flooded southern Korean cities—drove USAMGIK to favor the entrepreneurial nationalists of the Posong faction (Kim Song-su and Song Chin-u) in battling inflation (300 percent in 1945) and unemployment, which affected nearly a million people or 20 percent of the potential industrial workforce. Meanwhile, the People's Republic shadow and hollow government kept sliding left under the aggressive leadership of its Communist organizers, who followed Pak Hon-yong's urging to build a radical urban-proletariat from the now-legalized labor unions. Yo Un-hyong saw his left-middle supporters fade from the fight or defect to the Communists; he spent three critical weeks in September 1945 in hiding while he recovered from a beating. The communist lawyer Ho Hon assumed de facto control of the People's Republic. Moderates like Kim Kyu-sik and An Chae-hong aligned themselves with the USAMGIK and the Posong faction's elitist Korean Democratic Party, formed in late September. Desperate to identify some sort of centrist coalition that could form a majority electoral party, the Americans looked abroad for other acceptable leaders with Independence Movement credentials. Two absentee members of the People's Republic urged that they should come to Seoul to save Korea: Syngman Rhee and Kim Ku. They could go home only if they did so as individuals, not members of the Provisional Government in Exile or the People's Republic.[25]

Despite reservations by the Asian specialists in the State Department, General Hodge and his advisers—as well as the War Department's occupation supervisors—successfully argued that Rhee and Kim Ku might save USAMGIK from its "pro-Japanese" image and rally public support for rationing, land reform, and curbing inflation and draw the survivors of the Independence Movement into the governing process. Rhee also benefited from the loyalty of a coterie of American supporters and Korean expatriates in Washington. With their help and MacArthur's approval, Rhee returned to Seoul on 16 October and enjoyed a special press conference, hosted by Hodge. Kim Ku and his group arrived four weeks later and pledged their cooperativeness with Rhee and the Korean Democratic Party. Rhee interviewed fifty factional leaders and announced he had formed a special unity commission to advise USAMGIK, but Kim Ku remained aloof and instead courted other leaders, including Yo Un-hyong and even the Communists, focusing on the issue of land reform and expropriating Japanese assets. In the meantime, Yo formed his own People's Party and tried to escape the Communists' grasp. By December 1945 Hodge felt secure enough to announce that the Korean People's Republic no longer had a place in his plans "to establish a sound Korean economy and to stabilize and prepare Korea for its independence when a sovereign and unified government of the people, by the people, and for the people can be established."[26]

The State Department inadvertently brought a new focus and unity to the Seoul political circus by crafting an agreement with the Soviets and other allies to establish a five-year trusteeship to prepare Korea for independence as a unified country. The Moscow

Agreement (27 December 1945) decreed that a U.S.-Soviet Joint Commission (the military occupation authorities) would create a plan for establishing a Korean provisional government through national elections. This government would direct the continuing electoral and constitutional process toward full sovereignty. Hodge knew about the plan and opposed it to no avail. He reaped the whirlwind. The major political factions in southern Korea could not condemn the agreement fast enough and called their supporters into the streets for protest rallies. On 31 December the anti-trusteeship demonstrators ruled Seoul, and USAMGIK took a bank holiday because most of its Korean employees had already left work. Kim Ku considered seizing a radio station to announce that he had reestablished the Provisional Government to replace USAMGIK. The southern Communists, however, redirected the public ire by switching from a virulent anti-Moscow Agreement stand (1–3 January 1946) to equally strident support for trusteeship, as directed by Moscow via the Soviet consul in Seoul. On 3 January Pak proposed that Korea join the Soviet Union. A conference of ninety-one political, social, and religious organizations passed resolutions condemning the Communists and urging Pak Hon-yong's execution for treason. Such retributive furies had already struck the Korean Democratic Party; after expressing mild interest in trusteeship, founder Song Chin-u died from an assassin's bullet on 30 December. His successor, Chang Tok-su, was murdered two years later, also by a Kim Ku supporter. Syngman Rhee kept silent until the street rage subsided and thus won Hodge's gratitude and the chairmanship of another committee that USAMGIK quickly formed to advise it during the futile 1946–1947 negotiations with the Russians.[27]

In Pyongyang the Moscow Agreement strengthened the Kapsan (Kim Il-sung) and Yanan (Kim Tu-bong) factions in their struggles with the resident northern Communists (O Ki-sop) and drew the Soviet Koreans closer to Kim Il-sung. Urged on by his political advisers, General (later Ambassador) T. F. Shtykov and Colonel A. A. Ignatiev, Kim took a more aggressive stance in party matters. The most immediate impact, however, was to drive Cho Man-sik from any leadership role, to remake Cho's Choson Democratic Party into a Kapsan faction clique headed by Kim's comrade Choe Yong-gon, and to set off a wave of Communist economic policies that drove most of the remaining Christian-nationalists into impoverished and angry exile. A new and renamed Central Committee, chaired by Kim Il-sung, went quickly to work in February 1946. The committee nationalized all private banking, then published a land reform plan that confiscated and redistributed about half of North Korea's 2.5 million arable acres with debt forgiveness and lowered taxes. In August it nationalized all Japanese-owned industries, almost 90 percent of northern Korea's extractive and industrial infrastructure. The Kapsan-Yanan-Soviet coalition felt secure enough to organize the First Party Congress in Pyongyang. The Yanan faction, in fact, felt certain of its ascendancy, based on the popularity of its Maoist New People's Party and its freedom from Russian diktat. Kim Il-sung, however, now had the money and much of the bureaucracy and security forces behind him, and he demanded that there be only one Korean Communist Party, the North Korean Workers' Party, formed at the First Party Congress. He threw Kim Tu-bong a sop, the chairmanship, while he became vice chairman. Within a year Kim claimed that nearly a million Koreans had qualified as party members and that four million people belonged to party auxiliary associations. Thus, almost every adult northern Korean had found a place in the all-embracing socialist system.[28]

In southern Korea the trusteeship issue created new opportunities for activism outside the personalist-court politics that characterized Korean-USAMGIK relations. Syngman Rhee probably benefitted most since his energy and public-speaking stamina (extraordinary in a man of seventy-two and very impressive to age-reverential Koreans) made him the most popular anti-trusteeship leader. Rhee and his associates formed the National Society for the Rapid Realization of Korean Independence (NSRRKI) in February 1946, which soon claimed seven million members and a network of offices in every province. To demonstrate his high-minded patriotic populism, Rhee did not allow NSRRKI members to stand for office as "political" leaders, although they did as members of the Korean Democratic Party. Rhee's rhetorical populism and new mass political base made him an essential member of General Hodge's new advisory council, although the Americans found Dr. Kim Kyu-sik a more appealing figure.[29]

Rhee did not monopolize the claim of national savior, however, since Yo Un-yong and Kim Ku kept their People's Republic and Provisional Government factions alive. Both looked for ways to counter Rhee's sudden popularity and grudging, distant support from the Korean Democratic Party. With nearly sixty registered political groups to accommodate, the negotiations for coalitions swept Seoul and confused everyone. Yet other developments reshaped the political landscape in the fall of 1946. One was the growing role of refugee northern Koreans as a political force; another was the growth and regimentation for the youth associations, some thirty of them in 1946–1947, as anti-leftist vigilante groups. One such group, the National Youth Association, claimed 100,000 members and received a $5 million subsidy from USAMGIK to serve as a police auxiliary. The group's leader was Yi Pom-sok, a Provisional Government stalwart, who championed authoritarian populism and shifted back and forth in allegiance between Rhee and Kim Ku. Yi's principal ultra-nationalist ideologue and eventual competitor was Dr. An Ho-sang, educated in China, and spiritual leader and director of the Student National Defense Corps (1949) and the two-million member Taehan Youth Corps (1949).[30]

Though wounded by their support of the Joint Commission's futile trusteeship negotiations, the southern Communists—still a legal political party—worked on building a mass, urban-based party of workers, students, and revolutionary middle-class idealists and opportunists. Communists sought places with success in the rapidly expanding Korean Constabulary, abetted by the KNP, which refused to do security checks for the rival Constabulary. The police also infiltrated the party and conducted two successful raids on the party leadership meetings of Pak Hon-yong's opponents, charging them with inciting labor violence, printing counterfeit money, and publishing newspapers that attacked USAMGIK's authority.

In October 1946, the political tension in southern Korea exploded in the Autumn Harvest Rebellion, an event that rattled General Hodge, USAMGIK, and the military-diplomatic communities shaping Korean policy in Washington. The Korean political factions were no less shocked and unprepared, including the communists. The broad signs of unrest could be seen everywhere in the summer of 1946: runaway inflation, a dry monsoon season and poor rice harvest, a cholera epidemic, and a rash of strikes. The catalyst for violence, however, was the rapid and heavy-handed rice collection scheme and the supporting anti-inflationary programs designed in good faith by USAMGIK bureaucrats, but enforced by the hated KNP and its youth auxiliaries. Street protests and supporting strikes broke out in the cities of Korea's four southern and most radical provinces, North and South Cholla and North and South Kyongsang. Police reaction, often hasty and panic-stricken, turned minor looting into major mayhem, including shooting into mobs. The rioters attacked police and police stations. Weak Constabulary companies and American infantry rushed in to save the KNP and stop the violence, but more than 1,000 people died, four times that many were wounded, and more than 10,000 people were jailed. Because some local communists had emerged as insurrectionary leaders, General Hodge focused on decapitating the Korean Communist Party. In the chaos and round-up of dissidents, Pak Hon-yong and Ho Hon escaped across the 38th parallel and with other surviving cadres declared themselves the South Korean Labor Party. They established their headquarters for revolution at the Kangdong Institute in Haeju, a border town in the Hwanghae province. Although not entirely thrilled by his new allies, Kim Il-sung sponsored Pak and Ho for key posts at the Second Party Congress (March 1948) and used them to drive out the O Ki-sop faction since they were now the "true" domestic Communists.[31]

For the Americans, the Autumn Harvest Rebellion added new urgency to the effort to find some formula for unifying the two occupation zones under an elected Korean government. In part to rid himself of Rhee and in part to strengthen his hand in another round of negotiations with the Russians, General Hodge rushed (October–December 1946) to create a Korean Interim Legislative Assembly, whose laws Hodge and the State Department agreed would be applied in the American zone. Half of the ninety representatives would be elected and half would be appointed by Hodge. Definitions of suffrage and a confused administration allowed the nationalist factions to take thirty-two of the forty-five elected seats; Hodge tried to balance the assembly with thirty of the forty-five appointed delegates drawn from independent moderates and socialists, including Yo Un-hyong. Kim Kyu-sik, USAMGIK's favorite progressive politician, chaired the assembly, which spent a year and a half in balanced paralysis, passing eleven laws of no consequence.

Another round of U.S.-USSR Joint Commission meetings (June–September, 1947) produced no agreement on how to form a national government. The Russians, for example, proposed suffrage definitions that would have disenfranchised all the Korean political factions except the socialists and communists because of "national traitor" collaboration with the Japanese. To appease the Russians, the Americans accepted a proposal that all opponents of the Moscow Declaration and the work of the Joint Commission should be excluded from further negotiations; as the *quid pro quo* the Soviets promised to consult southern Korean leaders who had opposed the Moscow Agreement but who would now accept any political solution crafted by the Joint Commission. This position (Joint Communique No.1, Second Session, Joint Commission, 12 June 1947) marginalized Syngman Rhee and, in theory, empowered Kim Kyu-sik, who supported the work of the Joint Commission by late 1946. It also strengthened Rhee's claim that he was the only national leader who would not appease the communists and would challenge American policy. Within months the Americans realized that the Russians would not allow free elections in their zone but wanted the Korean Democratic Party and other non-cooperationist groups denied the franchise in southern Korea. The Americans had no enthusiasm for recognizing the South Korean Labor Party. In desperation, the State Department turned to the United Nations as the optional trustee-of-choice.[32]

Meanwhile, USAMGIK moved quickly to strengthen its Korean security forces, the KNP and Korean Constabulary, while it adjusted to the reduction of XXIV Corps from three wartime divisions to two understrength divisions, both scheduled to leave Korea no later than 1948 as an army economy move. The KNP, directed by ultra-nationalists Cho Pyong-ok and Chang Taek-sang, grew to 30,000 by the end of 1947 and improved its public behavior, at least to reduce itself as a terrorist target. It passed some of its tax-collecting and public health duties to other agencies. It also built a Japanese-like system of undercover operatives, informers, and para-military youth auxiliaries designed to match the communists in the streets and back alleys. Targeting unemployed northern refugees as potential recruits simplified the search for loyal officers but complicated relations with the non-Christian southern population.

The Constabulary endured even sharper growing pains when it expanded from 25,000 (1946) to 50,000 (early 1948) with plans to double that force again if and when all American troops departed. The U.S. Army planners already believed that there would be no unified, neutralized Korea; they feared that a southern Korean army, however, would not survive internal subversion and North Korean military pressure. American officers switched from commanders to advisers in 1947, their principal mission was to manage weapons and equipment transfers from departing American units and to arrange joint tactical training with those that remained. The Constabulary's expansion, however, made it an attractive safe-haven for communist fugitives, who penetrated the officer corps and enlisted ranks with impunity. The second, third, and fourth groups of officers commissioned in 1946–1947 numbered 583, of whom nearly half were shot, jailed, or discharged for treason and incompetence before June 1950. American advisers received no cooperation from KNP investigators; they compensated by transferring officers from unit to unit and by relocating Constabulary regiments away from their provincial bases if there were hints that subversive cells (ultranationalist and communist) had formed an alliance with the local factional organizers. Such personnel problems made training difficult, as did assuming property-protection duties from the U.S. troops in 1947. Moreover, the Russians insisted that the Constabulary resembled a national army—a Japanese national army—because the executive agency that supervised it used the name (in Korean) *Kuk Bang Kungbidae* or National Defense Force. The fact that some former Japanese officers wore their sabers, pistols, and riding boots did not help counter the Russian propaganda attacks in the newspapers on the Constabulary's illegitimacy.[33]

Under constant attack to form a plan that would end the American military occupation, the State Department proposed that the United Nations General Assembly create a United Nations Temporary Commission on Korea (UNTCOK) that would supervise the election of a second and more representative interim assembly. The optimal plan would halt the development of two separate regimes on either side of the 38th parallel. As an ultimate option, the United States would accept a neutralized, demilitarized, unified Korea under international protection. Moving the question of trusteeship to the United Nations created new opportunities for Korean politicians, especially Syngman Rhee. Rhee turned the UNTCOK option to his advantage. By moving the critical decisions to New York and Washington—and making them transparent—the State Department allowed Rhee to revive the Korean Commission. The Korean members—Henry Chung, Louise Yim, Ben Limb, Hugh Cynn, and John Chang—knew how to lobby Congress, to encourage the media, to rally Christian pressure groups, and to persuade other endangered regimes like those in the Philippines and the Chinese Nationalists to see mutual advantage in adopting the Korean cause. Within Korea Rhee argued that he was the only independent political leader of stature. He claimed that Kim Kyu-sik was America's favorite Korean, not him, and he aggravated General Hodge with threats to use his NSRRKI network to frustrate UNTCOK. Rhee also claimed that he could split the Korean Democratic Party. Rhee's major concern, shared by his competitors, was that India, a pseudo-neutralist with communist sympathies, would define UNTCOK's mission. That UNTCOK's chair became K. P. S. Menon, a pliable Indian diplomat, reassured no one. Even when UNTCOK arrived in Seoul in January 1948, its charge was not clear. A month later, the Interim Committee of the General Assembly authorized UNTCOK to supervise elections in only the American zone if the Russians continued to insist on impossible preconditions.[34]

As the southern Korean factions maneuvered to prepare for UNTCOK-supervised elections, the marginalization and elimination of the leading figures continued. USAMGIK was not the problem. General Hodge responded to every UNTCOK demand for him to improve the electoral "atmosphere" by issuing orders that neutralized the police interference, improved electoral procedures, and widened the franchise. He pardoned more than 3,000 prisoners, including the leaders of the Autumn Harvest Rebellion mobs. An assassin had eliminated a major figure when another Kim Ku admirer emptied a pistol into the dapper socialist Yo Un-hyong in July 1947. Convinced that Rhee had won UNTCOK's favor when he had decided to support UN-sponsored elections even if they divided Korea, Kim Ku and Kim Kyu-sik announced their opposition to the elections and went to Pyongyang in April 1948 for an all-Korean political conference. Their popularity immediately sagged. Nine days after Kim Ku and Kim Kyu-sik returned to southern Korea, the northern Koreans stopped the flow of hydroelectric power to the southern provinces, for which the two Kims drew public ire. With elections scheduled for May 1948, the southern Koreans regarded the police, the Constabulary, and the youth associations as essential voter precinct guards. Convinced that UNTCOK would have to depend on his own system of poll-watchers and managers, Rhee urged UNTCOK to continue with the elections as rapidly as possible. His opponents had other plans.

The joint occupation of Korea by the United States and the Soviet Union provided ambitious Korean politicians with an unusual opportunity to seek foreign endorsements and assistance. This hectic period of political organizing, however, did not produce any modification of the extreme goals of the communists and the capitalist-evangelical-nationalist leaders. Compromise was no more possible in Korea than it was in Poland and Czechoslovakia. The result of the Korean political maneuvering was polarization, with the security forces north and south of the 38th parallel under the control of the most extremist cliques. As the two Koreas moved toward permanent division as sovereign states, the Korean people prepared to subvert the new nations. The communists held the advantage, as they had survived in southern Korea and their competitors in northern Korea had not.

The People's War in South Korea, 1948–1950

Even though their own political houses were not in order, Kim Il-sung and Syngman Rhee attempted to wage one war against each other in 1948–1950 and to prepare for another war if their rival looked vulnerable to instant conquest. Since both sought control of all Korea and professed to lead the only legitimate national government, the Republic of Korea and the Democratic People's Republic of Korea should be viewed as "enclave regimes" or "political basecamps" like Mao Zedong's Yanan socialist republic in China. The relationship was asymmetrical, however, since Kim Il-sung's grip was far stronger; his Soviet patrons more helpful; and his influence in South Korea greater than Rhee's influence in the north. Both regimes used partisan war to strengthen their relative positions. Kim Il-sung, well tutored by his Soviet advisers, saw his advantages and ruthlessly exploited them. By driving his noncommunist opponents to the south, he reduced demands on his limited food supply, confiscated more land and real property for his supporters, and integrated his natural resources (hydro-electric power, water, coal, and minerals) into the economic development of Manchuria, Siberia, and the Maritime Province. In March 1948, Kim organized a Second Party Congress, which expanded Central Committee membership from forty-three to fifty-nine. The new committee included thirty survivors of the first committee; the twenty-nine new members helped shift the effective leadership of the committee to a

Kapsan-Soviet Korean coalition of leaders, but accommodated the southern Communist faction (Pak Hon-yong) and the Yanan faction (Kim Tu-bong, Kim Mu-chong). Both groups contributed military muscle to the communist cause through their southern Korean partisans, subversives in the Korean Constabulary, and ethnic Korean units in the People's Liberation Army (PLA).[35]

Kim Il-sung's political dominance required clear and consistent Soviet support, ardently provided by Ambassador Shtykov and Colonel Ignatiev. In addition to economic leverage, the Soviets supplied military training (including tank crew and pilot instruction in the Soviet Union) and weapons and equipment for a modern army. The Soviets also provided leverage on the Chinese Communists, trading military assistance for the PLA's eventual release of its Korean divisions to Kim as well as access to the Sino-Korean population of Manchuria for military recruits. In March 1949, Kim Il-sung and Pak Hon-yong visited Joseph Stalin in Moscow, their first "official" call after creation of the Democratic People's Republic the preceding September. Their purpose was to convince Stalin that South Korea could be easily taken. Stalin disagreed, but his *nyet* was conditional. He wanted more proof of Rhee's vulnerability, of American disinterest in Korea, and some surety that Kim's own political base was secure. He also wanted tangible proof that China would back Kim's play, like the transfer of the PLA's Korean units to the Korean People's Army. In addition, Pak needed to prove that his southern guerrillas posed a serious threat to the Republic of Korea (ROK), so serious that the South Korean army would face a two-front war, a partisan conflict at its rear and a conventional invasion to its front. For his part, Stalin would order his military staff to study the requirements for a Korean campaign, including enough artillery and tank battalions to transform an army of infantry and border constabulary. Impatient but not discouraged, the two Korean leaders brought the news to Pyongyang: put more pressure on Rhee's government.[36]

Stalin's caution reflected his knowledge that Rhee had stolen a political march on his communist competitors. Between 1 March 1948, when UNTCOK announced it would conduct elections, until 15 August 1948, when Syngman Rhee became the president of the independent ROK, the nationalist revolutionaries swept the field. Rhee's Korean Commission made sure that the Truman administration and the United Nations heard good news from Korea. General Hodge, though no champion of Rhee, provided good news as well. The USAMGIK had finally produced a workable land reform scheme that would give nearly a half a million acres of land to a like number of tenant farmers; a new tax system that discouraged more tenancy; and new agricultural cooperatives that provided seed and fertilizer at affordable prices. Hodge also pardoned an additional 3,000 imprisoned dissidents. The electoral process continued despite terrorism and sabotage; between March and May, almost 600 Koreans died in incidents directly linked to the elections. Backed by the one remaining American division, the KNP, the Constabulary and the paramilitary youth associations held their ground and ensured that Korean adults registered to vote for the 10 May election of a 200-man Constituent Assembly.

The national voter registration program produced an electorate of 8.4 million (about 80 percent of the estimated eligible voters), and they turned out with only 5 percent absenteeism to elect delegates with whom Rhee could be comfortable. In late May the Assembly chose Rhee as its chair, voting 189 to 9, and then produced a constitution, signed on 17 July. The constitution created a quasi-parliamentary system, but actual power remained in the hands of the president. The president also had the power to declare martial law, grant appointments, rule by administrative fiat, and dominate the judicial and legislative branches. The Assembly elected the president, and Rhee had no effective opposition, winning the office with 180 votes. Kim Ku received a mere sixteen votes. By the time he was murdered in June 1949, Kim Ku was no longer politically viable. On 15 August 1948, Rhee, flanked by Generals Hodge and MacArthur, established the First Republic.[37]

Among the problems he faced, Syngman Rhee inherited a guerrilla war. Although the strikes, demonstrations, and scattered acts of violence did not halt the 1948 electoral process, the members of the South Korean Labor Party (SKLP), with other armed oppositionists, formed guerrilla bands throughout the provinces of North and South Cholla, North and South Kyongsang, and Cheju island. On 1 April 1948, the Cheju-do guerrillas, pressed by an aggressive governor and his enthusiastic police force, launched a coordinated attack upon twenty-four police substations and other government facilities. Defecting soldiers of the Ninth Constabulary Regiment joined the rebels. Neither side, however, gained the upper hand. The guerrillas created base camps in the mountains while the police and loyal soldiers held the seacoast towns and made limited forays into the hills. The farming villages between the coast and the mountains became a battlezone with neither side concerned about civilian casualties. Not until late in 1948 did government forces, reinforced and commanded by effective Constabulary officers and American advisers, start to reduce the number of guerrillas.[38]

Although the Rhee administration could contain the Cheju-do revolt, the Yosu-Sunchon Rebellion of October 1948 was another matter. In this case, the 14th Constabulary Regiment mutinied under the command of its SKLP junior officers and senior sergeants; other dissidents rallied to the cause of eliminating the police in Yosu and Sunchon cities. The rebel army grew to between 2,000 and 3,000. The Cholla partisans made their political preferences clear by massacring "rightist" families and Christian youth groups, not just policemen and pro-government vigilantes. Rhee ordered a Constabulary task force of 5,000 to quickly retake the cities, which allowed at least 1,000 rebels to escape to the nearby Chiri-san mountain range. Supported by two additional mutinies in the Sixth Constabulary Regiment in North Kyongsang province, the guerrillas established base camps and conducted partisan warfare throughout southern Korea during the winter of 1948–1949. Expatriate southern Korean communists crossed the 38th parallel into Kangwon province and established four partisan operational zones in the Taebaek and Odae mountain ranges. In February 1949, a careful American intelligence assessment identified ten partisan operational zones, controlled by 5,000 to 6,000 guerrillas. More than twenty Korean cities had enough communist underground groups to mount urban terrorism, protests, and sabotage.[39]

The guerrilla war in South Korea eventually strengthened the Rhee regime. The threat to independence posed by the SKLP shifted public ire away from the collaborators of the Japanese colonial period to the communists. In one of its first acts, the Assembly passed the National Traitors Act (September 1948) and used the law to begin purging former colonial officials from Rhee's bloated and rapacious bureaucracy. Some of the prime targets were Rhee's strongest constituents: the National Police, the Constabulary, the youth associations, the entrepreneurial elite, northern refugees, educational and religious leaders, and government banking and economic development officials. Prosecutions numbered in the thousands, trials and punishments in the hundreds. The Rhee government, however, stopped the modest Reign of Terror by February 1950 and used the communist insurgency to pressure the National Assembly to pass a draconian National Security Law (December 1948) that essentially made dissenters vulnerable to legal action and made a more effective mean for administrative intimidation. No one, including members of the judiciary and Assembly, enjoyed immunity. By the summer of 1949, more than 90,000 South Koreans had been arrested or detained, and nearly 20,000 jailed, the vast majority under the loyalty provisions of the National Security Act. In the spring of 1950, Rhee's jails held 58,000 Koreans, the majority for anti-government activity. Although it had a different self-policing authority, the Republic of Korea Army *(Hanguk Gun)*, founded in December 1948, purged more than 4,000 dissident officers and men, a quarter of them jailed or executed for mutiny and treason. As many as 6,000 more deserted or defected to North Korea. The army in 1949 also doubled in size to 65,000 and continued to grow in 1950 to a planned strength of 100,000. The KNP increased its numbers to more than 50,000, and by 1950 it had formed "combat police" battalions for counterinsurgency operations.[40]

The partisan war spawned another more conventional conflict along the 38th parallel, a war that sent Rhee and Kim Il-sung on arms-buying expeditions to their American and Soviet patrons. Kim Il-sung won the arms race. The war had its origins in Pak Hon-yong's efforts to reinforce the southern guerrillas. Eleven separate guerrilla columns of 2,000 men penetrated the border from November 1948 to March 1950. The principal routes came through the mountains at Kaesong and Chunchon and along the coast, but the base area remained the Haeju Institute, just across the border on the Ongjin Peninsula. The KNP tried to stop the guerrillas but were driven from the ill-defined border by the North Korean *Boandae* (Border Constabulary), who in turn fell back from cross-border raids by the South Korean army. Regular regiments of the KPA struck back, benefiting from the advantages of real artillery (not just mortars) and ample machine guns. Between May and December 1949, the North Korean army not only dominated the border zones (Kaesong was regularly shelled) but also pushed south in strength, thus drawing the South Korean army into ill-considered counterattacks. Despite bold talk of "marching north" from Rhee's favorite generals, it was Kim Il-sung who in late August 1949 submitted a plan for a campaign to capture the Ongjin Peninsula. Again Stalin did not like the timing and balance of forces, but he agreed to examine more plans to expand the North Korean army and consider a future campaign.[41]

Heartened by the final withdrawal of American combat units in July 1949, Kim Il-sung found Mao Zedong ready to transfer Korean troops from the PLA to the KPA after the creation of the People's Republic of China in October 1949. The Soviets had detonated their first nuclear weapon in August, another triumph of socialism. After extended negotiations in Beijing and Pyongyang, two PLA divisions (about 33,000 men) joined the North Korean army by the end of 1949, bringing the KPA to seven divisions. Another Sino-Korean division formed in March 1950. Kim and Ambassador Shtykov sent a series of weapons requisitions to Moscow. The arms order of 20 April 1949 reflected the changed size and structure of the KPA; in addition to small arms for three or four new divisions, the request included ninety combat aircraft, eighty-seven T-34 tanks, and 102 self-propelled artillery pieces, all with ample ammunition. Stalin approved the request on 4 June as submitted and added more towed artillery, ordnance, and engineering equipment. According to an arms transfer protocol signed in March 1949, the Koreans would pay Stalin in raw materials and rice. By the end of 1949, the KPA had received most of its tanks, some artillery, and most of its aircraft. Stalin later doubled the heavy weapons transfers when he approved Kim's revised war plans in April 1950. The largest uncertainty was the readiness of Pak's partisans; Pak promised that at least 3,000 guerrillas would be prepared to start a popular uprising. South Koreans and Americans put the number of guerrillas at less than 1,000 by early 1950.[42]

Protected by an army plagued by lack of training, purges and defections, and the turmoil of expansion, the Rhee regime could not persuade the United States to enhance its combat capability to equal the KPA. The State Department countered requests for heavy weapons by stating that Rhee might authorize a "march North" campaign, at least to Haeju. This oft-repeated complaint masked concern about Rhee's use of his emergency powers to crush opponents in the press and the National Assembly as well as his inability to shape a fiscal and monetary policy that offered hope for economic development. Rhee understood the power of patronage and the lure of printing currency, but little else. The U.S. Army's Korean Military Advisory Group (KMAG), numbering 500 officers and men in early 1950, did not think "marching North" was a real threat. The American officers knew the South Korean infantry regiments were not well-trained, and they could not maintain more howitzers and anti-tank guns, let alone tanks, unless they received more trainers and more money; neither were forthcoming from the Pentagon. The U.S. Army, stung by Chinese nationalist equipment losses in 1949–1950, would not send scarce weapons to Asia when it had the U.S. Seventh Army to build in Germany and its own strategic reserve divisions in the United States to supply. Even the four U.S. divisions in Japan (U.S. Eighth Army) received little materiel above the World War II equipment and ordnance they brought to Japan in 1945.[43]

Confronted by his lack of success through official channels, Rhee resorted to unofficial solicitations. He urged his representatives in Washington to lobby with Congress to no avail, until a military aid bill could be linked to aid for Chiang Kai-shek. Even then the aid program, shaped by a KMAG-State team, included no heavy weapons. Rhee recruited his former OSS contact, M. Preston Goodfellow, to buy ordnance abroad, but Goodfellow, a newspaper editor and a marginalized Republican, had no real power. Goodfellow failed as an arms buyer and fund-raiser. The only success came in Canada, where the government sold Rhee ten unarmed AT-6 "Texan" training aircraft. The only other purchase was a surplus Navy patrol boat (PC 823) owned by the U.S. Maritime Commission. The U.S. Mutual Defense Assistance Act (1948) did allow South Korea to arm the planes and PC 823 with appropriated funds. The total outlay was $279,470. Rhee also turned to General MacArthur for assistance: "We are fighting for our lives!"[44] MacArthur was sympathetic but not helpful as the Eighth Army did not have mines, tanks, aircraft, or artillery to share. The Rhee government had no better success in lobbying for aid money from the U.S. Economic Cooperation Administration. Frustrated that the Koreans had done so little to curb inflation and corruption, American officials would not support Rhee's request for additional subsidies. In 1949–1950 Rhee's government borrowed 40 percent of the revenues necessary pay its bills, and it borrowed from itself, the Bank of Korea. The Korean aid program dropped from $116 million to $58 million in 1949–1950. Syngman Rhee's international influence had evaporated, and his presidency suffered accordingly.[45]

Having failed to curb Rhee by constitutional revision, the opposition factions—dominant in the National Assembly—changed their names and some faces before the biennial election in May 1950. With limited supporters in the Assembly, Rhee faced two uneasy coalitions of excluded office holders. The Korean Nationalist Party, whose heritage was Kim Ku and the Provisional Government, rallied around Shin Ik-hui, who also appealed to survivors from the camp of Yo Un-hyong and the People's Republic. The Democratic Party, essentially the party of Kim Song-su and the murdered conservative spokesman Song Chin-u, was still one of property but shifting from rural landlords to urban real estate investors. The cosmetics produced nothing. Two-thirds of the 2,209 candidates claimed no party affiliation. On 30 May with 90 percent of the electorate participating, the Koreans voted all the rascals out, or at least rewarded those who were untarnished. Only 31 incumbents were reelected. The Democratic Party's seats fell from 68 to 24, the Korean Nationalist Party from 71 to 24. The Independents took 126 seats. The returns did not weaken Rhee since he had already lured some Nationalists and nominal independents into a pro-government faction, but only 57 seats. He now embraced land reform and tax relief. Nevertheless, he recognized his vulnerability, especially when one of Pyongyang's notables called for a new north-south movement for reconciliation, the National Front for the Unification of the Fatherland, on 8 June 1950. Rhee needed a sign that he had not lost the mandate of heaven.[46]

Syngman Rhee looked to an unlikely American friend of Korea, John Foster Dulles. Recently appointed to ambassadorial rank after service in the United Nations delegation, Dulles had taken charge of the Japanese peace treaty negotiations. On his way to Tokyo in June 1950, he first visited Korea to bolster the confidence of his fellow Princetonian with a ringing pledge of American support and a much-photographed pilgrimage to the tense Uijongbu front. Rhee stressed that his army's intelligence staff feared an invasion, and he argued for a preemptive attack, which his generals and the KMAG advisers thought unrealistic. Dulles posed with binoculars, a dapper diplomat playing a military expert, on 18 June. A week later, Kim Il-sung remade Korea's political landscape by playing Napoleon.[47]

The Expanded Internationalized War, 1950–1953

Although Syngman Rhee and Kim Il-sung spent many anxious days and sleepless nights in 1950, the war they both sought left them in a dominant political position in 1953 when it ended in a military armistice. A year later, their political control was secure, founded on the support of their armies and police and their single party-bureaucratic governments. Kim's system, however, has lasted fifty years, Rhee's only seven. The two leaders had several common wartime successes. They outmaneuvered their foreign patrons to enlarge their powers; they kept their armies under control; and they eliminated their domestic challengers through the manipulation of factions and their control of patronage and administrative power.

The North Korean invasion of June 1950 almost destroyed the Rhee regime, which fell back with its own shattered divisions and the U.S. Eighth Army through Taejon to Taegu toward Pusan. Basically, the South Korean ministeries could function only as junior partners of American military organizations and private welfare agencies, both working under United Nations sanction. The initial disaster of June–September 1950, followed by six weeks of euphoric victory, and then followed by the Chinese intervention provided Rhee with a popular image of the outraged victim, the national champion of a unified Korea, and the stubborn opponent of foreign-imposed compromise. The communists improved Rhee's position by their massacre and deportation of 200,000 South Koreans in 1950; the flood of 800,000 North Korean refugees fleeing the Chinese People's Volunteers Force in the winter of 1950–1951 added more supplicants to Rhee's popular base among the dispossessed. Rhee even had one day of sublime triumph, visiting a liberated Pyongyang on 30 October.[48]

The Syngman Rhee of 1950, twice victimized and twice saved, never surrendered his declared policy of unifying Korea by military force, but his minimum goal remained the preservation of the Republic of Korea and his personal grip on his nation's future, however bleak. By July 1951, he could be reasonably sure that the United Nations Command would not surrender more territory below the 38th parallel by battle or by negotiation. That did not mean Rhee was safe. Although the communist occupation of South Korea had resulted in executions, deportations, and military impressments measured in the tens of thousands, the KNP, the Korean army's military police, and the paramilitary youth associations had extracted comparable vengeance in type if not in numbers during the same six month period—and in front of western witnesses. United Nations soldiers, civilian officials, western newsmen, and relief agencies reported anti-communist pogroms from Pusan to Pyongyang. The U.S. Eighth Army ordered its KNP combat battalions out of North Korea to halt the vigilantism. United Nations resistance to Rhee—and its own doubts—forced the Truman administration to announce that the Rhee government did *not* automatically replace Kim Il-sung's regime, but Chinese intervention ended this crisis.

Rhee created more crises almost immediately as the Chinese army drove the United Nations Command south of Seoul in January 1951. Determined to form a government of no-compromise nationalists, the president turned to his most violent retainers such as Yi Pom-sok (Home Minister, May 1951). Rhee gave General Kim Yoon-gun, head of the Taehan Youth Corps, the responsibility of forming the National Defense Corps, established on the power of universal conscription. Kim was supposed to take all potential soldiers south out of communist reach and put them into the service of the Republic of Korea. Haste, corruption, and mismanagement made the National Defense Corps such a scandal that Rhee eventually had Kim and four of his cronies tried and executed. Had such enthusiastic prosecutions been extended to the rest of the government, there would have been no end of revealed scandals of profiteering.

Rhee turned on the National Assembly instead, declaring it a barrier to victory in a speech in August 1951. He pushed for constitutional amendments that would destroy the Assembly's mild power to criticize and obstruct his rule-by-fiat. In January 1952, the Assembly refused to commit suicide by a vote of 143 to 19. Rhee's aggressiveness encouraged Dr. Chang Myon (John Chang), an American favorite, to break with Rhee and join Shin Ik-hui in the opposition. The Assembly then found another cause: the massacre of 719 villagers of Kochang, South Kyongsang province by South Korean soldiers during a guerrilla hunt in February 1951 and the subsequent army cover-up. When an Assembly investigating team tried to pursue its inquiry, it was attacked by an army "special operations" team led by Colonel Kim "Tiger" Chong-won, a notorious administration "enforcer" in the Provost Marshal Command. In a related incident, Kim entrapped a leading assembly-man, Shin Chung-mok, in a bar room brawl and arrested him for "murdering" an army captain in a gunbattle. The assemblyman was convicted by an army court-martial and sentenced to death. The National Defense Corps scandal and Kochang Affair gave Rhee an excuse to replace Defense Minister Sin Song-mo. It also proved that the president's martial law authority would be enforced by at least part of the army, even in dubious causes.[49]

His continuing war with the National Assembly hanging in the balance, Rhee decided to strip the Assembly of its power to elect the president, its ultimate political leverage. To change the electoral system, which could deny Rhee a second term, the president advocated a constitutional amendment that provided for the popular election of the president and vice president. To advance his campaign of constitutional revision, Rhee, in December 1951 announced the creation of the Liberal Party, headed by his longtime protege, Yi Ki-bung, who left the National Assembly to be Defense Minister.

Rhee envisioned the Liberals as a true "ruling party" with a mass popular base tied to a corporatist administrative state. Korea would be governed by a political elite who worked at the president's bidding, backed by a politicized police and army and ever-faithful youth associations. The first test of the new party would be the Assembly election of 1952. The grand prize was the presidency, for the newly elected Assembly would elect a president unless the First Republic's Constitution could be changed before August 1952.

Rhee concluded that the Liberal Party ploy left too much to chance. He renewed his call for constitutional reform in April 1952, initiating five months of political crisis. Rhee asserted that a cabal of closet communists had poisoned the Assembly. He linked his political fate to the continuing troubles of the rear-area war effort: prisoner violence on Koje-do Island, communist guerrilla warfare, rampant inflation and money problems with U.S. economic aid officials, subversion of his regime by United Nations representatives and American diplomats, and potential abandonment of South Korea in the Panmunjom armistice negotiations. Again his Assembly supporters introduced constitutional amendments that would sever the presidential election from future Assembly elections. And again the majoritarian opposition refused to comply, regardless of Rhee's disingenuous promise to not run again.[50]

In late May 1952, President Rhee organized a campaign of direct intimidation on the Assembly when it convened in the temporary capital of Pusan in another special session. Yi Pom-sok organized street demonstrations and other forms of harassment of oppositionist Assemblymen. Rhee declared the Pusan area and all of North Kyongsang province under martial law and ordered Major General Won Yong-dok, a Rhee loyalist and Provost Marshal General, to govern the martial law territory. General Won promptly arrested forty-five Assemblymen and then pursued other oppositionists who tried to destroy a quorum by flight. American and United Nations protests had no impact. Rhee then challenged his opponents in the U.S. mission by ordering his Army Chief of Staff, Lieutenant General Lee Chong-chan, to remove two divisions from Eighth Army operational control to reinforce Martial Law Command's military police. General Lee refused, backed by his commanders and Generals James A. Van Fleet and Mark W. Clark, the senior American commanders. American diplomats then encouraged General Lee—allied with Chang Myon, Cho Pyong-ok and Shin Ik-hui—to consider a coup. Not pleased with the possibility of the South Korean army fighting some of its own units, Van Fleet had his staff draft Operation Plan Everready, a set of contingency plans that assumed a second civil war between Rhee's loyalists and opponents. American diplomats wanted the plan to include removing Rhee, something neither the Truman administration nor United Nations Command was ready to risk.

Rhee resolved the crisis by ordering General Won to produce an Assembly quorum on 2 June 1952 and to keep the Assembly in continuous session (backed by Yi Pom-sok's mobs) until the constitution had been amended. With no expectation of external support, the Assembly approved the direct election of the president by a vote of 163 to 0 on 4 July 1952. One month later, Syngman Rhee retained his office, receiving five million of the seven million votes cast for the four presidential candidates. He cemented his triumph two years later (1954) when the Liberal Party became the first Korean party to form a true majority (114 seats, with 12 independents in coalition) in the Assembly. The oppositionist Korean Nationalist Party (born the Korean Democratic Party) held only fifteen seats. Rhee also cast loose Yi Pom-sok and had the Assembly bar youth associations from political activity (September 1953). For good measure, Rhee relieved General Lee Chong-chan in July 1952, and General Lee, having received death threats, fled first to

General Van Fleet's quarters and then to the United States to attend a U.S. Army school, the usual safe haven for supernumerary ROKA generals.[51]

With his political base more secure than ever, Rhee launched his most assertive attack on the armistice terms being negotiated at Panmunjom. His intransigence prolonged the war since the Chinese and North Koreans hoped that the United States (urged by the United Nations) might accomplish in 1953 what the National Assembly had failed to do in 1952: send the seventy-seven year old president into permanent retirement. Despite the urging of the collective Russian leadership, emboldened by Stalin's death in March 1953 to settle on terms, the Chinese were in no hurry to stop fighting. From May through July, Chinese ground forces and the Russian-Chinese air forces went on the offensive and dealt heavy blows to the Eighth Army's American and international units and even heavier blows upon the ROKA. Rhee remained obdurate against an armistice until the United States provided several pre-truce assurances:

1. A mutual security treaty with the United States alone, not tied to United Nations approval
2. A military assistance program that would provide South Korea with a twenty-division army and modern air and naval forces
3. A promise to station American troops in Korea as long as Chinese troops remained
4. An economic aid and reconstruction program with American and United Nations funding of several billion dollars
5. A favorable settlement of *won* borrowed by United Nations Command to pay the U.S. bills for Korean goods and services
6. A promise of draconian United Nations military action if the Communists broke the truce
7. A formula for processing POWs that allowed prisoners to reject repatriation and kept the neutralist UN forces (the Indian army) confined to the proposed Demilitarized Zone

Rhee made his point in June 1953 by releasing 27,000 Korean prisoners who had passed their loyalty tests but had been retained in United Nations custody, in Rhee's view, as hostage bargaining chips.[52]

When the armistice was signed on 27 July 1953, Syngman Rhee publicly denounced the compromise with communism and pledged to continue the struggle, if not immediately on the battlefield, then by other means. His bold talk reflected his most impressive achievement: the Americans had agreed to almost all his preconditions for accepting (but not signing) the armistice. His domestic political victory of 1952 made his intransigence in 1953 effective and bound the United States to the future survival of the Republic of Korea.

In Pyongyang, then at his rump capital-in-exile at Kanggye, and then back to the rubble of Pyongyang, Kim Il-sung survived, flourished, and finished the war on the road to the cult of personality and his Stalinesque version of *juche* or self-sufficiency. Like Rhee, he survived because his international patrons refused to give full backing to his rivals. The war thinned the upper ranks. In 1948 Kim had posed with his four closest Kapsan comrades, all bearing new PPSh41 submachine guns; by 1951, two of them (Chae Yong-gun and Nam Il) were in temporary disgrace, and two (Kim Chaek and Kang Kon) had been killed in action. Kim's alter ego, the shadowy Colonel Ignatiev, had also perished. In December 1950, Kim removed the military darling of the Yanan faction, General Kim Mu-chong, as part of his purge of defeated generals.

With the Chinese People's Volunteers Force fully committed to stopping the United Nations Command, Kim could focus on political reconstruction since the U.S. Air Force had made any other rebuilding impossible. The Eighth Army's temporary conquest of North Korea had thrown Communist party organization into chaos. Many North Koreans had thrown away their party cards; those who had not often faced a KNP firing squad. Kim recruited First Party Secretary Ho Kai-i, the organizing genius of the Soviet faction, to rebuild the party, but instead, Ho chose a more restricted model of party membership and purged 400,000 members in 1950–1951. With Ignatiev dead and Ambassador Shtykov recalled, the Soviet Koreans slipped their leashes, but Kim stopped the pre-coup organizing with an outburst of forgiveness and recruitment, rebuilding a mass party in 1952 that reached 1.2 million members (half of them were new) in 1956. In 1953, Kim announced that Comrade Ho had committed suicide.[53]

In 1952, as the Soviet faction fell back in line, the southern Communists mounted a coup attempt against Kim Il-sung. Given Kim's unslackened thirst for scapegoats for the failed invasion of 1950, the Pak Hon-yong faction may have been motivated by a preemptive strategy rather than awaiting passive elimination. The key figure, Minister of Justice and Party Secretary Yi Sung-yop, would have been high on Kim's list of sacrifices since he had been the 1950 communist "mayor" of Seoul and the southern Communist party secretary. Yi rallied his surviving party cadres and the Haeju guerrillas to create a new network of agents and partisans behind United Nations Command's lines in 1951. His agents and those from the Korean People's Army political department provided the leadership for the POW resistance campaign. Yi's special operations forces provided a useful disguise for plotting. Kim may have drawn Pak Hon-yong into his scheme, although Pak's later confessions had the taint of torture and a desperate bargain to spare his family from Kim's wrath. Kim's security services penetrated the plotters' inner circle, and the southern communist leadership perished after a series of show trials that would have warmed Stalin's heart. Of the twelve tried, ten died. Pak survived until 1955 after he confessed to having been an American and Japanese agent since 1946 and a traitor in 1950. His execution ended the gallant career of Korea's Kirov.

Kim Il-sung used the postwar reconstruction period to continue his political cleansing. He paraded his political muscle at the Third Party Congress; the new Central Committee grew to seventy-one members, forty-two were first-time appointments and Kim Il-sung supporters. The Yanan faction (Kim Tu-bong) challenged Kim's policy of investment in heavy industry. Kim struck back and arrested or exiled the Yanan leadership. Kim Tu-bong died in 1961 as an exhausted farm laborer. Kim Il-sung took pity on no one outside of his Kapsan comrades, regardless of their wartime services. Army officers with service in the People's Liberation Army or the Red Army lived the remainder of their lives in exile or in trivial appointments. Before his second and final removal in 1978, General Kim Ung, KPA frontline commander, 1951–1953, served as ambassador to South Yemen. General Lee Sang-cho, Panmunjom negotiator and political-intelligence chief, died in Minsk, Russia. As a rule, however, KPA generals fared better than their political peers.[54]

Summary

The internationalized People's War in Korea, 1950–1953, may have ended in a strategic draw, but it resulted in the clear political dominance of the two Koreas' wartime leaders, Syngman Rhee and Kim

Il-sung. As their American, Chinese, and Russian sponsors fought one another, the two Koreas quintupled the size of their armies, ruined each other's social fabric and economic structure, and transformed the politics of faction into one-party, one-leader corporative states. If there were two revolutions in Korea in 1945, there were also two betrayed revolutions a decade later. The two authoritarian successor regimes had more in common with each other than the revolutionary visions of 1945–1948. The war of 1950–1953 actually strengthened Rhee and Kim, who were battered and discredited by their failures and dependency in 1950. Four years later, their positions were unassailable. Their patrons had been tamed. Although the U.S. diplomatic mission tried to curb Rhee's slide into autocracy, the Russians and Chinese did nothing to unseat Kim, whom they underestimated and patronized while he eliminated the Soviet and Yanan factions. In a strange twist of fate, both Koreas could claim victory, if not over each other, then over the Great Interventionist Powers. Neither Korea had won a battle or a diplomatic conference against a foreigner since the French had foundered at Kanghwa-do in 1866. Now, at the cost of two million Korean lives, the Korean political leadership had manipulated three major powers as well as the United Nations into guaranteeing the independence of *two* Koreas, not just one. The Korean War may have been limited for the intervening nations, but it was a struggle to the death for Koreans on either side of the 38th parallel. The winners, mostly self-defined, were the Korean politicians, not the Korean people. Their struggle is ongoing.

Notes

1. George Trumbull Ladd, *In Korea with Marquis Ito* (New York: Charles Scribner's Sons, 1908), 8–9.

2. Ibid., 463. In 1909, a Korean patriot assassinated Ito in Manchuria.

3. Peter Hyun, *Koreana* (Seoul: Korea Britannica, 1984); John H. Koo and Andrew C. Nahm, eds., *An Introduction to Korean Culture* (Seoul: Hollym, 1997); Donald Stone Macdonald, *The Koreans: Contemporary Politics and Society* (Boulder, Colo.: Westview Press, 1988), 44–52, 67–111; Alexander C. Nahm, *Korea: Tradition and Transformation: A History of the Korean People* (Elizabeth, N.J.: Hollym, 1988), 223–325.

4. *Korea Herald*, 10–15 August 2000; Koo and Nahm, *Korean Culture*, 194–217.

5. Chong-sik Lee, *The Politics of Korean Nationalism* (Berkeley: Uni-

versity of California Press, 1963); Dae-yeol Ku, *Korea Under Colonialism* (Seoul: Royal Asiatic Society, 1985).

6. Kim Han-kyo, "The Declaration of Independence, March 1, 1919: A New Translation," *Korean Studies* 13 (1989): 1–4. Choe Nam-son did not sign the Declaration, but was jailed anyway. He was imprisoned in the ROK in 1949 for collaboration with the Japanese despite his valiant efforts to preserve Korean language and culture. For the personal perspectives of lives of nationalists, see Henry Chung [Chang Han-gyong] *Korea and the United States through Peace and War, 1943–1960* (Seoul: Yonsei University Press, 2000). Biographical information in this essay comes from several reliable sources: G-2, HQ, U.S. Armed Forces in Korea (USAFIK), "Who's Who in Korea," 15 October 1947, copy in Charles H. Donnelly Papers, U.S. Army Military History Institute (USAMHI), Carlisle Barracks, Pennsylvania; James I. Matray, ed., *Historical Dictionary of the Korean War* (Westport, Conn.: Greenwood Press, 1991); Keith Pratt and Richard Reett with James Hoare, *Korea: A Historical and Cultural Dictionary* (Richmond, Surrey, UK: Curzon Press, 1999).

7. In addition to the biographical entries cited above, see also "Syngman Rhee," *Current Biography, 1947*, copy in Syngman Rhee Subject File, M. Preston Goodfellow Collection, Hoover Institution Archives. In addition to the Rhee-Goodfellow correspondence, the best source of material on Rhee is the papers and book notes of Dr. Robert T. Oliver, Professor of Communications, Pennsylvania State University Library. Oliver was Rhee's sympathetic biographer in *Syngman Rhee: The Man Behind the Myth* (New York: Dodd Mead, 1955) and *Syngman Rhee and American Involvement in Korea, 1942–1960* (Seoul: Panmun, 1978). The unsympathetic biography is by Richard C. Allen, *Korea's Syngman Rhee* (Rutland, Vt.: Charles E. Tuttle, 1960). Rhee's correspondence in languages other than English is collected by the Syngman Rhee Papers Editorial Committee, Institute for Modern Korean Studies, Yonsei University, *Syngman Rhee Papers* (18 vols., Seoul: Yonsei University Press, 1998).

8. See especially Chong-Sik Lee, "The Personality of Four Korean Political Leaders: Syngman Rhee, Kim Ku, Kim Kyu-sik, and Yo Un-hyong," reprinted in Dr. Mark C. Monahan, *Korean Studies Reader*, Yonsei University, 1998.

See also the memoir of the Nationalists' leading female colleague, Louise Yim, *My Forty Year Fight for Korea* (Seoul: Chungang University, 1967).

9. Suh Dae-sook, *The Korean Communist Movement, 1918–1948* (Princeton, N.J.: Princeton University, 1967), 4–52.

10. Ibid, 117–211, 256–93; "Pak Hon-yong," in "Who's Who in Korea," USAFIK mss., cited in note 6.

11. Nam Koon-woo, *The North Korean Communist Leadership, 1945–1965* (Tuscaloosa: University of Alabama Press, 1974).

12. Dae-sook Suh, *Kim Il-sung* (New York: Columbia University Press, 1988), 1–57. See also Adrian Buzo, *The Guerrilla Dynasty: Politics and Leadership in North Korea* (Boulder, Colo.: Westview Press, 1999); Sydney A. Stiles, *Kim Il-Song: The Creation of a Legend, The Beginning of a Regime* (Lanham, Md.: University Press of America, 1994). Stiles prints a translation of Yu Song-chol, "Testimony," nineteen installments in *Hanguk Ilbo* (November 1990).

The "real" Kim Il-sung was probably another Korean partisan leader from North Kyongsang province who had deserted from the Japanese army, was driven out of Korea, and had died in Manchuria in the 1930s.

13. For an overview, see Sir Robert Thompson and John Keegan, eds., *War in Peace: Conventional and Guerrilla Warfare since 1945* (London: Orbis, 1981); and D.M. Condit et al., *Challenge and Response in Internal Conflict*, vol. 1, *The Experience in Asia*, 3 vols., Center for Research in Social Systems for the U.S. Army (Washington, D.C.: American University, 1968).

14. For the "liberation politics" of Korea, see Won-sul Lee, *The United States and the Division of Korea, 1945* (Seoul: Kyung Hee University Press, 1982); George McCune, *Korea Today* (Cambridge, Mass.: Harvard University Press, 1950); and Bruce Cumings, *The Origins of the Korean War*, vol. 1, *Liberation and the Emergence of Separate Regimes, 1945–1947* (Princeton, N.J.: Princeton University Press, 1982).

15. James I. Matray, *The Reluctant Crusade: American Foreign Policy in Korea, 1941–1950* (Honolulu: University of Hawaii Press, 1985), 1–51.

16. David M. Glantz, *August Storm: The Soviet 1945 Strategic Offensive in Manchuria* (Leavenworth, Kansas: Combat Studies Institute, 1984).

17. Memoirs of Richard F. Underwood, 1995–1998, Urbana, Illinois, retired headmaster, Seoul Foreign School, provided to the author by Mr. Underwood. In 1945, Mr. Underwood was one of three American soldiers in the USAFIK liaison mission to the Soviet military government in Pyongyang. Mr. Underwood, the third generation of his family to serve as a Presbyterian missionary in Korea, was an army CIC agent and a Korean interpreter and returned to that role in 1950–1953 as an army lieutenant. He and his older brother, Dr. Horace G. Underwood (Lt., USNR), served as interpreters-translators during the armistice negotiations, 1951–1953.

See also Henry Chung, *The Russians Came to Korea* (New York: J.J. Little, 1947), which is based on interviews with Korean refugees; Erik van Ree, *Socialism in One Zone: Stalin's Policy in Korea, 1945–1947* (New York: Berg, 1989); and Charles K. Armstrong, *The North Korean Revolution, 1945–1950* (Ithaca, N.Y.: Cornell University Press, 2003).

18. Office of Intelligence Research, Report No. 5550, "North Korea: A Case Study of a Soviet Satellite," 2 April 1951, Korean War File, Presi-

dential Secretary's Files, Harry S. Truman Papers, Truman Library. This study is based on North Korean documents captured in Pyongyang in October 1950 and then translated and analyzed by an intelligence team. A public, censored version was later published as Department of State, *North Korea: A Case Study in the Techniques of Takeover* (Washington, D.C.: Government Printing Office, 1961).

19. Eric Van Ree, *Socialism in One Zone: Stalin's Policy in Korea, 1945–1947* (Berg Publishers, 1990), 85–186; Andrei N. Lankov, "The Demise of Non-Communist Parties in North Korea (1945–1960)," *Journal of Cold War Studies* 3 (winter, 2001): 103–25; and Armstrong, *The North Korean Revolution*, 63–64.

20. Suh, *The Korean Communist Movement*, 294–329.

The development of the Southern Korean Communist movement may be followed in detail in the party newspapers, *Haebang Ilbo* (September–December 1945), *Hyong myong sinmun*, and *Kongsandang* for 1945–1946, reprinted in Chong-sik Lee (trans. and ed.), *Materials on Korean Communism, 1945–1947* (Honolulu: University of Hawaii, 1977). The papers often printed party resolutions, minutes, and announcements. See also Lee, *The United States and the Division of Korea, 1945*, 21–58.

21. Cumings, *The Origins of the Korean War*, I, 81–91.

22. Col. Kenneth C. Strother, USA (Ret.), "The Occupation of Korea, September–December," unpublished history, 1984, Strother Papers, U.S. Army Military History Institute (USAMHI).

Maj. Gen. Sugai Toshimoro, IJA, principal operations officer for the Japanese forces in Korea, 17th Area Army, proved especially helpful in advising the Americans; he reported that the People's Government was a Russian creation.

23. XXIV Corps, FO 55, 1 September 1945, copy in XXIV Corps Historical File, Records of U.S. Theaters of War, World War II, RG 332, National Archives and Records Administration (NARA).

See also Donald W. Boose, Jr., "Portentous Sideshow: The Korean Occupation Decision," *Parameters* 25 (winter, 1995–1996): 112–29.

24. Capt. Robert K. Sawyer, "United States Military Advisory Group to the Republic of Korea," vol. 1, *1945–1949*, 4 vols., mss. History, 1953–1957, copies at USAMHI and 8th Army History Office, Yongsan U.S. Army Base, Seoul, ROK.

See also Lee Young-woo, "The United States and the Formation of the Republic of Korea Army, 1945–1950," Ph.D. dissertation, Duke University, 1984; Huh Nam-sung, "The Quest for a Bulwark of Anti-Communism: The Formation of the Republic of Korea Officer Corps and Its Political Socialization, 1945–1950," Ph.D. diss, The Ohio State University, 1987; and Allan R. Millett, "Captain James H. Hausman and the Formation of the Korean Army, 1945–1950," *Armed Forces and Society*

23 (summer, 1997): 503–39. I have also drawn on my own interviews and those conducted by John Toland and Huh Nam-sung with Generals Paik Sun-yup, Kang Mun-bong, Chung Il-kwon, Yu Jae-hung, Min Ki-sik, Kang Yoon-hoon, Lim Sun-ha, Kim Ung-soo, and Lee Chi-op. I have had access to General Lee Chi-op's mss., "The Korean Army Founders Association," 2000, personality sketches of the first 110 officers commissioned in the Korean Constabulary, part of a forthcoming memoir.

25. "Korea," Annex B, Military Intelligence Division (MID), War Department General Staff (WDGS), *Review of Far East*, 28 January 1946 [Secret], author's possession. The *RFE* ceased publication the next month, a serious loss of analysis. See also Central Intelligence Group, Situation Reports, No. 2, *Korea* (1947), Intelligence Files, President's Secretary's Files, Harry S. Truman Papers.

26. Quoted in Lee, *The United States and the Division of Korea*, 229.

27. Statistical Research Division, Office of Administration, Military Government, USAMGIK, "History of United States Military Government in Korea," September 1945–June 1946," 2 vols., Eighth Army Historical Files, HO, Eighth Army, Yongsan.

28. Joungwon Kim, *Divided Korea: The Politics of Development, 1945–1972* (Cambridge, Mass.: Harvard University Press, 1975), 86–114; Nam, *North Korean Communist Leadership*, 26–83.

29. Transcript, interviews, Maj. Gen. A. E. Brown with Korean political leaders, 5–7 March 1947, General Thomas W. Herren Papers, USAMHI.

HQ, Far East Command, "History of the U.S. Army Forces in Korea," 1947, copy in HO, Eighth Army, Yongsan. The author was Col. Frederick P. Todd, AUS, a professional historian.

Rhee made himself especially useful by halting (by his account) a potential "coup" by Shin Ik-hui and Yi Pom-sok. USAMGIK officers thought Rhee had invited the threat.

30. "An Ho-sang" and "Yi Pom-sok" in Matray, ed., *Historical Dictionary of the Korean War*, 17–18, 538–39.

31. AC/S, G-2, HQ, 6th InfDiv, "Kongsang Communist Uprising of October 1946," 1 December 1946, File 720.009-2, HO, Eighth Army; AC/S, G-2, HQ, Sixth InfDiv, "Cholla-South Communist Uprising of November 1946," 31 December 1946, File 720.009-1, HO, Eighth Army; n.a., "The Quasi-Revolt of October, 1946" in "History of the U.S. Army Forces in Korea," cited above.

32. HQ, USAFIK, "The Joint Commission on Korea," 1948, General A. E. Brown Papers, USAMHI; notes and transcript of conference, Generals Hodge and Brown with General Albert C. Wedemeyer, USA, 27 August 1947, Brown Papers; USAFIK/USAMGIK, National Economic Board, "South Korean Interim Government Activities," no. 27, December 1947, RG 9, MacArthur Papers.

The National Economic Board (U.S.-Korean) was USAMGIK's analytic agency and produced reports superior to those of the intelligence agencies.

33. Interview with Maj. Gen. Lim Sun-ha, ROKA (Ret.), Seoul, ROK, August 2000. General Lim served as the Constabulary adjutant and G-1, 1946–1947. His account is confirmed by Maj. Gen. Kim Ung-soo, ROKA (Ret.), a retired professor at Catholic University.

34. Oliver, *Syngman Rhee and American Involvement in Korea,* 119–39; Yim, *My Forty Year Fight for Korea,* 245–76; General Assembly, UNO, *First Part of the Report of the United Nations Temporary Commission on Korea,* 3 vols. (Lake Success, N.Y.: United Nations Organization, 1948) and *Second Part of the Report of the United Nations Temporary Commission on Korea,* 2 vols. (Paris: United Nations Organization, 1948); Matray, *The Reluctant Crusade,* 99–150. In 1949 UNTCOK dropped "temporary," but I have not to avoid confusion.

35. Suh, *Kim Il Sung,* 74–105.

The public face of North Korean Communism, 1946–1950, may be found in Kim Il-sung, *Selected Works,* 6 vols. (Pyongyang, DPRK: Foreign Language Publishing House, 1971–1972), I, 68–203, a collection of Kim's speeches to varied party audiences.

36. Kathryn Weathersby, ed. and trans., "Korea, 1949–1950: To Attack or Not to Attack? Stalin, Kim Il Sung, and the Prelude to War," *Cold War International History Project Bulletin* no.5 (Washington, D.C., spring 1995): 1–9, seven documents on USSR-DPRK communications about strategy and defense cooperation, 1949–1950.

37. The best analysis of Korean electoral politics in the Rhee era is Donald S. Macdonald, "Korea and the Ballot: The International Dimension in Korean Political Development as seen in Elections," Ph.D. diss., MIT, 1977. Dr. Macdonald came to Korea in 1945 as a military government officer and stayed as a foreign service officer and until his death became one of America's premier Koreanists. The best source of reliable data and information on Korean politics, 1948–1950, is the monthly reports of the National Economic Board, MacArthur Papers. See also HQ USAFIK, "Summary and Conclusions: Technical Report on Elections of 10 May 1948," May 1948, Herren Papers.

38. National Economic Board, reports, "South Korean Interim Government Activities," March–August 1948, Nos. 30–34, covering KNP and Constabulary activities in detail; Colonel Rothwell H. Brown, USA, "Report of Activities on Cheju-do Island, 22 May 1948 to 30 June 1948," Rothwell H. Brown (Interim governor of Cheju-do and CO, 20th Infantry) Papers, USAMHI; HQ, USAFIK, "The Police and National Events, 1947–1948," vol. 2 in "History of USAFIK," previously cited; John Merrill, "The Cheju-do Rebellion," *Journal of Korean Studies* 2 (1980): 139–97.

39. My reconstruction of the partisan war is based on two document collections: HQ, USAFIK, G-2 Periodic [Daily] Reports [1948.12.13–1949.6.17], reprints of the original USAFIK reports, USAFIK Command Records, RG 338, published by the Institute of Asian Cultural Studies, Hollym University Press, 1989, and HQ PMAG and KMAG, weekly reports, July–December 1948, copies in archives, Korean Institute of Military History, Seoul, ROK. Additional sources are Capt. James H. Hausman, "History of Rebellion, 14th Constabulary Regt.," November 1948, James H. Hausman Papers, Korea Institute, Harvard University; G-2, HQ, HSAFIK, "History of the Rebellion of the Korean Constabulary at Yosu and Taegu, Korea," 10 November 1948, provided by Col. J.W. Finley, USA (Ret.), 1995–1996; 971st CIC Detachment, "Annual Progress Report 1948," December 1948, Unit Historical File and Occupied Areas Reports, 1948–1954, Records of the Adjutant General's Office, RG 407.

The only careful printed account is John Merrill, *Korea: The Peninsular Origins of the War* (Newark: University of Delaware Press, 1989).

40. Interviews with Colonel Hausman and General Paik Sun-yup; semiannual reports, USMAG to ROK, December 1949 and June 1950, copies in archives, KIMH; Col. W.H.S. Wright [Deputy Cmdr., KMAG] to Maj. Gen. C. L. Mullins Jr., 28 July 1949, Colonel Jay D. Vanderpool Papers, USAMHI; Merrill, *Korea*, 130–67.

41. Radiograms, Chief KMAG to CINCFE (General Douglas MacArthur), July 1949–June 1950, KMAG Files, RG 9, MacArthur Papers; Soviet documents, Nos. 2–5, 3–24 September 1949, in Weathersby, "Korea, 1949–1950," previously cited; Kim Kook-hoon, "The North Korean People's Army: Its Rise and Fall, 1945–1950," Ph.D. diss., University of London, 1989; MIS, G/S, FECOM, "History of the North Korean Army," July 1952, File 330.008, HO, Eighth Army.

Both Ambassador John J. Muccio and Brig. Gen. William L. Roberts, USA, Chief KMAG, kept General MacArthur fully informed on Korean affairs.

42. Docs. 6 and 7, Shtykov to Vyshinsky, 19 January 1950, and Stalin to Shtykov, 30 January 1950 in Weathersby, "Korea, 1959–1950," previously cited; KMAG Semi-annual Report, 1950, previously cited; Kathryn Weathersby, ed. and trans., "New Russian Documents on the Korean War," CWIHP *Bulletin* Nos. 6–7 (winter 1995–1996) 30–35, which provides thirteen documents (telegrams and messages), 31 January–25 April 1950 between Stalin or his representatives with Kim Il-sung and Ambassador Terenti F. Shtykov; appendices 3–10 on DPRK-USSR and ROK-US estimates on arms transfers and material readiness, Korean People's Army and the ROK Army, 1950, provided by Dr. Alexandre Mansourov from his forthcoming book.

43. Kelly C. Jordan, "Three Armies in Korea: The Combat Effective-

ness of the United States Eighth Army in Korea, July 1950–June 1952," Ph.D., diss., The Ohio State University, 1999.

44. Syngman Rhee to Gen. Douglas MacArthur, 22 May 1949, MacArthur Papers.

45. The basic American position on Korea until the spring of 1950 is best expressed in 9th Meeting, National Security Council, 2 April 1948, memo, "Consideration of SANACC 176/39, Korea Policy," a memo that became NSC 8, "The Position of the United States with Respect to Korea," 2 April 1948 and revised as NSC 8/1 and 8/2 in 1949. Copy in President's Secretary's Files, Truman Papers. The American relationship with Syngman Rhee is outlined in Lt. Gen. John R. Hodge, USA, to William Randolph Hearst, January 1948, CG USAFIK Office Files, USAFIK Records, RG 332. The erratic course of U.S. aid to Korea before June 1950 is summarized in John H. Ohly, "Steps in United States Military Activities as an Aid to the Republic of Korea," 25 June 1950, and memo, W. Galbraith to J. H. Ohly, "Acquisition by the Republic of Korea of Military Equipment on a Reimburseable Basis under Section 408(a) of MDAA," 27 June 1950, John H. Ohly Papers, Truman Library; OSD, Memorandum for the JCS, "Additional Military Assistance to Korea," 26 May 1950, JCS 1950 Geographic File and CCS 383.21 (Korea), Records of the Joint Chiefs of Staff, RG 218; Secretary of State Dean Acheson to Charles Ross, 20 January 1950, "Korean War" Collection, President's Secretary's Files, Truman Papers.

The "Mutual Defense Program" Subject file, White House Confidential Files, Truman Papers, contains many documents on Korea.

46. Cumings, *Origins of the Korean War*, II, 466–507.

47. Shytkov to Comrade Zakharov, 26 June 1950, Doc. 14 in Weathersby, "New Russian Documents," previously cited.

48. The overview of the war I have used MIS, G/S, GHQ, United Nations Command, "One Year in Korea: A Summary, 25 June 1950–25 June 1951," and HQ, US 8th Army, transcript, "Year-End Tactical Briefing," 25 December 1952, copies in Gen. James Van Fleet Papers, George C. Marshall Library, Lexington, Virginia. The experience of the Republic of Korea may be found in Korean Institute of Military History, *The Korean War*, 3 vols. (Seoul, ROK: Ministry of National Defense, 1997–1999).

I have used Evgeniy P. Bajanov and Natalia Bajanova, "The Korean Conflict, 1950–1953," 1998, Institute for Contemporary Problems, Russian Foreign Ministry for the Soviet perspective.

49. The most complete set of documents on the crisis of 1952 is in Part II, "May 1–July 14, 1952: The South Korean Political Crisis and Third Party Approaches to End the War," in John P. Glennon, ed., for the Office of the Historian, Department of State, *Foreign Relations of the United States, 1952–1954*, vol XV, *Korea* (Washington, D.C., 1984) Pt. 1,

187–408. Macdonald, "Korea and the Ballot," covers the two 1952 elections in detail. Documentation that does not appear in *FRUS* may be found in File 47, "The Political Crisis in Korea, 1952," in the Special State-Defense Korean War Subject Files, Truman Papers.

50. S. Rhee to H. S. Truman, 21 March 1951, "Political Crisis" File, Truman Papers; memo, Muccio conversation with Rhee, 12 February 1952, *FRUS 1952–1954*, XV, 1, 47–50; S. Rhee to H. S. Truman, 25 June 1952, Ibid., 354–55; AC/S, G-5 (Civil Affairs) HQ UNC, papers, briefings and conference notes, Unified Command Mission to the ROK, Tokyo, 9–12 April 1952, Herren Papers; Syngman Rhee to Gen. M. B. Ridgway, 16 January 1952, CINCFE Confidential Files, Matthew B. Ridgway Papers, USAMHI.

51. Deputy Assistant Secretary of State to Secretary of State, 2 June 1952 *FRUS 1952–1954*, XV, 1, 281–85; Lt. Gen. Lee Chong-chan to Gen. J. A. Van Fleet, 25 May 1952, Van Fleet Papers.

The crisis may be followed in detail in CIA, daily Korean summaries, April–August 1952, President's Secretary's Files (Intelligence), Truman Papers.

The UN perspective (opposing Rhee) is found in United Nations Commission for the Unification and Reconstruction of Korea (UNCURK), "Report" to Seventh Regular Session, General Assembly, from Pusan, ROK, August 1952, File 90/33, Van Fleet Papers.

52. Full text, NSC 147, "Analysis of Possible Courses of Action in Korea," 2 April 1953, NSA with abridged NSC 147 reprinted in *FRUS: Korea, 1952–1954XV*, 383–57 with excerpts for NIE-80 (pp. 865–77) and SE-41 (pp. 886–92), supporting intelligence assessments of 3 and 8 April. The Eisenhower quote and discussion are in memorandum of discussion, 139th Meeting, NSC, 8 April 1953, White House Office, National Security Council Papers, 1948–1961, Whitman File: ANSC Series," Eisenhower Papers, Eisenhower Library, also excerpted in *FRUS: Korea: 1952–1954, XV*, 838–57.

Deputy Assistant Secretary of State (Far Eastern Affairs) to Secretary of State, 8 April 1953, and memorandum of conversation, "Korean Armistice Developments" 8 April 1953, *FRUS: Korea, 1952–1954, XV*, 896–900; Syngman Rhee to James Van Fleet, 25 May 1953, Van Fleet Papers; Gen. Paik Sun Yup, *From Pusan to Panmunjom* (Washington, D.C.: Brassey's, 1992), 214–34; Amb. Briggs to Deptartment of State, 15 April 1953, *FRUS: Korea, 1952–1954, XV*, 910–12.

Memo, HQ, UNC, "ROK Opposition to Armistice," General Mark W. Clark Papers, The Citadel Archives and Museum. The critical phase of the armistice negotiations and Chinese campaign of 1953 is described in detail in United Nations Command Reports No. 55 (October 1952) to No. 73 (July 1953), Clark Papers.

For secondary accounts, see John Kotch, "The Origins of the American Security Commitment to Korea," in Bruce Cumings, ed., *Child of Conflict: The Korean-American Relationship, 1943–1953* (Seattle: University of Washington Press, 1983), 239–59; and Edward C. Keefer, "President Dwight D. Eisenhower and the End of the Korean War," *Diplomatic History* 10 (summer 1986): 279–89.

On the truce negotiations, see Sydney D. Bailey, *The Korean Armistice* (New York: St. Martin's Press, 1992).

53. Suh, *Kim Il Sung*, 111–57.

54. Kim Il-sung, "Everything for the Postwar Rehabilitation and Development of the National Economy," 6th Plenary Meeting, Central Committee, Workers Party of Korea, 5 August 1953, *Selected Works* I, 413–62. For a review of the war's impact, see Akira Iriye, ed., "The Impact of the Korean War," a special issue of *The Journal of American-East Asian Relations* 2 (spring 1993).

Chapter 2

The Soviet Role in the Korean War

The State of Historical Knowledge

KATHRYN WEATHERSBY

The release of a substantial body of Russian archival documents on the Korean War, a gradual and halting process begun in late 1991, has brought a sea change in our knowledge of the Soviet role in that pivotal conflict. Until this evidence became available, the discussion of Moscow's part in the war focused almost exclusively on the question of the extent of Soviet involvement in the outbreak of the war on 25 June 1950. Most early accounts of the war assumed that North Korea could not have mounted the attack on South Korea without Moscow's support, but revisionist literature of the 1970s and 1980s challenged that assumption, drawing on American and British documents released in the 1970s. Since the trend of later scholarship was to depreciate the significance of the Soviet role in the war, the release of a large body of Russian records showing the centrality and the breadth of that role has caused a sharp change of course in the historical literature.

The new sources first became available in November 1991, when the archive of the Ministry of Foreign Affairs of the Russian Federation began to grant access to a large portion of its records on Soviet relations with North Korea. In September 1992, the Archive of the Central Committee of the Communist Party of the Soviet

Union opened its files on Korea, and in late 1992 President Boris Yeltsin furthered the process by ordering the relevant archives in Moscow to catalog and declassify their documents on the war in order to present a portion of them as a gift to South Korean President Kim Young Sam. As a result of Yeltsin's order, in the summer of 1994 the Archive of the Ministry of Defense released some of its vast holdings on the war. In December 1994, after President Yeltsin had presented to President Kim a collection of documents revealing high-level decision making on the war, largely from the Presidential Archive, the Foreign Ministry Archive granted access to photocopies of that collection. In 1995 a larger collection of approximately twice as many documents that were declassified from the Presidential Archive became available to researchers through an agreement between the Cold War International History Project of the Woodrow Wilson International Center for Scholars, the Korea Research Center of Columbia University, and the Diplomatic Academy of the Russian Foreign Ministry. In 1999, the director of the Diplomatic Academy published additional documents from the Presidential Archive that filled in key gaps left by the original collection. Other gaps were filled with the release in January 2000 of a collection of Presidential Archive documents on the war found in the Dmitri Volkogonov Papers held in the Library of Congress in Washington, D.C. In addition to the archival documents, a number of Russians and North Koreans who played military or political roles in the war have published their memoirs or granted extensive interviews.

This wealth of new material has shed much light on the central question of the extent of Soviet involvement in the outbreak of the war, in the process providing substantial documentation of the decision making behind the offensive and the chronology of its preparation. The Russian sources have also broadened the range of inquiry into the Soviet role. The extensive record of Moscow's relations with Pyongyang prior to the war, along with memoirs and interviews published over the last decade, makes it possible to examine in some detail the evolution of Soviet leader Joseph Stalin's aims regarding the Korean peninsula from 1945 to 1950. These documents also reveal the nature of the relationship between the North Korean leadership and the Soviet officials in Pyongyang and Moscow, laying the groundwork for an analysis of the Moscow/Pyongyang/Beijing alliance during the war.

For the wartime period, the Russian sources illuminate Stalin's response to the American intervention, to the early North Korean success and to its sudden reversal following the Inchon landing. Particularly when combined with Chinese sources, these new materials make possible a much more detailed analysis of the intra-bloc dynamics that shaped the Chinese intervention. The Russian sources also provide important evidence of Stalin's approach to the armistice negotiations, the Soviet Air Force participation in the war, and the role of the post-Stalin Soviet leadership in concluding the armistice. This essay will survey the main conclusions regarding the Soviet role in the war that have been drawn thus far on the basis of this new evidence, pointing out gaps in the documentation and identifying the most important questions that remain obscure.

The Outbreak of War

The North Korean attack on South Korea on 25 June 1950 was widely viewed at the time as a Soviet action that if left unchecked would lead to another world war. The desire to avoid repeating the disaster of the appeasement of Nazi aggression in the 1930s was so keen that sixteen nations agreed to intervene to repel the invasion, fighting under the flag of the United Nations. The question of Soviet responsibility for the attack has therefore rightfully been at the center of historical analysis of the war's origins. Writings on the war in the 1950s and 1960s, most prominently David Rees' history of the conflict,[1] followed policy makers in assuming that the Soviet client state in Korea had neither the physical means nor the political autonomy to launch a large-scale military offensive on its own. The journalist I. F. Stone challenged that view as early as 1952,[2] but until the release of Western documents in the 1970s prompted a new wave of literature on the war, his remained a minority view.

The most influential of the revisionist historians whose work dominated the field in the 1980s, Bruce Cumings, concluded on the basis of newly released American documents that although Kim Il Sung probably consulted with Stalin, he planned and carried out the attack largely on his own. Cumings also concluded that the North Korean action may in fact have been a response to a Southern attack, as the communist countries had always maintained, a provocation perhaps orchestrated by Chinese nationalists and by Americans eager to reassert a U.S. military presence in East Asia.

At any rate, he argued, the war can best be explained as a civil war, a continuation of the violent struggle between the political right and left in Korea that had begun with the collapse of Japanese colonial rule in 1945. In the late 1980s, Callum MacDonald and Gye-Dong Kim made similar arguments.[3]

A more centrist position was taken by John Merrill, Burton Kaufman, and Peter Lowe, who agreed with Cumings that the civil nature of the war had been inadequately appreciated but argued that the war must nonetheless be seen as both a great power struggle between the United States and the Soviet Union and a civil war between North and South Korea.[4] The strongest dissent from the growing revisionist consensus minimizing the Soviet role in the conflict came from William Stueck, who argued that the origins of the war must be found in Stalin's calculations of its probable benefits to his own international and domestic position. While North Korea may have been "an assertive pawn in an international chess game," Stueck concluded, "it was a pawn nonetheless."[5]

The documents from the Presidential Archive have resolved the question of Soviet responsibility for the decision to attack South Korea. They have also provided substantial evidence of Stalin's reasons for taking this step, but the important question of his rationale and of how this action related to the larger aims of Soviet foreign policy remains open to differing interpretations. The documents show that the idea of gaining control over South Korea by means of a conventional military offensive—as opposed to internal sabotage, which had been tried and failed—originated with Kim Il Sung. The North Korean leader first requested permission to invade the South in March 1949, during conversations with Stalin while the North Korean leader was in Moscow to conclude a formal alliance following the establishment of the Democratic People's Republic of Korea (DPRK). At that time Stalin refused permission, informing Kim Il Sung that while he should be prepared to counterattack in case of an invasion from the South, he must not mount an offensive.[6]

The records of the Soviet Foreign Ministry and Central Committee of the Communist Party of the Soviet Union make abundantly clear why North Korea could not attack the South on its own. Because Moscow had brought its occupation zone in Korea into the Soviet economic system, severing its ties with the rest of Korea, Japan, and Manchuria, and because Korea had been economically devastated by Japanese colonial rule and Tokyo's wartime exactions, the new state in the North was profoundly dependent on economic support from the Soviet Union. Except for very limited trade with Hong Kong and two Manchurian ports, in the period prior to the Korean War the Soviet Union was the only source of supply and the only market for North Korean goods. Moreover, because Japan had permitted only a small number of Koreans to gain higher education or management experience and most of those had fled to the South to avoid persecution as Japanese collaborators, North Korea was dependent on the Soviet Union for the technical expertise it needed to manage its economy. Foreign Ministry files are filled with requests from Kim Il Sung for technical advisers to train his new administration in everything from railroads to banking to health care.[7] Cumings argues that China always offered an alternative source of support to North Korea, but the Soviet and Chinese sources show that prior to the war this interaction was limited, as Sergei Goncharov, John Lewis, and Xue Litai emphasize as well.[8] In any case, in the early years of the People's Republic, the Chinese were themselves dependent on the Soviet Union for their economic and military development.[9]

In addition to its physical reliance on the Soviet Union, Kim Il Sung's government was constrained by its political dependence on Moscow. With little support base of his own within Korea, Kim Il Sung faced challenges to his leadership from Communist party leaders who had remained in Korea and from those who had returned there from China. Because Kim owed his position solely to Moscow's patronage, he could not afford to flout Stalin's wishes. It was also natural that he would depend on the Soviet Union for guidance in building his new socialist state. Most importantly, perhaps, for a young communist leader of the late 1940s, Stalin was an awesome and fearsome figure. Although in his later years Kim attained considerable stature of his own, in 1949 and 1950 the inexperienced North Korean leader could hardly have contemplated taking a major step without Stalin's approval.

In any case, the documents are clear that it was Stalin who made the decision about whether or not to invade South Korea. In August 1949, Kim Il Sung requested permission a second time and was again refused. In January 1950, he pleaded for an audience with Stalin to discuss the possibility once more, particularly in light of the recent victory of the Chinese Communist Party (CCP).[10] At the end of that month Stalin informed Kim that he would, at last, "help him in this matter." This decision was taken without consultation with Mao Zedong. Allegedly for security reasons, Stalin instructed Kim to limit knowledge of the plan to the highest officials within North Korea.[11]

In late March, Kim and Foreign Minister Pak Hon-yong traveled to Moscow for discussions, during which Stalin emphasized that Soviet troops would not intervene should North Korea need reinforcements. In such an eventuality, Kim would have to rely on China. Given this limitation, Stalin stipulated that the operation could go forward only if Kim secured Mao Zedong's approval. The North Korean leader accordingly traveled to Beijing in May, where Mao, after confirming Kim's message with Stalin, approved the plan.[12] Strictly speaking, therefore, the decision to invade was made by Mao as well as Stalin. However, there was in actuality little chance for Mao to disagree, given his recently concluded alliance with Moscow, and little likelihood as well, given his natural desire to support revolution in neighboring Korea. Mao's revolutionary enthusiasm and his calculation that the campaign could succeed were thus components of the war's origins, but the essential decision was nonetheless Stalin's. It was furthermore Soviet, not Chinese, advisers who planned the campaign and Soviet shipments of armaments and supplies that made it possible.

While the new Russian sources have resolved the question of Stalin's complicity in the attack on South Korea, a lively debate has arisen among Korean scholars over how to weigh the relative responsibility of Stalin and Kim Il Sung. In the most comprehensive history of the war's origins thus far produced in South Korea, Park Myung Lim concludes that Kim should be seen as the initiator and Stalin the facilitator.[13] Soh Jin-Chull, on the other hand, argues that Stalin was the sole initiator.[14] Kim Yongho agrees, concluding that Stalin's rollback policy in Korea should be seen as the "efficient cause" of the war.[15] Lee Wan-bum adopts a middle position, arguing that because both North Korea and the Soviet Union were indispensable actors in the outbreak of the Korean War, they should be seen as co-initiators.[16]

Because the Western response to the attack on South Korea, and hence the escalation of the war, resulted not only from the presumption of Soviet support for the action but also from the perception that the attack signaled a new Soviet willingness to use military force to bring additional territory under Soviet control, the question of Stalin's rationale in approving the offensive has been central to analyses of the war. Interpretations of his reasoning have varied widely. Writing when only a small number of Soviet documents had become available, Goncharov, Lewis, and Xue concluded that Stalin took the decision in order to widen his buffer zone in the East, to acquire political leverage over Japan and perhaps a springboard for an attack against it, to test American resolve and capabilities, and to divert American power away from Europe.[17] Drawing on many of the Russian documentary sources along with an extensive examination of the international context of the war, Stueck argues that the decision was taken to shore up Stalin's hold on power at home, to strengthen his influence over communist governments on the Soviet periphery, particularly China's, and to draw American attention and resources away from Europe.[18]

The Russian documents have shed considerable light on Stalin's rationale, but the question remains open to interpretation. The archival sources reveal that Stalin viewed Korea in light of the long-term security threat he believed the Soviet Union faced from Japan. Because he assumed that Japan would eventually rearm and again threaten the Soviet Far East, using the Korean peninsula as its bridgehead, he considered it essential to ensure that the entire peninsula be under the control of a government "friendly" to the Soviet Union. Washington's lenient occupation policy in Japan, its support for a rightist government in Seoul, and its failure to eradicate remnants of Japanese rule from South Korea led him to conclude that an American-backed government in Seoul would at some point support a Japanese or Japanese/American attack on the Soviet Far East.

Stalin's anxieties on this score were heightened in the spring of 1949, when he received reports of South Korean forays into DPRK territory. Erroneously assuming that the South Korean actions reflected American intentions, Stalin reached the false conclusion that the imminent withdrawal of U.S. forces from South Korea was designed to free the southerners to invade the North. The issue was not, therefore, whether to support Kim Il Sung's fervent desire to gain control over the remainder of the peninsula, but when and how to do so without risking war with the United States. While Stalin seemed to assume that the Soviet Union would eventually fight a war with the United States, he wanted above all to avoid doing so until the USSR was prepared to win it.[19]

The key factor in the decision for war was therefore Stalin's assessment of whether an attack on the South would prompt the Americans to intervene. In the fall of 1949, after U.S. troops had withdrawn from the peninsula and no attack on the North had ensued, he was willing to consider Kim's request for a limited campaign against the South. In the end, however, he concluded that since the DPRK lacked clear military superiority over the Republic of Korea and the partisan movement in the South was insufficiently strong, the North Koreans would be unable to win a quick victory. The Americans would thus have time to intervene.

In late January 1950, Stalin concluded that the international environment had changed in such a way as to make it possible to proceed with an invasion of South Korea. He explained his reasoning to Kim Il Sung and Pak Hon-yong while they were in Moscow in April, in a series of three conversations. Stalin's explanations to the North Korean leaders may not, of course, have been an exhaustive account of his thinking. For example, his omission of European factors may have reflected the junior standing of the Koreans rather than any lack of linkage between the two fronts in Stalin's thinking. It is unlikely, however, that he misled Kim and Pak, because he had no reason to do so and his explanation of the "changed international situation" is consistent with other evidence.

The first element of the changed international situation, Stalin explained, was the victory of the Chinese Communist Party, which was important for two reasons. First, Chinese troops were now available to fight in Korea, if necessary. Second, giving some validity to the "who lost China" debate within the United States, Stalin explained that the CCP victory in China proved that the United States was weak. Thus, because the Americans had not fought to prevent a Communist victory in China, they would not fight for the smaller prize of Korea. Moreover, because the People's Republic of China (PRC) and the USSR had concluded a defensive alliance, the Americans would be even more hesitant to challenge the communists in Asia. In an apparent reference to the U.S. security policy statement NSC 48, whose substance he was in a position to know through the British spy Donald McLean, and from public statements such as Secretary of State Dean Acheson's National Press Club speech of 12 January, Stalin told Kim and Pak that "according to information coming from the United States, it really is so. The prevailing mood is not to interfere." The final component of the changed situation was the Soviet possession of the atomic bomb and the "solidification" of the military position of North Korea.[20]

Despite these indications that the climate was at last favorable for an attack on South Korea, Stalin nonetheless remained worried about a possible American intervention. He emphasized that the war must be won quickly so that the United States would not have time to intervene. He also made it clear to the Koreans that the Soviet Union would not participate directly in the war, especially if the United States sent troops to Korea. Moscow would provide the necessary advisers, weapons, and supplies, but Kim would have to rely on Beijing if he needed additional troops.

Were Western political leaders therefore correct to view the North Korean attack as constituting a new level of aggression that if not resisted would have emboldened Stalin to attack other countries as well? The question of whether Stalin's foreign policy was defensive or offensive has been central to the debate over the origins of the cold war as a whole, and the interpretive positions on his Korean decision generally follow those of the larger debate. Alexandre Mansourov argues for a defensive motivation, emphasizing Stalin's and Mao's anxieties regarding the supposed threat of an attack on North Korea. He concludes that both Stalin and Mao decided to initiate hostilities in Korea in the summer of 1950 because they believed that the window of opportunity for the spread of communist revolution in Korea that had been opened in 1945 would soon close as the United States shifted to a policy of rollback. This insecurity made them susceptible to pressure from Kim Il Sung, who played the two powers' interests in the peninsula off one another, highlighted "the reputational cost they would have to pay if they did not vigorously support the cause of communist-led Korean unification," and persuaded them in the spring of 1950 that "offense had gained a strategic advantage over defense, in contrast to the situation in 1949."[21]

While Stalin's insecurity was indeed at the root of his decision to attack, I would argue that this action was in essence aggressive. His insecurity was of such depth and nature that no action by the United States could have persuaded him that the Soviet Union was tolerably secure.[22] Believing that he must defend against future attacks by constantly expanding the territory under his control, he adopted what was in essence an offensive position. Those contemporaries who believed that he was testing American resolve preparatory to taking action elsewhere were mistaken; he took the action in Korea only because he believed the United States would not intervene. However, even though he did not intend the invasion to be a test of resolve, it in fact became one. Just as he had concluded from American non-intervention in China that he had an opportunity to advance in Korea, had the United States and its allies not intervened in Korea, he would have drawn the same conclusion about opportunities elsewhere.

Regardless of the interpretation placed on Stalin's rationale, however, the possibility of American intervention clearly continued to worry him as the invasion date drew near. On 20 June he agreed to allow the Korean People's Army to use Soviet ships for amphibious landings, but he refused to allow Soviet personnel on the ships "because it may give the adversary a pretext for interference by the USA."[23] Stalin's fear that the war might not be won quickly enough to avoid U.S. intervention led him to modify the invasion plan on 21 June in such a way as to make such intervention far more likely. The initial plan was to deploy the Korean People's Army (KPA) along the entire border but begin the attack only on the Ongjin Peninsula in order to disguise who initiated the hostilities. After the South counterattacked on Ongjin, the troops would move across the rest of the border, claiming they were responding to ROK aggression. However, when told on 21 June that the South had learned of the invasion plan and was reinforcing its defenses in the area of Ongjin, Stalin agreed with Kim Il Sung's suggestion to attack along the entire border at once. Whatever merits this decision may have had on a purely military basis, it reflected a disastrous misapprehension of how a World War II–style attack across the South Korean border would be perceived by most of the world—a lack of sensitivity all the more striking since Stalin had himself been among the chief victims of a German surprise attack.

Stalin's failure to break the Soviet boycott of the United Nations Security Council in time to block its resolutions to send troops to defend South Korea has long puzzled historians of the war. Andrei Gromyko recorded in his memoirs that he had recommended to Stalin that the Soviet representative return to the Security Council in order to veto such a vote, but Stalin rejected the idea—a decision Gromyko describes as having been "guided for once by emotion."[24] Cumings concludes that Gromyko's report suggests that the Soviets did not have advance knowledge of the attack.[25] Goncharov,

Lewis, and Xue offer two possible explanations—either that Stalin believed that the war would still be won quickly and the UN resolution would therefore be irrelevant, and/or that anticipating eventual Chinese intervention, he calculated that he could avoid having the Sino-Soviet mutual defense pact invoked if U.S. forces fought under the UN, rather than the American, flag.[26] Vojtech Mastny notes that Stalin explained to the Czechoslovak Communist leader Klement Gottwald in August 1950 that Soviet representatives could not return to the Security Council because Moscow had to maintain the boycott to protest the UN exclusion of the government of the PRC from the UN.[27]

The Russian archival sources do not provide direct evidence of Stalin's reasons for failing to return to the UN. They do suggest, however, that two reasons were paramount. First, because Stalin was counting on Chinese intervention should North Korea run into difficulty and because the alliance with Beijing was important to him for many reasons, he would be hesitant to damage his relations with the Chinese by ending the UN boycott. Second, and more importantly, because Stalin's strategy was to present the North Korean action as strictly independent of the Soviet Union, his initial reaction to the American intervention was to distance Moscow from the events in Korea. A dramatic return to the UN in time to veto the Security Council vote would have vividly connected the Soviet Union with the attack on South Korea. Besides, Stalin's main concern was whether the United States would intervene in Korea; judging from his correspondence with his allies and with his representatives in the field, he cared little about whether the Americans were fighting under the UN flag or their own.[28]

Stalin and the Chinese Intervention

There has long been much speculation about the dynamics within the Moscow/Beijing/Pyongyang alliance as the three states faced the threat of a North Korean defeat following the Inchon landing of 15 September. Adam Ulam wondered how Stalin persuaded Mao to pay such a high price to solve a problem Moscow had created, concluding that the main factor must have been the Soviet Union's dominant position in world communism.[29] Using the flood of Chinese memoir accounts that became available in the late 1980s and early 1990s, Goncharov, Lewis, and Xue outlined Stalin's attempts to prod the Chinese into intervening and his alleged reneging on his promise to provide air cover for Chinese troops. They conclude that Stalin remained firm in his determination not to face the United States in Korea and viewed Beijing's delay in committing its forces as a deliberate ploy to force a more direct Soviet participation in the war.[30] Looking at the broader international context, Stueck argued that the determination to avoid a direct confrontation with the Soviet Union shown by President Harry S. Truman and his West European allies since the outbreak of the war diminished Stalin's fear of such a confrontation because it showed the Western alliance to be weak militarily and fragile politically. As a result, the Soviet leader was confident enough to take the risks associated with a Sino-American conflict, particularly because it would tie down a large number of U.S. forces in Asia and place a serious strain on North Atlantic Treaty Organization (NATO).[31]

The Russian documentary sources provide for the first time solid evidence of the complex negotiations that preceeded the Chinese entry into the war. They reveal the extent of Stalin's personal involvement in managing the crisis, his manner of interacting with the North Koreans and the Chinese, the nature of the relations between the two junior partners, and the differing goals each ally had in Korea. On some key points, the documentary sources contradict Chinese memoirs and published documents, showing Stalin to have been more consistent and the Chinese to have been more vacillating than they had been represented in recent accounts based on the Chinese sources.

The Russian documents reveal that as early as the first week of July, Stalin began to encourage the Chinese leadership to prepare for possible entry into the war. He approved Beijing's proposal to move nine divisions to the Korean border, promising to send a division of fighter planes to provide air cover for those units, and then prodded the Chinese to proceed with the deployment. Holding to the division of responsibilities he had laid out in April, he attempted to minimize Soviet air involvement, informing Beijing that Soviet pilots would train Chinese airmen to take over their mission within two to three months, after which the Soviet Air Force equipment would be transferred to China.[32]

The Russian record also shows that the allies failed to prepare for the contingency of Chinese entry into the war. Mao Zedong agreed in May 1950 to send troops to North Korea if necessary, but no preparations for such assistance were made before the invasion was launched. Soviet military advisers had not been dispatched to Northeast China, Beijing had no military representative in Korea, and Stalin had not informed Mao of the date of the invasion or any of the operational plans, allegedly to safeguard secrecy. Blaming Mao for this absence of alliance infrastructure, Stalin brusquely informed him on 8 July that he should immediately send a military representative to Korea in order to have a reliable communications channel between Pyongyang and Beijing.[33] None was in place by the time of the Inchon landing, however, leaving the Chinese with no information on the landing other than what was reported in Western newspapers or over Pyongyang radio.[34] Soviet support for the defense of Northeast China was also slow to arrive. The Soviet 151st Fighter Air Division reached Manchuria by 10 August,[35] and it was only late in that month that Stalin informed Beijing that Soviet advisers in anti-aircraft defense and air operations would be sent to China, as Beijing had requested.

As Alexandre Mansourov has discussed, in the wake of the Inchon landing Stalin began personally to manage the operations in Korea. On 18 September he told Kim Il Sung to move four divisions from the Pusan area to Seoul and ordered the Soviet Defense Minister, Marshal A. M.Vasilevsky, urgently to develop a plan for providing air cover for Pyongyang with fighter squadrons based in the Soviet Maritime Province. As the military situation deteriorated, Stalin dispatched to Korea the Deputy Chief of the General Staff of the Soviet Army, General M. V. Zakharov, to order Kim Il Sung to redeploy all his forces to defend Seoul and pressed Vasilevsky to set up an air defense system around Pyongyang.[36]

When Seoul fell to the rapidly advancing UN and Republic of Korea (ROK) forces on 26 September, Stalin blamed the debacle on the KPA's tactical mistakes and poor command and control, but his main fury was directed against the Soviet military advisers in Korea. In a Politburo resolution of 27 September he excoriated them for failing to implement orders for the withdrawal of four divisions to Seoul, for using tanks without preliminary artillery strikes and for "strategic illiteracy" and "incompetence in intelligence matters" in failing to grasp the strategic significance of the landing at Inchon. He then issued guidelines for conducting the withdrawal of remaining forces to DPRK territory, while Zakharov oversaw the reorganization of the KPA's command and control structure.[37]

Stalin did not, however, call on Mao to provide his promised assistance until he received a request to do so from the North Koreans. Moreover, the North Koreans did not turn first to China, as the terms agreed to in April obliged them to do. Instead, on 29 September Kim Il Sung and Pak Hon-yong made a restrained appeal for direct Soviet intervention, explaining to "dear Iosif Vissarionovich" their desperate military situation and stating that "at the moment when enemy troops cross over the 38th parallel we will badly need direct military assistance from the Soviet Union." They immediately added, however, that "if for any reason this is impossible, please assist us by forming international volunteer units in China and other countries of the People's Democracy."[38] Kim and Pak, in their desperation, may have simply been turning to the more powerful of their two allies as the better guarantor of their survival. They may also have reflexively vetted their request through Stalin, since they had been doing so since 1945. The routing of the request may also, however, have reflected a reluctance to accept Chinese intervention in Korea because of the long history of Chinese interference in Korea, and/or because of Kim Il Sung's fear that Chinese intervention would strengthen the China-oriented faction within the Korean Communist Party that threatened his hold on power.

Stalin's hesitation in requesting Chinese intervention was consistent with the tone he took toward Beijing throughout the war, and was in sharp contrast to his blunt commands to the Koreans. Immediately after the Inchon landing he solicited the Chinese leadership's opinion regarding what should be done about the military situation in Korea and attempted to smooth over the awkward situation of Beijing's prior exclusion from the operational planning.[39] On 1 October, after receiving Kim's and Pak's request for direct intervention, he sent a delicately worded message to Mao Zedong and Zhou Enlai indirectly asking the Chinese to provide the assistance they had promised in May. After first blaming the disastrous situation on the Koreans' failure to follow Moscow's advice to withdraw their forces to Seoul, Stalin stated that "if in the current situation you consider it possible to send troops to assist the Koreans, then you should move at least five to six divisions toward the 38th parallel at once so as to give our Korean comrades an opportunity to organize combat reserves north of the 38th parallel under the cover of your troops. The Chinese divisions could be considered as volunteers, with Chinese in command at the head, of course." Making it clear that he was not again presenting Mao with a plan worked out in advance without his participation, he added that he had not informed and was not going to inform their "Korean friends" about this idea, but that he had no doubt "that they will be glad when they learn of it."[40] In his analysis of these documents, Mansourov concludes that Stalin offered Mao a power-sharing arrangement in exchange for shouldering so much of the burden of defending North Korea, thus signaling the end of the unilateral control Moscow had exercised in Korea since 1945.[41]

Mao's reply to Stalin's request has been a matter of contro-versy, because Chinese documents published in 1987 included a telegram informing Stalin that the PRC would send troops to Ko-rea. The Russian documents reveal, however, that a different tele-gram was actually sent to Moscow. On 2 October Mao replied to Stalin that after originally planning to send several divisions to North Korea, the leadership was now reconsidering the advisability of such action. The reasons cited were that their troops were poorly equipped in comparison to the Americans, that the intervention would ruin their plans for rebuilding their country after the long years of civil war, and that their intervention would likely lead to an open conflict between the United States and China, which might drag the Soviet Union into war as well. A final decision had not been taken, however; Mao stated that the leadership wished to send Zhou Enlai and Lin Biao to Stalin's vacation home for consulta-tions.[42]

Nikita Khrushchev later recalled that when Stalin discussed the situation with his top entourage, he was resigned to the demise of the North Korean regime. "So what? If Kim Il Sung fails, we are not going to participate with our troops. Let it be. Let the Ameri-cans be our neighbors in the Far East."[43] Stalin's telegram to Mao on 3 October, however, indicates that he went to considerable lengths to persuade the Chinese to intervene to prevent a North Korean defeat. He reminded Mao of the previous assurances of support given by "leading Chinese comrades" and of the risk that an Ameri-can-controlled Korea would provide a springboard for a future Japa-nese attack on China. He then boldly prodded Mao to intervene by claiming to be unconcerned about the risk of war with the United States. American actions in the war had shown that the USA is not ready for a major war, he argued, while Japan is not yet able to assist the Americans. Because China is backed by the Soviet Union, the United States will be forced to yield to the Chinese, abandoning Taiwan and its plans to conclude a separate peace with Japan and turn that country into its springboard in the Far East. He warned, however, that China "could not extract these concessions . . . without serious struggle and an imposing display of force." Stalin admitted that despite all these conditions, the United States might still be drawn into a major war, pulling China and the Soviet Union in as well. "Should we fear this?" he asked rhetorically. "In my opinion, we should not, because together we will be stronger than the USA and England, while the other European capitalist states (with the exception of Germany, which is unable to provide any assistance to the United States now), do not present serious military forces." Invoking Mao's greatest fear, he concluded that "if a war is inevitable, then let it be waged now, and not in a few years when Japanese militarism will be restored as an ally of the USA and when the USA and Japan will have a ready-made bridgehead on the continent in the form of the entire Korea run by Syngman Rhee."[44]

This sensational passage has often been quoted since its publication in 1996 in the *Cold War International History Project Bulletin*, but if taken out of context it can easily be misunderstood. Stalin's actions in October and November 1950 show that he had not abandoned the caution that had marked his approach to the possibility of a new world war. The recollections of Stalin's talks with Zhou Enlai on 9–10 October provided by two of the participants, Mao's interpreter Shi Zhe and a Soviet participant Nikolai Fedorenko—the only sources available to date—show Stalin continuing to argue that China could intervene without risking an American attack on Chinese territory and that preventing a North Korean defeat was essential for the PRC's own security.[45] But when Zhou did not yield to Stalin's pressure, the Soviet leader remained firm in his determination to avoid entering the war. Instead, he ordered Kim Il Sung to evacuate his troops from Korea. "Continuation of the resistance is hopeless," he wrote. "Chinese comrades refuse to get involved militarily. Under these circumstances you must prepare for total evacuation to China and/or the USSR."[46] This order was revoked the following day after Stalin received a telegram confirming that the Chinese would, after all, send their troops to Korea, but its issuance provides the clearest evidence of the Soviet leader's determination to avoid war with the United States at all cost.

A Chinese official who accompanied Zhou Enlai in his talks with Stalin later recalled that after the discussions ended with an apparent agreement on the terms of Chinese intervention, Stalin reneged on his promise to provide air cover for Chinese troops entering Korea, prompting Mao to suspend his decision to intervene.[47] On the basis of his interview with Fedorenko and other Soviet officials, Mansourov strongly rejects the Chinese account, arguing that Zhou Enlai intentionally misrepresented Stalin's statements in order to discourage Mao from intervening, believing it would not be in China's national interest to do so.[48]

The debate over whether Stalin at one point reneged on his promise to provide air cover remains unresolved, but documents released from the archive of the Russian Ministry of Defense provide more support for the Chinese account than for Mansourov's interpretation. As Mark O'Neill has discovered, throughout October, Stalin's order to the commander of the 151st Fighter Air Division stationed in Northeast China remained unchanged. Soviet aircraft and tanks sent to Manchuria were to be used only to defend Chinese industrial cities and to train Chinese crews; their use at the front and to cover troops and targets near the Chinese-Korean border was categorically forbidden. Repeated requests from the commander of the 151st Air Division to attack U.S. planes that violated Chinese airspace were turned down. It was only on 1 November, apparently in response to a UN attack on the airfield at Andong, on the Chinese side of the border, that Soviet MiG-15s were at last allowed to enter the war. O'Neill also notes that in October Stalin declined to protect Soviet, as well as Chinese, airspace. When two US F-80s strafed the Soviet Fifth Fleet's airbase at Sukhaya Rechka, less than twenty-five miles southwest of Vladivostok and sixty-six miles from the Soviet-Korean border, Stalin took no retaliatory measures. Of course, his actions in the field may not have conformed with his statements to Zhou Enlai, but the reality on the ground nonetheless suggests that the Chinese may well have had good reason to believe that Stalin was failing to deliver the air cover he had promised in July.[49]

The Soviet Air War and Supply Mission

Once Soviet pilots and ground air defense crews entered the war, their mission remained sharply limited. They were to prevent U.S.

bombers from destroying the bridges across the Yalu at Andong and the vital hydroelectric plant at Suiho. They were forbidden from flying over enemy-held territory or over the sea, in order to prevent their presence from being exposed in case they were shot down. This restriction was immensely frustrating to Soviet pilots, who were consequently unable to pursue attacking American jets, but the success of the Soviet Air Force in accomplishing its limited objective nonetheless played a critical role in the war. Not only were the US B-29s unable to destroy the railroad bridge between Andong and Sinuiju, but the MiG-15s proved to be effective enough against the B-29 that after their last and most pronounced victory on 23 October 1951, the UN Bomber Command was forced to abandon daylight operations in "MiG Alley." U.S. fighter-bombers finally succeeded in destroying the Suiho hydroelectric facility in the summer of 1952, but O'Neill concludes that the success of the Soviet Air Force in interdicting American bombers over the Sino-Korean border in the earlier stages of the war played a major role in persuading the Truman administration not to attempt to drop nuclear weapons on China.[50]

The Soviet Air Force contribution grew to substantial proportions over the course of the war. According to General Georgii Lobov, who commanded the 64th Fighter Aviation Corps—formed after the 28th and 50th Fighter Air Divisions were added to the 151st—approximately 70,000 Soviet pilots, technicians, and gunners served in the corps over the course of the war.[51] Stalin's priority, however, continued to be to transfer the burden of the air war to the Chinese and North Koreans as quickly as possible. Chinese pilots flew their first combat mission on 3 January 1951,[52] but Stalin was nonetheless dissatisfied at the pace of the training effort. In June 1951 he excoriated his military representative in China for apparently intending "to make professors rather than battle pilots out of the Chinese pilots. . . . If Russian pilots were trained during the war [World War II] in five to six months, then why is it impossible to complete the training of Chinese pilots in seven to eight months? . . . The Chinese troops will not fight without air cover. Therefore it is necessary to create more quickly a group of eight Chinese air fighter divisions and send them to the front. This is now your main task."[53] While there may have been some resentment among the Chinese military leadership of Stalin's eagerness to end his air engagement in Korea, the rapid construction by the Soviet Union of a modern air force, as well as a navy, for the PRC was a significant legacy of the Korean War.

In addition to providing military training and air defense, the Soviet Union provided the bulk of arms, ammunition, and supplies used by the communist allies throughout the war. According to Chinese records, Moscow sent enough arms for sixty-four infantry divisions and twenty-two air divisions as well as most of the replacement munitions.[54] The Russian documents released by the Presidential Archive include extensive correspondence between Mao and Stalin regarding the kind, quantity, shipment dates, and terms of payment for this materiel. It is noteworthy that Stalin and Mao themselves negotiated these agreements, and that their exchanges on this subject were a source of intra-alliance tension. The Chinese later resented the amount of money they were forced to pay to the Soviet Union for supplying the intervention after having been excluded from planning the initial campaign.[55]

Stalin and the Armistice Negotiations

The literature on the lengthy armistice negotiations that prolonged the war for two years has focused on the formation of the UN negotiating position, particularly the issue of POW repatriation, and on Washington's atomic diplomacy.[56] With the exception of Zhang Shu-guang's groundbreaking work on the Chinese role in the war, the Communist side has emerged only as reflected in the Western sources and only as related to the debates among Western policy makers and scholars. The Russian sources supplement the Chinese sources used by Zhang to provide a substantial documentary record of high-level decision making concerning the negotiations on the Communist side, illuminating particularly the question of Stalin's approach to a negotiated settlement of the war.

Once the Chinese People's Volunteers entered the war, Chinese commanders took over responsibility for the day-to-day management of the fighting. Although Stalin closely followed events on the ground, periodically intervening with specific military instructions, and his advisers continued to manage the North Korean contribution to the war, the locus of operational decision making shifted to China. Moscow retained greater control, however, over the diplomatic side of the war. Stalin solicited Mao's opinion, and to a lesser extent that of Kim Il Sung, on matters involving relations with outside powers, but, as was the case with regard to initiating the operation, the voice of the senior alliance partner dominated on matters involving negotiations to end the war.

In the wake of the American intervention, Stalin instructed his officials to respond positively to British and Indian peace overtures, but he did not seriously pursue the possibility of a negotiated settlement until the situation on the ground deteriorated following the Inchon landing. This initiative was quickly cut short, however, by the remarkable success of the Chinese in turning back the UN advance in November and December 1950. In January 1951, at the high point of the Chinese advance, Stalin agreed with the Chinese proposal to call for a cease-fire, but on terms that the United States would never accept.[57]

When the spring offensive of 1951 failed to push UN forces farther south and moreover resulted in very high casualties among Chinese and North Korean troops, the three allies finally agreed to pursue a negotiated settlement. Kim Il Sung was reluctant to abandon hope for a total victory, but Mao persuaded him of the need to adopt a new strategy. In meetings with Stalin on 13 June, Kim Il Sung and Mao's representative Gao Gang—who relayed and received messages from Mao via telegram—agreed with his plan to open armistice negotiations in order to avoid an enemy offensive until fall. The Chinese calculated that it would take two or three months to reinforce their position and be ready to make a new assault on enemy positions. The debate between hawks and doves in Washington over whether opening the armistice negotiations gave up an opportunity for the UN forces to push further north is thus brought to the fore by the new evidence. This issue had become less prominent in the 1970s and 1980s, as Western sources revealed the considerable opposition among the UN allies to a new northward offensive, rendering the question moot. However, whether or not the UN could have mounted a new offensive, the Russian sources suggest the hawks had good reason to argue against opening negotiations on the grounds that this would give the enemy time to build up its strength in order to resume the fight.

In August 1951 the Communist side suspended the negotiations after alleging that UN troops bombed and strafed the conference site, but the Russian sources show that Beijing did not wish a permanent rupture in the talks. Stalin also wished the negotiations to continue, but for different reasons. On 28 August he informed

Mao that he agreed with his opinion about the need to receive a satisfactory answer to the bombing incident before resuming the talks, but pressured him to maintain a hard line toward the negotiations, declaring that the Americans have a greater need to resume the talks. He rejected Mao's proposal to invite neutral states to participate as monitors and witnesses, because "the Americans will view it as [an indication] that the Chinese-Korean side has more need to quickly reach an agreement about an armistice than do the Americans." Making his point clear, he ended with the blunt message that if Mao agrees with such an [American] view, he must communicate this to Comrade Kim Il Sung.

Stalin continued to insist on a hard line toward the negotiations for the remainder of the war until his death in March 1953. The Russian sources provide no explicit explanation of his reasoning, but it appears that he considered it in the Soviet interests for the war to continue as long as there was no danger that UN troops would resume an advance into North Korea. The war tied down American forces, rendering the United States less likely to engage in military action in Europe; it drained American economic resources; and it caused political difficulties for the Truman administration. It also provided the Soviet Union with a superb opportunity to gather intelligence on U.S. military technology and organization and to inflame anti-American sentiment throughout Europe and Asia. Russian documents indicate that Stalin's main concern regarding the negotiations was to ensure that the Chinese/North Korean side not give an impression of weakness, as the benefits to the Soviet Union would accrue only if the war remained a stalemate.

By the fall of 1952, the Chinese were more eager to reach an armistice settlement, and the North Koreans had been ready for some months to negotiate an end to their suffering from the American bombardment. Stalin cavalierly dismissed Kim Il Sung's desire for peace, commenting that the North Koreans "have lost nothing but their casualties." With the Chinese, however, he was less blunt. In conversations with Zhou Enlai in August and September 1952 over a wide range of issues involving the alliance, the two leaders circled warily around the matter of a negotiated settlement in Korea, trying to avoid open disagreement without compromising their individual aims. Stalin framed the POW issue as a question of whether Mao would give in to the Americans and asserted that the

Americans are not capable of waging a large-scale war at all. "America cannot defeat little Korea. One must be firm when dealing with America. The Chinese comrades must know that if America does not lose this war, then China will never recapture Taiwan." The lengthy talks included many rounds of back and forth on the issue, without any agreement on a strategy for ending the war, which appeared to be Stalin's objective.

While Stalin's bombast about American weakness was designed primarily to pressure Zhou to hold firm in the negotiations, it also seems to have reflected a real shift in his attitude toward the danger of war with the United States. Romanian archives have revealed that in January 1951, at the high point of the Chinese success over the Americans, Stalin called the party leaders and defense ministers of his client states in Europe to a meeting in Moscow to order them to rearm speedily in light of the new international environment created by the American failure in Korea. "The opinion arose in recent times that the United States is an invincible power and is prepared to initiate a third world war," Stalin began. "As it turns out, however, not only is the U.S. unprepared to initiate a third world war, but it is unable even to cope with a small war such as the one in Korea. It is obvious that the U.S. needs several more years for preparation [for a third world war]." Predicting that the United States would remain bogged down in Asia for two to three years, creating "a very favorable circumstance for us," Stalin instructed the East Europeans to use this respite to create modern and powerful military forces in their countries. "China has created a better army than those of the People's Democracies. It is abnormal that you should have weak armies. This situation must be turned around." Promising to provide the necessary assistance, he explained that the East Europeans needed to arm themselves well because the imperialists "are in the habit of attacking unarmed or weakly armed countries in order to liquidate them, but they keep away from well armed countries."[58]

Within the Soviet Union itself, Stalin accelerated rearmament with conventional and nuclear weapons and created a psychological climate geared toward preparation for war.[59] According to Sergei Khrushchev, the son of Stalin's successor Nikita Khrushchev, the Soviet leader went so far as to order the building of airfields on Arctic Ocean ice to deploy 10,000 tactical bombers close to American territory. This impractical scheme was never carried out, but

Khrushchev states that 100,000 men were stationed in tents on the Chukotsk tundra in order to resist an invasion from Alaska.[60] The Russian archivist Oleg Naumov claims to have seen evidence in the archives—which he has not been allowed to make public—that in the spring of 1952 Stalin ordered the production of bombers capable of striking the northwestern parts of the United States and started preparations for an airborne as well as amphibious assault on Alaska.[61] Whatever war-making encouragement Washington's policy of limiting the war in Korea may have given Stalin, this effect did not outlast the dictator. But it does suggest that prolonging the war in Korea may have been a high priority for Stalin from early 1951 until his death.

The Allegations of Biological Weapons Use

Intriguing but very fragmentary evidence has emerged from the Presidential Archive regarding the extensive campaign the Soviet Union waged worldwide during the last year of the war accusing the United States of using biological weapons in Korea and China. The campaign met with considerable success. The charges were widely believed in China, North Korea, and Eastern Europe, and in Western Europe elicited protests strong enough to disrupt meetings of the rapidly evolving NATO. The Unites States categorically denied the charges and called for an international investigation, but because the United States was at that time developing biological weapons and had shielded the Japanese officers in charge of Tokyo's former biological weapons laboratory in Manchuria, the question remained unresolved. Jon Halliday and Gavan McCormack, writing in the 1980s, gave credence to the charges,[62] but most scholars considered the evidence inconclusive. Stephen Endicott and Edward Hagerman brought the issue to the fore in 1999, with their book arguing on the basis of U.S. archival records that the United States had, in fact, used biological weapons in Korea on an experimental basis.[63] In a book on the American air war in Korea published in 2000, Conrad Crane persuasively refutes the Endicott and Hagerman argument, drawing on American archival records of its BW program and on records of the Air Force participation in the Korean War.[64]

The texts of the Russian documents, obtained by the Japanese newspaper *Sankei Shimbun* and subsequently made available to scholars, document in part the way that accusations about responsibility for the charges against the Americans were used in the fierce infighting within the Soviet leadership following Stalin's death. They show that the Council of Ministers sent a harshly worded message to Mao Zedong in May 1953 blaming China for misleading the Soviet government about alleged American use of biological weapons and "recommending" that the Chinese cease all such accusations. They informed Beijing that Soviet "workers" who participated in the "fabrication of the so-called 'proof' of the use of bacteriological weapons will receive severe punishment." The documents include statements by some of these "workers" detailing how they falsified evidence of biological weapons use in preparation for the visit of two Soviet-sponsored international delegations that investigated the charges. They also include a statement by the Soviet ambassador in Pyongyang outlining the Chinese and North Korean initiatives on the issue, the conclusions of Soviet specialists that the claims were not valid, and the contribution that Soviet advisers nonetheless made to creating false zones of contamination.[65]

The Russian documents provide only a tiny fraction of the record of this extensive operation, and thus raise more questions than they answer. But they show persuasively enough that the campaign was based on manufactured evidence. If fuller documentation becomes available, it will provide important insights into how Stalin and Mao viewed the utility of "agitation and propaganda" and how the alliance orchestrated this massive campaign.

The Soviet Role in Ending the War

The Russian documents confirm that Stalin's death on 5 March 1953 was the impetus for the Communist side finally to conclude an armistice. The new collective leadership in Moscow, prompted primarily by their anxiety over whether they could retain power in their European empire and in the Soviet Union itself, unanimously wished to end the war. On 19 March, only two weeks after Stalin died, the Council of Ministers adopted a lengthy resolution on the war in Korea, with attached letters to Mao Zedong and Kim Il Sung. The letters outlined statements that were to be made by Kim, Peng Dehuai, the government of the People's Republic and the Soviet delegation to the United Nations to indicate their willingness to resolve the outstanding issues in order to reach an armistice agreement. According to a Soviet Foreign Ministry report written in 1966, while Zhou Enlai was in Moscow for Stalin's funeral he "urgently proposed that the Soviet side assist the speeding up of the negotiations and the conclusion of an armistice." As we have seen, the Chinese and North Koreans had been eager for some time to bring the war to an end; Moscow's directive must have been welcomed in both Pyongyang and Beijing. Whatever concerns the Chinese leadership may have had about avoiding loss of face in the agreement, since neither Beijing nor Pyongyang could continue the war without Soviet support, Moscow's decision meant that an agreement would soon be reached.

The 19 March Council of Ministers decision indicates that the threats made by the Dwight D. Eisenhower administration in May 1953 to use nuclear weapons against China if the issue of POW repatriation were not soon resolved—which President Eisenhower and Secretary of State John Foster Dulles often claimed had brought the Communists to an agreement—were not, in fact, what broke the stalemate at Panmunjom. Fear that China might be subjected to a nuclear attack apparently contributed to Beijing's hesitation to intervene in the fall of 1950, and Moscow's fear of U.S. use of nuclear weapons prompted it to launch the massive "Peace Initiative" in the fall of 1950. But the longer the United States refrained from using such weapons, even while being unable to defeat North Korea through conventional means, the more the fear of a nuclear attack seems to have receded among the Communist allies. There is no evidence that this fear increased after the new administration took office in Washington, but because the documentary evidence from both Russia and China is very sketchy for the spring of 1953, we know little about how Stalin viewed the Eisenhower administration. At any rate, the decision to end the war was made by the post-Stalin leadership several weeks before the new round of threats was made.[66]

Conclusion

The Russian documentary evidence that has become available from the Presidential Archive and the archives of the Ministry of Foreign Affairs, Ministry of Defense, and Central Committee of the Communist Party has led to a great increase in knowledge of the Soviet role in the Korean War. Several key questions that were hotly debated only a decade ago, especially the extent of Soviet involvement in the outbreak of the war, have now been resolved. Others, such as Stalin's rationale for supporting the invasion of South Korea, the content of his negotiations with the Chinese leadership over Beijing's intervention, and his reasons for urging his allies to hold to a hard line in the armistice negotiations, can now be discussed on the basis of substantial evidence. However, compared to the extensive literature on the U.S. involvement in the Korean War, the scholarly examination of the Soviet role is still limited.

The Presidential Archive documents have shed much light on Stalin's decision making, but as important as that issue is, it does not illuminate how his decisions were actually implemented. Soviet military advisers in Korea and China clearly played a key role in planning and directing the war, but we have no substantial analysis of how they operated or of their successes and failures in cooperating with their junior allies. Nor do we have an adequate understanding of the personal role played by the two most important Soviet officials in Pyongyang during the war—Ambassador Terentii F. Shtykov and his successor V. N. Razuvaev. Shtykov was instrumental as a liason between Kim Il Sung and Moscow, but despite extensive documentation of the ambassador's correspondence with Stalin and other Soviet officials, the nature of his relationship with the North Korean leadership remains elusive.

The impact of the war on Moscow's relations with China and North Korea is now better known from the Russian and Chinese documentary sources, but this important subject requires more analysis. The experience of jointly fighting the Americans and their allies in many ways solidified the Communist alliance. At the same time, however, it sowed the seeds of the eventual rupture between Moscow and Beijing and the sharp turn toward autarky in Pyongyang. Russian archival sources from the postwar period may shed light on the workings of the alliance during the war, but Chinese and North Korean sources are needed to adequately analyze this complex dynamic. Moscow's relations with its East European allies were also affected by the Korean War, but, while we have several substantial analyses of the war's impact on the development of NATO, our knowledge of its effect on Soviet military alliances in Eastern Europe remains limited.

On the operational level, Mark O'Neill's pioneering work on

the first year of the Soviet Air Force involvement in the war is an important first step, but much work remains to be done before we have an adequate military history of the Communist side in the war. In this case, much more documentation is available than has been used; only a small portion of the extensive records on the war declassified by the Ministry of Defense archive has thus far been examined. Among other questions, the American reliance on air power begs an examination of how the Communist side managed to continue to supply the rear and the front despite being subjected to massive and sustained bombardment.

The Soviet intelligence-gathering effort during the war was apparently large and systematic, but the impact of captured American weapons and interrogations of prisoners of war remains largely a matter of conjecture. Similarly, the impact on the Soviet Air Force of the return of large numbers of pilots and ground crews with experience fighting the Americans has not been examined. Nor has the impact on the Soviet economy of its supply of the Korean War been analyzed. The inner workings of the massive international campaign Moscow coordinated to charge the United States with using bacteriological weapons during the war likewise remains little understood.

In sum, the analyses of the Soviet role in the Korean War made thus far on the basis of Russian documents have begun to correct the striking imbalance in our knowledge of the two sides of the conflict. They have broadened the scope of inquiry, raising new questions and reexamining old ones on the basis—for the first time—of solid evidence. As substantial as this historiographical advance is, however, it represents only the first steps toward an adequate investigation of the Communist side of this important conflict. Now that we have gotten a glimpse of the riches contained in the Russian archives, the scholarly bar has moved that much higher.

Notes

1. David Rees, *Korea: The Limited War* (New York: St. Martin's, 1964).

2. I. F. Stone, *The Hidden History of the Korean War* (New York: Monthly Review Press, 1952; paperback 1970).

3. Bruce Cumings, *The Origins of the Korean War, Volume I, Liberation and the Emergence of Separate Regimes, 1945–1947* (Princeton,

N.J.: Princeton University Press, 1981) and *The Origins of the Korean War, Volume II: The Roaring of the Cataract, 1947–1950* (Princeton, N.J.: Princeton University Press, 1990); Callum A. MacDonald, in *Korea: The War Before Vietnam* (London: Macmillan, 1986) and Gye-Dong Kim, in "Who Invented the Korean War?" in James Cotton and Ian Neary, eds. *The Korean War in History* (Manchester, U.K.: University of Manchester Press, 1989). Earlier revisionist arguments included Frank Baldwin, ed., *Without Parallel: The American-Korean Relationship since 1945* (New York: Random House, 1973); John Gittings, "Talks, Bombs and Germs— Another Look at the Korean War," *Asia* 5 (1975): 205–17; Jon Halliday, "The Korean War: Some Notes on Evidence and Solidarity," *Bulletin of Concerned Asian Scholars* 11 (July–September 1979): 2–18; and idem, "What Happened in Korea? Rethinking Korean History, 1945–1953," *Bulletin of Concerned Asian Scholars* 5 (November 1973): 36–44; Joyce Kolko and Gabriel Kolko, *The Limits of Power: The World and United States Foreign Policy, 1945–1954* (New York: Knopf, 1972); and Robert Simmons, *The Strained Alliance: Peking, Pyongyang, Moscow and the Politics of the Korean Civil War* (New York: Free Press, 1975).

4. John Merrill, *Korea: The Peninsular Origins of the War* (Newark: University of Delaware Press, 1989); Burton Kaufman, *The Korean War: Challenges in Crisis, Credibility, and Command* (Philadelphia: Temple University Press, 1986); and Peter Lowe, *The Origins of the Korean War* (London: Longman, 1986).

5. William Stueck, "The Korean War as International History," *Diplomatic History* 10 (fall 1986): 294.

6. Kathryn Weathersby, "To Attack or Not To Attack? Stalin, Kim Il Sung, and the Prelude to War," *Cold War International History Project Bulletin*, 5 (spring 1995): 1–9.

7. For a discussion of some of this documentation, see Kathryn Weathersby, "Making Foreign Policy Under Stalin: The Case of Korea," in Niels Erik Rosenfeldt, Bent Jensen, and Erik Kulavig, eds. *Mechanisms of Power in the Soviet Union* (London and New York: Macmillan Press/ St. Martin's Press, 2000): 224–40.

8. Sergei N. Goncharov, John W. Lewis, and Xue Litai, *Uncertain Partners, Stalin, Mao, and the Korean War* (Stanford, Calif.: Stanford University Press, 1993), 134.

9. See the discussion of the early years of the Sino-Soviet alliance in Odd Arne Westad, ed., *Brothers in Arms, the Rise and Fall of the Sino-Soviet Alliance* (Washington and Stanford, Calif.: Woodrow Wilson Center Press and Stanford University Press, 1998).

10. Haruki Wada argues that Stalin's change of policy toward the Japanese Communist Party in early January 1950, demanding that they abandon their earlier moderation in favor of aggressive struggle against

the U.S. occupation forces, signaled to Kim Il Sung that Stalin might be willing to reconsider his cautious approach to Korean reunification. See "The Korean War, Stalin's Policy, and Japan," *Social Science Japan Journal*, vol. I, no. 1 (1998): 5–29.

11. Weathersby, "To Attack or Not to Attack?" *CWIHP Bulletin* Issue 5, and "New Russian Documents on the Korean War," *CWIHP Bulletin* 6–7: 30–84; and Evgenii P. Bajanov and Natalia Bajanova, "The Korean Conflict" unpublished manuscript (copy in author's possession).

12. For documentation on Kim's April visit to Moscow and his May visit to Beijing, see Bajanov and Bajanova, "The Korean Conflict."

13. Park Myung Lim, *The Korean War: The Outbreak and Its Origins, Volumes I and II* (Seoul: Nanam, 1996). For the discussion of the literature on the war produced by South Korean scholars, I am indebted to the paper by In-Taek Hyun of Korea University, "Korean War Studies Revisited: Third Wave and Beyond," presented at the conference "The Korean War, Forgotten No More" at Georgetown University, 23–25 June 2000.

14. Soh Jin-Chull, *The Origins of the Korean War* (Yiri: Wonkang University Press, 1996).

15. Kim Youngho, "The Origins of the Korean War: Civil War or Stalin's Rollback?" *Diplomacy and Statecraft*, vol. 10, no. 1 (March 1999): 186–214.

16. Lee Wan-bum, "The Organic Interpretation of the Cause of the Korean War," *The Korean Journal of International Relations*, vol. 39, no. 1, 1999.

17. Goncharov, Lewis, and Xue, *Uncertain Partners*, 139.

18. William Stueck, *The Korean War, An International History* (Princeton, N.J.: Princeton University Press, 1995), 33–34.

19. Kathryn Weathersby, "Should We Fear This?: Stalin and the Danger of War with America," in *Stalin and the Cold War* (Woodrow Wilson Center Press and Stanford University Press, forthcoming).

20. The text of a report on Stalin's conversations with Kim Il Sung and Pak Hon-yong in Moscow in April 1950 prepared by the Central Committee of the Communist Party of the Soviet Union can be found in Evgenii P. Bajanov and Natalia Bajanova, "The Korean Conflict."

21. Alexandre Y. Mansourov, "Communist War Coalition Formation and the Origins of the Korean War" (Ph.D. diss., Columbia University, 1997).

22. For an extensive exposition of this argument, see Vojtech Mastny, *The Cold War and Soviet Insecurity: The Stalin Years* (New York and Oxford: Oxford University Press, 1996).

23. Bajanov and Bajanova, "The Korean Conflict."

24. Andrei A. Gromyko, *Memories* (London: Hutchinson, 1989): 102.

25. Cumings, *The Origins of the Korean War, Volume II,* 637.

26. Goncharov, Lewis, and Xue, *Uncertain Partners,* 161–62.

27. Vojtech Mastny, *The Cold War and Soviet Insecurity: The Stalin Years,* 99.

28. Stalin referred to the intervention of American troops, and sometimes of those of the Anglo-American bloc. I cannot recall any instance when he referred to the adversary's forces as the United Nations Command.

29. Adam Ulam, *Expansion and Coexistence, The History of Soviet Foreign Policy, 1917–1967* (New York and Washington: Frederick A. Praeger, 1968), 529.

30. Goncharov, Lewis, and Xue, *Uncertain Partners,* 168–202, 216.

31. Stueck, *The Korean War, An International History,* 105.

32. Weathersby, "New Russian Documents on the Korean War," *Cold War International History Project Bulletin* 6–7: 31.

33. Ibid.

34. Alexandre Y. Mansourov, "Stalin, Mao, Kim and China's Decision to Enter the Korean War, September 16–October 15, 1950: New Evidence from the Russian Archives," *Cold War International History Project Bulletin* 6–7: 96.

35. Mark O'Neill, "The Other Side of the Yalu: Soviet Pilots in the Korean War, Phase One, 1 November 1950–23 October 1951" (Ph.D. diss., Florida State University, 1996), citing a document from the Central Archive of the Ministry of Defense.

36. Alexandre Y. Mansourov, "Stalin, Mao, Kim and China's Decision to Enter to Korean War, 16 September–15 October 1950: New Evidence from the Russian Archives," *Cold War International History Project Bulletin* Issues 6–7: 94–119.

37. Mansourov, "Stalin, Mao, Kim and China's Decision to Enter the Korean War," *Cold War International History Project Bulletin* 6–7: 97, 109.

38. Mansourov, "Stalin, Mao, Kim and China's Decision to Enter the Korean War," *Cold War International History Project Bulletin* 6–7: 112.

39. Mansourov, *CWIHP Bulletin* 6–7: 96.

40. Mansourov, *CWIHP Bulletin* 6–7: 114.

41. Mansourov, *CWIHP Bulletin* 6–7: 99.

42. Mansourov, *CWIHP Bulletin* 6–7: 114–15.

43. Jerrold L. Schecter with Vyacheslav V. Luchkov, eds. *Khrushchev Remembers, The Glasnost Tapes* (Boston: Little, Brown and Co., 1990): 147.

44. Mansourov, *CWIHP Bulletin* 6–7: 116.

45. See CHEN Jian, tr. and ed., Shi Zhe, Fedorenko's recollections are

taken from an interview conducted by Alexandre Mansourov in June 1995, described in Mansourov, *CWIHP Bulletin* 6–7: 102–3.

46. The evacuation order is found in the Dmitri Volkogonov Papers, Library of Congress, Reel 18.

47. Goncharov, Lewis, and Xue, *Uncertain Partners*, 190–92.

48. Mansourov, *CWIHP Bulletin* 6–7: 103.

49. O'Neill, "The Other Side of the Yalu."

50. O'Neill, "The Other Side of the Yalu."

51. "Blank Spots in History: In the Skies Over North Korea," an interview with General Georgii Lobov, 1991. JPRS Report, JPRS-UAC-91-004, p. 3.

52. O'Neill, "The Other Side of the Yalu."

53. Weathersby, "New Russian Documents on the Korean War," *Cold War International History Project Bulletin* 6–7: 60.

54. Goncharov, Lewis, and Xue, *Uncertain Partners*, 201.

55. Weathersby, "New Russian Documents on the Korean War," *Cold War International History Project Bulletin* 6–7: 30–84.

56. For a review of this literature, see Rosemary Foot, "Making Known the Unknown War: Policy Analysis of the Korean Conflict in the Last Decade," *Diplomatic History* 15 (summer 1991): 411–31.

57. The following account of Stalin's approach to a negotiated settlement comes from Kathryn Weathersby, "Stalin, Mao, and the End of the Korean War," in Odd Arne Westad, ed., *Brothers in Arms, The Rise and Fall of the Sino-Soviet Alliance, 1945–1963* (Washington and Stanford, Calif.: Woodrow Wilson Center Press and Stanford University Press, 1998): 90–116.

58. Alexandru Osca and Vasile Popa, "Stalin a decis: Lagarul socialist se inarmeaza" [Stalin Decided: The Socialist Camp Arms Itself], *Document* (Bucharest) 1, nos. 2–3 (1998), 71–76.

59. See David Holloway, *Stalin and the Bomb* (New Haven, Conn., and London: Yale University Press, 1994).

60. Sergei Khrushchev, "The Cold War Through the Looking Glass," *American Heritage* (October 1999): 36.

61. Vojtech Mastny, "Stalin as Cold War-Lord," paper prepared for the conference "Stalin and the Cold War, Yale University, 23–26 September 1999.

62. Jon Halliday, "Anti-Communism and the Korean War, 1950–1953," in *The Socialist Register*, Ralph Miliband et al. eds. (London, 1984): 151; Gavan McCormack, *Cold War, Hot War: An Australian Perspective on the Korean War* (Sydney: Hale and Iremonger, 1983), 154–56.

63. Stephen Endicott and Edward Hagerman, *The United States and Biological Warfare: Secrets of the Early Cold War and Korea* (Bloomington and London: Indiana University Press, 1999).

64. Conrad C. Crane, *American Airpower Strategy in Korea, 1950–1953* (Lawrence: University Press of Kansas, 2000), 143–54.

65. Kathryn Weathersby, "Deceiving the Deceivers: Moscow, Beijing, Pyongyang, and the Allegations of Bacteriological Weapons Use in Korea," *CWIHP Bulletin* 11 (winter 1998): 176–85; and Milton Leitenberg, "New Russian Evidence on the Korean War Biological Warfare Allegations: Background and Analysis," *CWIHP Bulletin* 11 (winter 1998): 185–99.

66. For a discussion of the debate over the utility of nuclear threats in the Korean War, see Roger Dingman, "Atomic Diplomacy During the Korean War," *International Security* 13:3 (winter 1988/89): 50–91; and Rosemary Foot, "Nuclear Coercion and the Ending of the Korean Conflict," *International Security* 13:3 (winter 1988/89): 92–112.

Chapter 3

In the Name of Revolution

China's Road to the Korean War Revisited

CHEN JIAN

When China entered the Korean War in October 1950, the newly established People's Republic of China (PRC) had just celebrated its first anniversary. Mao Zedong's revolutionary regime faced enormous challenges at home and abroad, having to deal with such problems as achieving political consolidation, rebuilding a war-shattered economy, and finishing reunification of the country by "liberating" Taiwan, which was still under the control of the Guomindang (GMD or the Nationalist party). Why then did the Beijing leadership decide to send troops to Korea? How was the decision made? What were the immediate and long-range causes leading to Beijing's decision to enter the Korean War? How should the significance of Beijing's participation in the war be evaluated? Using newly available Chinese and, to a certain extent, Russian language sources, I will try to synthesize my answers to these questions in this essay.[1]

"Beating American Arrogance"

In analyzing Beijing's reasons for entering the Korean War, previous scholarship usually followed a "China under threat" thesis, emphasizing that Beijing's decision on intervention was a response to the threat to China's "vital security interests" caused by U.S./ UN forces' aggressive advance toward the Yalu River in the wake

93

of the Inchon landing.[2] While it is apparent that the defense of China's physical safety represented a crucial element in Beijing's decision to enter the Korean War, the reasons behind China's intervention were much broader and more complicated than the simple defense of China's northeastern border. In a deeper political sense, China's intervention has to be understood in terms of Mao Zedong's determination to create new momentum for pushing forward his "continuous revolution" and to defeat "American arrogance."

In retrospect, three fundamental and interrelated rationales shaped the PRC's foreign policy and security strategy: the Chinese Communist Party (CCP)'s revolutionary nationalism, its sense of responsibility toward an Asia-wide or worldwide revolution, and its determination to maintain the inner dynamics of the Chinese revolution after its nationwide victory. Beijing's management of the Korean crisis cannot be comprehended properly without an understanding of these rationales and the mentality related to them.

Mao Zedong and his fellow CCP leaders grew up in an age when China had lost the status as the "Central Kingdom" and even the very survival of the Chinese nation was at stake. Their conception of China's national interests was deeply influenced by the perceived unequal exchanges between China and the foreign powers during modern times; and their commitment to a Communist revolution in China grew out of the belief that the revolution would revitalize the Chinese nation while at the same time leading to the destruction of the "old world," and that China's position as a "Central Kingdom" would be revived in the emergence of a "new world." Mao's conception of revolution reflected his generation's emotional commitment to China's national liberation, as well as of their longing for China to take a *central* (but not *dominant*) position in world politics.[3] Indeed, underlying this revolutionary nationalism was the unique Chinese "victim mentality"—during modern times, the Chinese people's perception of their nation's position in the world was continuously informed by a profound conviction that it was the political incursion, economic exploitation, and military aggression by foreign imperialist countries that had undermined the historical glory of Chinese civilization and humiliated the Chinese nation.[4] Consequently, a victim mentality dominated the Chinese conceptualization of China's relations with the outside world.[5] As far as China's relations with the United States are concerned, Chinese revolutionary nationalism, reinforced by the Chinese "victim mentality," led Mao and his comrades to emphasize persistently that the Chinese Communists would not tolerate Washington's disdain of China and the Chinese people. While Washington's hostility toward the Chinese revolution offended Mao and his comrades, the perceived American disdain for China as a weak country and the Chinese as an inferior people made them angry. Mao and his fellow CCP leaders were more than willing to challenge this "American arrogance."[6]

Closely related to the CCP's revolutionary nationalism was the Chinese Communists' lofty aspiration to promote an "Eastern Revolution" or even a world revolution that would follow the Chinese model. With the victory of the Chinese Communist revolution in 1949, Mao and his fellow CCP leaders were more confident than ever before that their revolution had established for other "oppressed peoples" in the world a brilliant example of national liberation. Mao believed that it was the Chinese Communists' lofty duty to support communist revolutions and national liberation movements in other countries. China's foreign policy was in essence revolutionary: Mao and his fellow CCP leaders made it clear that the "new China" would not inherit any of the diplomatic legacies of the "old China," that China would lean to the side of the Soviet Union and other "world revolutionary forces," and that, in the final analysis, China would not be bound by any existing norms and codes of behavior in international relations (which the Chinese Communists saw as of Western origin and inimical to the Chinese revolution). [7] Again, Mao's perception of the significance of the Chinese revolution was interwoven with Chinese ethnocentrism and universalism. He believed that the rejuvenation of China's position as a central world power would be realized through the promotion of Asian and world revolutions following the Chinese model. The Korean crisis presented a crucial test for this rationale.

In a deeper sense, the CCP's foreign policy in general and its attitude toward the Korean crisis in particular were shaped by the determination on the part of Mao and his fellow CCP leaders to enhance the inner-dynamics of the Chinese Communist revolution. When the Chinese Communists achieved nationwide victory in 1949, Mao and many of his comrades were worried that their revolution, which had merely accomplished the "first step" in its "long march," might lose its momentum.[8] How to maintain and to enhance the inner-dynamics of the great Chinese revolution thus became Mao's central concern—and would remain so until the last days of the Chinese chairman's life. When Mao first encountered this problem as China's new ruler in 1949, among other things, his train of thought developed in terms of emphasizing the continuous existence of outside threats to the revolution. While identifying the United States as China's primary enemy, Mao and the CCP leadership did not necessarily perceive Washington as an immediate threat to China's physical security in the early days of the People's Republic (as a matter of fact, after the summer and fall of 1949, they began to believe that the United States lacked the capability to engage American forces in major military conflicts in East Asia in the near future);[9] yet they continued to emphasize the seriousness of the "American threat" and prepared for a long-range confrontation with the United States.[10] After the outbreak of the Korean War, Mao and the CCP leadership found that the Korean crisis challenged China's national security and at the same time offered them a new means to mobilize the entire Chinese nation under the CCP's terms. That the CCP's understanding of China's national security interests was defined by the perceived necessity of maintaining and promoting the momentum of the Chinese revolution explains to a large extent the uncompromising character of Beijing's management of the Korean crisis.

Indeed, Mao's "new China" was a new type of international actor. In international relations, it intended to break with the existing principles and codes of behavior, which, in the minds of Mao and his comrades, were the product of the Western dominance. In domestic affairs, Mao and his fellow CCP leaders always related the management of international crisis to the mobilization of the Chinese people for the sake of China's continuous revolution. Therefore, the PRC's foreign policy had its own language and theory, and behaved according to its own values and logic. Accordingly, the CCP leadership consistently treated the United States as China's primary enemy and prepared throughout 1949 and 1950 for the coming of an inevitable confrontation with it.[11]

Within the context of the escalating global cold war in the late 1940s and early 1950s, the Chinese Communists encountered an America incapable of understanding either the rationales or the mentality galvanizing Mao and the CCP leadership. Profound differences in political ideology and perceived national interests existed between Beijing and Washington; and suspicion and hostility between the CCP and the United States were further crystalized as the result of Washington's continuing support to the Guomindang regime and the CCP's determination to "make a fresh start" in China's foreign policy. But American policy makers' superpower mentality made the situation more complicated. President Harry S. Truman, Secretary of State Dean Acheson, General Douglas MacArthur, and other key American policy makers and military planners of their generation came to the political scene as the United States emerged as a prominent world power with continuously expanding interests abroad. This fact, combined with a long-existing belief in America's special destiny in the world and traditional hostility toward revolutionary changes, led this generation of American policy makers to assume that American values held universal significance.[12] This assumption was further supported by the notion of America's "special relationship" with China based on the "Open Door" ideology. American policy makers, who had fundamental problems adjusting to the realities created by the Chinese revolution, were also unwilling to understand the environment in which Beijing's leaders made decisions. Consequently, a stage was set for Chinese-American confrontation in East Asia.

The Sino-Soviet Alliance

China entered the Korean War only eight months after the signing of the Sino-Soviet alliance treaty. What role did the Sino-Soviet alliance play in Beijing's decision to enter the Korean War? With the opportunities to access new Chinese and Russian materials, we are now in a better position to answer this question than ever before.

The new materials available in the past decade do not completely overturn the views long held by many scholars that the development of CCP-Soviet relations had been tortuous during the course of the Chinese revolution. In the 1920s and early 1930s, the CCP, as a branch of the Soviet-controlled Comintern, had to follow Moscow's instructions. As a Communist leader in China who had never studied or worked in the Soviet Union, Mao Zedong had long been stifled by members of the international section within the CCP, who enjoyed the support of Stalin and the Comintern. After Mao emerged as the CCP's top leader in the mid- and late 1930s, he continued to face heavy pressure from the Comintern and the Soviet Union on many important issues. For example, in the early 1940s, when Mao refused to follow Moscow's order to use the CCP's military forces to attract more Japanese troops in China for the purpose of "better protecting the safety of the Soviet Union," Moscow severely criticized Mao and his fellow CCP leaders.[13] After Japan's surrender at the end of World War II, Stalin cabled Mao twice in August 1945, warning the Chinese Communists not to risk a civil war with the Guomindang because "it would bring the danger of the complete destruction of the Chinese nation." Mao was extremely upset with these warnings and would repeatedly complain about them after Stalin's death.[14] During the 1946–1949 Chinese civil war, CCP-Soviet relations were again inharmonious from time to time. While contingently offering the CCP assistance in the war against the GMD government, especially in the Northeast, Stalin generally doubted the CCP's ability to win.[15] Certainly it was not easy for Mao and the CCP to establish a close strategic relationship with Stalin and the Soviet Union.

But new Chinese and Russian materials clearly indicate that CCP-Soviet relations had another, and, in my judgment, more fundamental side. In the final analysis, Mao and his fellow CCP leaders were communists. In the long process of the Chinese revolution, the CCP leadership always kept (or tried to keep) an intimate relationship with Moscow. Except for a short period during the Chinese Red Army's Long March, the CCP central headquarters maintained daily telegraphic communication with Moscow. Mao and the CCP leadership kept Stalin well informed of nearly all of their important decisions.[16] Even when the CCP leadership strongly disagreed with Stalin and the Comintern, they avoided any open disputes with Moscow. Indeed, Mao and the CCP leadership believed that the divergences between themselves and Moscow were no more than the ones that would sometimes emerge between brothers.[17]

Both the Chinese and Soviet Communists felt the need to strengthen their relations when it became clear that the CCP was going to win the civil war. From late 1947, Mao actively prepared to visit the Soviet Union to "discuss important domestic and international issues" with Stalin.[18] The extensive telegraphic exchanges between Mao and Stalin resulted in two important secret missions in 1949. From 31 January to 7 February 1949, Stalin sent Anastas Mikoyan, a Soviet Party Politburo member, to visit Xibaipo, the CCP's headquarters at that time. Mao and other CCP leaders had extensive discussions with Mikoyan, introducing to him how and why the CCP made its strategies and policies. Mao particularly explained to Mikoyan the CCP's foreign policy of "making a fresh start" and "cleaning the house before entertaining guests."[19] In May and June 1949, the CCP kept Moscow well informed of the meetings between Huang Hua and John Leighton Stuart (American ambassador to China).[20] From late June to mid-August 1949, Liu Shaoqi, the CCP's second in command, led a top CCP delegation to visit Moscow. During the visit, in a rare gesture Stalin apologized for failing to give sufficient assistance to the CCP during the civil war, promising that the Soviet Union would provide the Chinese Communists with both political support and substantial assistance in military and other fields. Moreover, the Soviets and the Chinese reached a "division of labor" agreement between them to promote world revolution: while the Soviet Union would remain the center of the international proletarian revolution, promoting revolutions in East Asia would become primarily China's duty. Liu left Moscow in mid-August, accompanied by a large group of Russian experts who were to assist China's military buildup and economic reconstruction.[21]

The CCP's effort to pursue a strategic alliance with Moscow culminated when Mao visited the Soviet Union from December 1949 to February 1950. The CCP chairman hoped to sign a new strategic alliance treaty with the Soviet Union. As revealed by new Chinese and Russian sources, however, the process of the visit was uneasy. During Mao's first meeting with Stalin on 16 December, the Soviet leader asked Mao what he hoped to achieve for his visit. Mao, according to his Russian language interpreter, replied that he wanted to "bring about something that not only looked nice but also tasted delicious"—an obvious reference to his wish to sign a new Sino-Soviet treaty.[22] However, initially Stalin disappointed Mao by emphasizing that it was not in Moscow's and Beijing's interests to abolish the 1945 Sino-Soviet treaty that Moscow signed with the GMD.[23] Consequently, the discussions between the Chinese and the Soviets encountered a temporary deadlock.[24]

Early in January 1950, almost three weeks after Mao's arrival in Moscow, Stalin's attitude suddenly changed, and he showed willingness to sign an alliance treaty with Beijing.[25] Zhou Enlai arrived in Moscow on 20 January to negotiate the details of the new alliance treaty. After a process of hard bargaining, the treaty was signed on 14 February, [26] according to which the two sides would "make every effort possible to stop Japan's aggression and the aggression by a third state which is directly or indirectly associated with Japan's act of aggression." [27] In addition, the Chinese agreed to allow the Soviets to maintain their privileges in China's Northeast and Xinjiang, and Stalin agreed to provide substantial military and other material support to China. During Mao's visit, China ordered 586 planes from the Soviet Union, including 280 fighters, 198 bombers, and 108 trainers and other planes. From 16 February to 5 March 1950, a mixed Soviet air-defense division moved into the Shanghai-Nanjing-Xuzhou area to take responsibility for the air defense of these cities under attack by GMD aircraft operating from nationalist-controlled offshore islands. From mid-March to mid-May, reportedly this Soviet division shot down five invading GMD planes over Shanghai, greatly strengthening China's coastal air defense capability. [28]

Stalin's eventual embrace of the Sino-Soviet alliance reflected his understanding that it would better serve the Soviet Union's strategic interests by enhancing Moscow's position in its global confrontation with the United States, especially in East Asia. In addition, the essence of the Sino-Soviet alliance must also be understood as a crucial step taken by Moscow and Beijing to formalize the "division of labor" agreement concerning how to promote the Eastern and the world revolution reached by Stalin and Liu Shaoqi. By signing the treaty, both Moscow and Beijing had committed not only to helping defend each other's security interests but also, and more importantly, to joining their forces to create a new revolutionary situation in East Asia as well as in the world.

It is within this context that Stalin brought the Korean problem to Mao's attention in Moscow. According to the recollections of Shi Zhe, Mao's Russian language interpreter who accompanied Mao on his visit to the Soviet Union:

> During Chairman Mao's visit to the Soviet Union, Stalin did talk with him about Kim Il-sung's plan to liberate the whole of Korea. Stalin told Chairman Mao that Kim had come to him with the ideas [of the plan] and he asked Kim if there existed any condition unfavorable to his plan, such as whether the Americans would intervene. He found that Kim was in a high mood. "He will only listen to the voice for his ideas, not the

voice against his ideas; he was really young and brave," commented Stalin. Then Stalin asked Chairman Mao's opinions about Kim's plan, especially if he thought the Americans would intervene. Chairman Mao did not answer immediately. After a while, he said: "The Americans might not come in because this is Korea's internal affairs, but the Korean comrades need to take America's intervention into account." As a matter of fact, Chairman Mao held reservations about Kim Il-sung's plan. Chairman Mao had anticipated that Kim Il-sung would attack the South no matter what happened.[29]

In the discussion, Mao did not commit China to Kim's plan of "liberating" Korea, but he touched upon Stalin's main concern: the possibility of American intervention, and made it clear that he believed the intervention unlikely. During Mao's stay in the Soviet Union, the CCP and the North Korean Communists reached an agreement to return all remaining ethnic Korean soldiers in the People's Liberation Army (PLA) to Korea with their weapons. (See discussions below.) These developments must have influenced Stalin's consideration of the Korean issue, pushing the Soviet leader toward making a decision to support Kim's plans. On 30 January 1950, for the first time in many months, Stalin, via the Soviet ambassador in Pyongyang, informed the North Korean Communist leader that he was now willing to discuss Kim's plans to unify Korea by force, and that "I am ready to help him in this matter."[30] Consequently, Mao's visit and the signing of the Sino-Soviet alliance treaty would produce a *de facto* Sino-Soviet green light to Kim Il-sung's plans to attack the South.

The Special Comradeship Between Beijing and Pyongyang

China's entry into the Korean War needs also to be understood in the context of the CCP-North Korean relationship. Historically, the Korean Communists had close ties with their comrades in China. During the 1930s, Kim Il-sung joined the Anti-Japanese United Army in Northeast China and was once a CCP member. In the late 1930s and early 1940s a group of Korean Communists, such as Pak Il-yu, came to Yanan to participate in China's war of Resistance against Japan. In the last stage of the war against Japan and during China's civil war, as many as 100,000 ethnic Korean residents in China joined Chinese Communist forces, especially in the Northeast. In the late 1940s, the Chinese People's Liberation Army's 156th, 164th, and 166th Divisions, three of the best units of the Fourth Field Army, were mainly composed of Korean-Chinese soldiers.[31]

What has been less known by scholars is that, during China's civil war from 1946 to 1949, North Korea served as the strategic base for Chinese Communist forces in the Northeast. In September 1945, the CCP leadership adopted a grand strategy of "maintaining a defensive posture in the South while waging the offensive in the North" in its confrontation with the GMD. A main reason CCP leaders made this decision was their belief that, with the Northeast bordering the Soviet Union to the north and Communist North Korea to the east, the CCP would occupy a more favorable position to counter the GMD there.[32]

In July 1946, the CCP forces, under great pressure from GMD forces, abandoned Andong and Tonghua, two of the last cities still under their control in southern Manchuria. Thousands of wounded CCP soldiers, family members of CCP troops, and other non-combat personnel crossed the Yalu River to take refuge in North Korea for the purpose of regrouping and rectification. Meanwhile, the Korean Communists helped the CCP to transport more than 20,000 tons of strategically important materials from North Korea to the Northeast. With the assistance of North Korean Communists, the CCP established two land transportation lines via North Korean territory, linking Communist forces in southern and northern Manchuria, which allowed the CCP forces in the Northeast to avoid being completely cut off from outside communication and supply.[33]

Indeed, North Korea's support dramatically changed the CCP's strategic position in China's civil war, making it possible for CCP forces in the Northeast to turn from defensive to offensive by late 1947 and early 1948. The CCP leaders would not forget the "brotherly support" they had received from the Korean Communists at a time of difficulty and crisis. As a matter of fact, CCP leaders, and Mao in particular, later used North Korean support of the Chinese revolution to justify their decision to send Chinese troops to "resist America and assist Korea."[34]

Within the context of CCP–North Korean cooperation, in late April 1949, a high-ranking North Korean delegation, headed by Kim Il, Director of the Political Department of the Korean People's Army (KPA), secretly visited China to meet CCP leaders (including

Mao Zedong). In addition to briefing his hosts on the situation on the Korean peninsula and discussing the possibility of establishing a "Communist Intelligence Bureau in the East," Kim Il asked the Chinese to return ethnic Korean soldiers in the PLA to Korea. Mao told Kim Il that the CCP definitely supported the Korean Communists' objective to unify their country, although he also expressed the hope that Pyongyang could wait until after the CCP had completely unified China to take the decisive action.[35] Following the agreement reached by Chinese and North Korean Communist leaders, two PLA units, the 164th and the 166th Divisions, the majority of whose soldiers were ethnic Koreans, returned to North Korea in summer and fall 1949. Together with several other groups of ethnic Korean PLA soldiers who were sent back to Korea around the same period, by the end of the year, the total number of returnees from China had reached 30,000 to 40,000.[36]

In January 1950, when Mao Zedong and Zhou Enlai were visiting the Soviet Union, the Chinese, the North Koreans, and the Soviets reached the agreement to return all remaining ethnic Korean PLA soldiers to North Korea.[37] Starting in February 1950, these soldiers, mainly from the PLA's 156th Division and several other units of the former Fourth Field Army, returned to North Korea. They were later organized as the KPA's Seventh Division, one of the KPA's main combat divisions in the early stage of the Korean War. It is estimated that as many as 50,000–70,000 (if not more) ethnic Korean PLA soldiers returned to Korea, bringing their military equipment with them, from late 1949 to mid-1950.[38]

However, the relationship between Beijing and Pyongyang was not always harmonious. First, as discussed earlier, Mao and the CCP leadership faced a dilemma on the Korean issue. Because the remaining Nationalist forces still occupied Taiwan, Mao and his fellow CCP leaders were reluctant to see a war break out in Korea, as they worried that such a development might complicate the situation in East Asia and jeopardize the CCP's effort to liberate Taiwan. Therefore, tension existed between Kim Il-sung's plans to attack the South and Mao Zedong's plans to occupy Taiwan. Second, the factional division among the Korean Communists proved to be a serious obstacle to a close cooperative relationship between Beijing and Pyongyang. In the late 1940s and early 1950s, Kim Il-sung's authority within the Korean Party still encountered challenges from both the southern section headed by Pak Hon-yong and, to a lesser degree, the Chinese section headed by Pak Il-yu, and he would feel extremely reluctant to tie himself too tightly to the Chinese. Not surprisingly, Kim seldom consulted with Chinese leaders in Beijing when he was striving to get Stalin's approval to attack the South in 1949–1950. Third, Kim's uneasiness in dealing with the Chinese had been further strengthened by his feelings as an intense Korean nationalist: the historical fact that the Korean peninsula had long been under the shadow of the "Central Kingdom" certainly made it less possible for Kim to give Beijing's leaders his full trust.

As revealed by new Chinese and Russian sources, the Korean War, in the final analysis, was the North Korean leader Kim Il-sung's war, which he initiated on the basis of his judgment (or misjudgment) of conditions existing on the Korean peninsula. Throughout 1949 and early 1950, he made extensive efforts to convince Stalin that there existed a real revolutionary situation in Korea so that he would get Stalin's support for his plans to unify his country by military means.[39] Stalin initially feared that such a war could result in direct military conflict between the Soviet Union and the United States, and he did not endorse Kim's idea of unifying his country by force until the end of January 1950. U.S. Secretary of State Dean Acheson's statement earlier in the month excluding Korea from America's western Pacific defense perimeter appeared to have convinced him that direct U.S. military intervention in the peninsula was unlikely.[40] In April 1950, Kim Il-sung secretly visited the Soviet Union to get Stalin's approval of his plans. After listening to Kim's opinions, Stalin finally gave the green light for Kim's plans to attack the South on the condition that the North Korean Communist leader receive Mao's blessing.[41] Kim Il-sung thus traveled to Beijing to meet Mao on 13–16 May. He told Mao that Stalin had approved his plans to attack the South. Mao cabled Stalin to confirm Kim's story, and Stalin's response was affirmative. Mao asked for Kim's assessment of possible American response if North Korea attacked the South, stressing that as Korea was close to Japan the possibility of an American intervention could not be totally excluded. Kim, however, seemed confident that the United States would not commit its troops, or at least that it would have no time to send in its troops because the North Koreans would be able to finish fighting in two to three weeks. Mao asked Kim if

North Korea needed China's military support and offered to deploy three Chinese armies along the Chinese-Korean border. Kim responded "arrogantly" (in Mao's own words, according to Shi Zhe) that North Korea's own forces and Communist guerrillas in the South could alone solve the problem, and thus China's military involvement was unnecessary.[42]

Although Mao seemed to have reservations on Kim's plans to attack the South at this moment, he never seriously challenged Kim. For Mao, to block Kim's plans would constitute a betrayal of China's "duty of proletarian internationalism," as well as a negation of Beijing's claim that China was to play a central role in promoting an Asia-wide or even worldwide revolution. Consequently, Mao's attitude was interpreted by Kim Il-sung as a kind of tacit permission to his plans, which allowed Kim to inform Stalin as well as other Korean Communist leaders in Pyongyang that he now had the support of his Chinese comrades. Indeed, after returning from Beijing, Kim accelerated preparations to attack the South. With the help of Soviet military advisers, North Korean military planners worked out the details of the operational plan for the attack in May and early June.[43] Kim, however, did not inform Beijing's leaders of the specifics of his plans, including the exact date of his attack.[44]

The Path toward Intervention

When the Korean War erupted on 25 June 1950, U.S. president Harry S. Truman quickly decided to come to the rescue of Syngman Rhee's South Korean regime and to dispatch the Seventh Fleet to "neutralize" the Taiwan Strait, decisions that turned the Korean War into an international crisis. Beijing's perceptions of the crisis were complicated. On the one hand, the Korean crisis threatened Beijing's key interests in a variety of senses: it presented potential threats to China's physical security, especially the safety of China's industrial bases in the Northeast; it questioned the correctness of Beijing's overall perception that East Asia represented "the weak linkage of the chain of international imperialism," which CCP leaders had held since 1946–1947; it changed the scenario of the CCP-GMD confrontation across the Taiwan Strait, forcing Beijing's leaders to postpone and, finally, to call off the military campaign to liberate Taiwan; it darkened the prospects for an ongoing East Asian revolution which, in Beijing's view, should follow the model of the Chinese revolution; and, last but not least, it created tremendous internal pressures on Mao and the CCP leadership as the rulers of the newly established People's Republic of China.[45]

On the other hand, the Korean crisis offered the CCP leadership potential opportunities. While evaluating how the Korean crisis might influence China, Mao and his fellow CCP leaders could clearly sense that, by firmly and successfully confronting the "U.S. imperialist aggression" in Korea and Taiwan, they would be able to translate the tremendous pressure from without into dynamics that would help enhance the Chinese people's revolutionary momentum, while at the same time legitimizing the CCP's authority as China's new ruler. This would help establish the basis for Mao to carry out his grand plans of transforming China's old state and society into a new socialist country.[46] In terms of its international impact, the Korean crisis challenged the international structure in the Asian-Pacific region. But as one of the main objectives of new China's foreign policy was to pound at the Western-dominated existing international order, Beijing's leaders realized that a North Korean victory (preferably, with China's support) could help a new order to emerge in East Asia. From Beijing's perspective, even an expansion of the conflict in Korea, certainly not desirable, might still be tolerable.[47] The relationship between the CCP and the North Korean Communists, as discussed earlier, had been intricate. Kim Il-sung, while endeavoring to maintain cooperation with his Chinese comrades, kept a high vigilance against Chinese influence. To Mao and the CCP leadership, expanding warfare in Korea would inevitably menace China's national security interests, but at the same time it could offer the Chinese Communists a possible opportunity to expand the influence of the Chinese revolution into an area at the top of the CCP's Asian revolutionary agenda.[48] Mao and the CCP leadership viewed the Korean War with mixed feelings: failure to eject the Americans from Korea could mean insecurity for China; success in "beating American arrogance" would advance revolutionary China's domestic mobilization and international reputation and influence.

Not surprising at all, Beijing's response to the Korean War was from the beginning comprehensive. By early July Beijing's leaders had decided to postpone the invasion of Taiwan to focus on Korea.[49] On 13 July, Beijing formally established the "Northeast Border Defense Army," assigning it with the task of preparing for military intervention in Korea in the event that the war turned against North Korea. By early August, more than 260,000 Chinese troops had taken position along the Chinese-Korean border.[50] On 18 August, after a series of deliberations and adjustments, Mao Zedong set the end of September as the deadline for these troops to complete preparations for military operations in Korea.[51]

On the home front, the Beijing leadership started the "Great Movement to Resist America and Assist Korea," taking "beating American arrogance" as its central slogan. Beijing's leaders used every means available to stir the "hatred of the U.S. imperialists" among common Chinese. They particularly emphasized that the United States had long engaged in political and economic aggression against China, that the declining capitalist America was not as powerful as it seemed to be, and that a confrontation between China and the United States was inevitable.[52] At the same time, the CCP leadership decided to promote a nationwide campaign aimed at suppressing "reactionaries and reactionary activities." The campaign would reach its climax a few months later, shortly before the Chinese troops were entering the Korean War.[53] All of these developments indicate that Beijing's management of the Korean crisis was comprehensive in nature. In the eyes of Mao and the CCP leadership, Communist China's security interests would be best served by guaranteeing the safety of the Chinese-Korean border, promoting the CCP's authority and credibility at home, and enhancing China's prestige on the international scene. Beijing's leaders were determined to achieve all of these goals.

From the beginning, Beijing based its handling of the Korean crisis on the assumption that if China entered the Korean War, the Soviet Union would honor its obligation in accordance with the Sino-Soviet alliance treaty and provide China with all kinds of support, including supplies of ammunition, military equipment, and air cover for Chinese land forces. Early in July, when Chinese leaders informed Stalin of the decision to establish the Border Defense Army, Stalin supported the plan and promised that if the Chinese troops were to fight in Korea, the Soviet Union would "provide air cover for these units."[54] Throughout July and August 1950, the Soviets accelerated military deliveries to China, and a Soviet Air Force division, with 122 MiG-15 fighters, entered Manchuria to help with air defense there.[55]

However, despite the intensive preparation for military intervention, Chinese troops did not enter Korea. One reason was that Kim Il-sung never issued an invitation for Chinese intervention. Beginning in early July, Mao Zedong repeatedly conveyed his concerns to Kim that, with the main force of the Korean People's Army becoming increasingly bogged down in the southern tip of the Korean peninsula, it was likely that U.S./UN forces might conduct landing operations in the KPA's rear. (Several times Mao particularly mentioned Inchon as a possible spot.) But Kim Il-sung paid little attention to Mao's warnings.[56] In the meantime, although Beijing dispatched a group of military observers to Korea, Kim basically kept them in Pyongyang without providing them with opportunities to learn about the development of the military situation at the front.[57]

On 15 September 1950, the U.S./UN forces waged a highly successful amphibious landing operation at Inchon, which immediately changed the entire course of the Korean War. With the gradual collapse of the North Korean resistance and the northward advance of the U.S./UN forces, and especially after Kim Il-sung formally asked for Chinese assistance on 1 October,[58] Mao and his comrades had to decide whether or not China should enter the Korean War.

Beijing reached the decision favoring intervention during the first three weeks of October. The process leading to the decision was complex. Top Chinese leaders were under intense pressures caused by cruel domestic and international conditions, and the party leadership was divided on the necessity of entering the fighting. On 1 October, following Kim Il-sung's request for direct Soviet and Chinese intervention in the Korean War, Stalin cabled CCP leaders, urging the Chinese to enter the war "to give the Korean comrades an opportunity to organize combat reserve under the cover of your troops." However, the Soviet leader failed to clarify what military support Moscow would give Beijing if the Chinese did send troops to Korea.[59]

Under these circumstances, members of the CCP Central Secretariat met on 2 October to discuss the Korean crisis and made the preliminary decision to send Chinese troops to Korea.[60] Mao personally drafted a long telegram to Stalin, informing the Soviet leader that Beijing had decided "to send a portion of our troops, under the name of [Chinese People's] Volunteers, to Korea, assisting the

Korean comrades to fight the troops of the United States and its running dog Syngman Rhee." Mao summarized the reasons for this decision, emphasizing that even though China's intervention might cause a war between China and the United States, it was necessary for the sake of the Korean and Eastern revolution.[61] Mao also made it clear that in order to defeat American troops in Korea, China needed substantial Soviet military support. He used plain language to ask Stalin to clarify "whether or not the Soviet Union can provide us with assistance in supplying weapons, can dispatch a volunteer air force into Korea, and can deploy large numbers of air force units to assist us in strengthening our air defense in Beijing, Tianjin, Shenyang, Shanghai, and Nanjing if the United States uses its air force to bombard these places."[62]

The CCP chairman, however, apparently did not dispatch this telegram, probably because the opinions among top CCP leaders were yet to be unified and he also realized the need to bargain with Stalin on the Soviet air support issue. According to Russian sources, Mao met with Nikolai Rochshin, the Soviet ambassador to China, late on 2 October, informing him that because dispatching Chinese troops to Korea "may entail extremely serious consequences," including "provoking an open conflict between the United States and China," many leaders in Beijing believed that China should "show caution" in entering the Korean War. Thus Mao told Stalin that the Chinese leadership had *not* decided whether to send troops to Korea.[63]

But Mao's heart was with intervention. Although the majority of CCP leaders hesitated to endorse sending troops to Korea when the Politburo met on 4–5 October to discuss the matter, Mao used both his political wisdom and authority to push his colleagues to support the war decision.[64] Mao's stand was further strengthened by Stalin's pressure. On 6 October, Stalin dispatched a telegram to Mao again urging him to enter the war, even at the risk of igniting World War III. "Need we fear this?" Stalin asked rhetorically; his answer was "no." He argued that the PRC and the Soviet Union were then stronger than the United States and Britain, while in a few years a rearmed Japan and West Germany would be able to contribute to the enemy's military cause. "If a war is inevitable," the Soviet leader reasoned, "then let it be waged now, and not in a few years when Japanese militarism will be restored as an ally of the USA and when the USA and Japan will have a ready-made bridgehead on the continent in the form of an entire Korea run by Syngman Rhee." Receiving Stalin's message, Mao immediately expressed his agreement, though he pointed out that Beijing would require massive technical aid and air support from Moscow. [65] On 8 October, Mao formally issued the order to establish the Chinese People's Volunteers with Peng Dehuai as the commander, and informed Kim Il-sung of the decision the same evening. [66]

Out of consideration of strengthening China's bargaining position in pursuing Soviet military support, however, Mao found it necessary to "play tough with" Stalin. [67] On 10–11 October, Zhou Enlai met with Stalin at the latter's villa on the Black Sea. Zhou, according to Shi Zhe, Zhou's Russian language interpreter, did not tell Stalin that China had decided to send troops to Korea but persistently brought the discussion around to Soviet military aid, especially air support, for China. Stalin finally agreed to provide China with substantial military support but explained that it was impossible for the Soviet Air Force to engage in fighting over Korea until two to two and a half months after Chinese land forces entered operations there. [68]

Stalin's ambiguous attitude led Mao again to order Chinese troops to halt preparations for entering operations in Korea on 12 October. [69] The next day the CCP Politburo met again to discuss China's entry into the Korean War. Pushed by Mao, the Politburo confirmed that entering the war was in the fundamental interests of the Chinese revolution as well as the Eastern revolution. [70] Mao then authorized Zhou Enlai, who was still in Moscow, to inform Stalin of the decision. At the same time, Mao instructed Zhou to continue to "consult with" Soviet leaders to clarify whether they would ask China to lease or to purchase the military equipment that Stalin agreed to provide, and whether the Soviet Air Force would enter operations in Korea at all. [71]

On 17 October, the day Zhou Enlai returned to Beijing, Mao again ordered the troops on the Chinese-Korean border to halt their movements to give him time to learn from Zhou about Stalin's exact position. [72] The next day, when Mao was convinced that the Soviet Union would provide China with all kinds of military support, including air defense for major Chinese cities and air cover for Chinese troops fighting in Korea in a later stage of the war, he finally ordered Chinese troops to enter the Korean War. [73] Although without direct Soviet air support until January 1951, more than a quarter million Chinese troops crossed the Yalu beginning on 19 October 1950.[74]

The Chinese Experience during the War

China's entry into the war immediately altered the balance of power on the Korean battlefield. On 25 October, the Chinese forces initiated their first campaign in Korea by launching sudden attacks on South Korean troops in the Unsan area. In less than two weeks, they forced the South Koreans to retreat from areas close to the Yalu to the Chongchun River.[75] This setback should have sent a strong warning signal to U.S./UN forces, but General Douglas MacArthur was too arrogant to heed it. In mid-November, he ordered his troops to start a new "end the war" offensive. In response, Peng Dehuai adopted a strategy of "purposely showing ourselves to be weak, increasing the arrogance of the enemies, letting them run amuck, and luring them deep into our areas," and ordered his troops to wait for the best opportunity to strike back.[76] In late November, when the advancing U.S./UN troops had fallen into the traps that the Chinese had prepared for them, Peng ordered a vigorous counteroffensive, causing the U.S./UN forces to undertake what the political scientist Jonathan Pollack has called "the most infamous retreat in American military history."[77] By mid-December, the Chinese and the reorganized North Korean troops had regained control of nearly all the territory north of the 38th parallel.

At this moment, Mao reemphasized the original goal of "eliminating the enemy troops and forcing the Americans out of the Korean peninsula." He refused to consider any proposal about ending the Korean conflict through negotiations, and was determined to solve the Korean problem by winning a clear military victory. On 21 December, he ordered Peng Dehuai "to fight another campaign" and "to cross the 38th parallel."[78] The Chinese troops started the third offensive campaign on 31 December 1950, and occupied Seoul four days later. Then the Chinese chairman pushed Peng to develop the offensive into one "to end the war by a glorious victory." With their supply lines extended and casualties increased, however, the Chinese offensive gradually bogged down. Peng had to order the Chinese-North Korean forces to halt offensive operations and consolidate their gains.[79]

Before the Chinese and North Koreans had the opportunity to

take a break, though, the UN forces began a counteroffensive in mid-January. On 27 January, Peng, with his troops exhausted and short of ammunition and food, proposed a tactical retreat to Mao. The chairman, however, was not willing to consider anything short of a total victory. The next day he ordered Peng to answer the American offensive with a Chinese counteroffensive. He even believed that the Chinese/North Korean forces had the strength to reach the 37th or even the 36th parallel.[80] Peng had to obey Mao's instruction; but the Chinese counteroffensive, as Peng had predicted, was quickly repulsed by the U.S./UN forces. In late February, Peng returned to Beijing to convey to Mao in person the real situation on the battlefield, arguing that the Chinese should shift to the defensive, and that new troops should be sent to Korea to replace those units that had suffered heavy casualties.[81] In the light of Peng's report, Mao began to acknowledge that the war would be prolonged and that the best strategy was to rotate Chinese troops in and out of Korea. Believing that the Americans lacked the heart to sustain heavy losses, the chairman, though, still held the view that the Chinese could force the U.S./UN forces out of Korea in a war of attrition.[82]

After two months of intensive preparations, the Chinese-North Korean high command gathered twelve armies to start an overall offensive in late April, planning to destroy the bulk of UN forces and to establish clear communist superiority on the battlefield. Without adequate air cover and reliable logistical supply, however, this offensive quickly failed. In the last stage of the campaign, several Chinese units that had penetrated too deeply behind the U.S./UN lines were surrounded by counterattacking U.S./UN forces. One Chinese unit, the 180th Division, was totally eliminated.[83]

The cruel reality forced Beijing's leaders to reconsider China's war aims. Becoming willing to conclude the war short of a total Chinese/North Korean victory, Mao and the Beijing leadership, after consulting with the Soviet leader Stalin, began to place tight controls on the scale of Chinese/North Korean operations on the Korean battlefield.[84] On 10 July 1951 Chinese and North Korean representatives and U.S./UN delegates met for the first time at Kaesong to discuss conditions for an armistice. Neither the Chinese nor the Americans, though, would trust the value of negotiations unless they themselves could be in a position of strength. Indeed, not a single issue on the negotiation agenda could be re-

solved easily. When the U.S./UN side proposed that the repatriation of prisoners of war be carried out on a voluntary basis (if this
principle was adopted, large numbers of communist prisoners would
not be repatriated), the POW issue immediately created a deadlock. Viewing this issue as a "serious political struggle" related to
the essence of China's intervention in Korea, Beijing's leaders were
determined not to make any concession on it. Consequently, an
unyielding communist approach toward the POW issue combined
with an equally rigid American policy to make the war last for
another two years. Not until after Stalin's death in March 1953 did
Beijing's attitude begin to change as the new Soviet leadership favored ending the war at an early date.[85] Fighting finally ended on
27 July 1953, with each side holding approximately the same positions as they had three years before.

Concluding Remarks

Beijing's leaders—and Mao Zedong in particular—decided to enter the Korean War in October 1950 not only to protect China's
physical security but also, and more importantly, to pursue a glorious victory over the American-led UN forces. Underlying this approach is the CCP leadership's desire—in particular Mao's desire—to
transform the challenge and threat brought about by the Korean
crisis into the dynamics for enhancing the Communist Party's control of China's state and society, as well as to promote new China's
international prestige and influence. Mao and his comrades hoped
to see the revival of China's central position in the international
affairs of East Asia.

   Indeed, it is of primary importance to make a distinction between the pursuit of "*centrality*" and "*dominance*" in international
affairs as a fundamental goal of Chinese foreign policy, as well as
its policy toward the Korean crisis. Simply put, what Mao and his
comrades hoped to achieve was the spreading of the influences of
the "minds and hearts" of the Chinese revolution, but not the expansion of China's political and military control over foreign territories (including Korea)—this was too inferior an aim for Mao and
his comrades to pursue. When Mao issued the order to send Chinese troops to Korea on 8 October 1950, he emphasized that in
order for the Chinese "volunteers" to fulfill their tasks in Korea, it
was essential for them to respect the "Korean Party, People, and

Comrade Kim Il-sung." The Chinese endeavored to follow Mao's order during the war. For example, although Kim Il-sung purged most of the prominent members of the "Chinese section" within the Korean Communist Party (such as Kim Mu Chong and Pak Il-yu) during and immediately after the Korean War, and major differences repeatedly emerged between Kim and the Chinese at different stages of the war, the Chinese tried very hard not to interfere with North Korea's "internal affairs." Mao longed for something bigger—he hoped that China's intervention in Korea would contribute to the strengthening of the inner dynamics of China's continuous revolution, as well as leading to other peoples' recognition of Revolutionary China's morally superior position. In this sense, underlying the Sino-American confrontation was the profound conflict between the modern, revolutionary version of China's age-old "Central Kingdom" mentality and America's "Manifest Destiny" tradition.

China's intervention in Korea caused the loss of hundreds of thousands of young Chinese lives on the battlefield, forced the expenditure of billions of dollars for military purposes at the expense of China's economic reconstruction, prevented Beijing from recovering Taiwan and entering the UN (until the early 1970s), and made Beijing, at least in the short-run, more dependent upon Moscow. But from Mao's perspective, China's gain from participating in the war was considerable. In particular, China's intervention in Korea had bolstered his plans for continuing the revolution at home. In the wake of China's entrance into the war, Mao's Communist regime found itself in a powerful position to penetrate into almost every area of Chinese society through intensive mass mobilization under the banner of "Resisting America and Assisting Korea." During the war years, three nationwide campaigns swept through China's countryside and cities: the movement to suppress counter-revolutionaries, the land reform movement, and the "Three Antis" and "Five Antis" movements.[86] When the war ended in July 1953, China's society and political landscape had been altered: organized resistance to the new regime had been destroyed; land in the countryside had been redistributed and the landlord class had been eliminated; the national bourgeoisie was under the tight control of the Communist state, and the "petit-bourgeoisie" intellectuals had experienced the first round of Communist reeducation. Consequently, the CCP effectively extended and deepened its organizational control of Chinese society and dramatically promoted its authority and legitimacy in the minds of the Chinese people. As far as the war's impact on China's international status is concerned, the fact that Chinese troops successfully forced the U.S./UN forces to retreat from the Chinese-Korean border to the 38th parallel allowed Beijing to call its intervention in Korea a great victory. Mao and his comrades thus believed that they had won a powerful position from which to claim that international society—friends and foes alike— had to accept China as a great power. China's intervention in Korea thus represented a crucial episode in its continuous emergence as a revolutionary country in East Asia and in the world.

Notes

1. In 1994, I published *China's Road to the Korean War: The Making of the Sino-American Confrontation* (New York: Columbia University Press, 1994). I will summarize some of my main findings in the book, and will go beyond the book to incorporate some of the new findings in light of the new sources that have been made available to scholars since the book's publication.

2. See, for example, Allen S. Whiting, *China Crosses the Yalu: The Decision to Enter the Korean War* (New York: Macmillan, 1960); Melvin Gurtov and Hwang Byoog-Moo, *China under Threat: The Politics of Strategy and Diplomacy* (Baltimore: Johns Hopkins University, 1980), esp. chap. 2; for a more detailed introduction of the "China under Threat" thesis, see CHEN Jian, "China and the Korean War: A Critical Historiographical Review," in *Korean and World Affairs*, vol. 19, no. 2 (summer 1995): 314–36.

3. I will provide a more detailed analysis of why "centrality" and "dominance" should be viewed as two distinctively different concepts in understanding the fundamental goals of Chinese foreign policy in the "Concluding Remarks" of this essay.

4. What should be emphasized is that while it is common for non-Western countries to identify themselves as victims in the Western-dominated international system, the Chinese perception of itself as a victimized member in the system is unique in the sense that it formed such a sharp contrast with the age-old Chinese "Central Kingdom" concept. Therefore, the Chinese consciousness of their country being a victimized member of the international community was stronger and, from a Chinese perspective, the experience was more painful.

5. For a more detailed discussion of the Chinese victim mentality and its impact upon Chinese attitude toward the rest of the world during

modern times, see CHEN Jian, *The China Challenge in the 21st Century: Implications for U.S. Foreign Policy* (Washington, D.C.: U.S. Institute of Peace, 1998), 5–6.

6. In fact, in Mao's telegrams prior to and during China's intervention in Korea, he repeatedly mentioned that it was necessary for the Chinese to "beat American arrogance." See, for example, telegram, Mao Zedong to Stalin, 2 October 1950, *Jianguo yilai Mao Zedong wengao* [Mao Zedong's Manuscripts Since the Founding of the People's Republic, hereafter *Mao wengao*] vol. 1, (Beijing: Zhongyang wenxian, 1987), 539–41.

7. Zhou Enlai, "Our Diplomatic Policies and Tasks," *Zhou Enlai waijiao wenxuan* [Selected Diplomatic Papers of Zhou Enlai] (Beijing: Zhongyang wenxian, 1992), 48–51; see also Xue Mouhong et al., *Dangdai zhongguo waijiao* [Contemporary Chinese Diplomacy] (Beijing: Dangdai zhongguo, 1988), 4–5; and Pei Jianzhang, *Zhonghua renmin gongheguo waijiao shi, 1949–1956* [A Diplomatic History of the People's Republic of China, 1949–1956] (Beijing: Shijie zhishi, 1994), 2–4.

8. Mao Zedong, "Report to the Second Plenary Session of the CCP's Seventh Central Committee," *Mao Zedong xuanji* [Selected Works of Mao Zedong] vol. 4, (Beijing: Renmin, 1965), 1439–40.

9. For a more detailed discussion, see CHEN Jian, *China's Road to the Korean War,* chap. 1.

10. For a more detailed discussion of the CCP leadership's changing perception of "American threat" in late 1949 and early 1950, see CHEN Jian, *China's Road to the Korean War,* chap. 1, esp. pp. 14–17.

11. For a more detailed discussion of the CCP's policy toward the United States in 1949 and early 1950 (prior to the outbreak of the Korean War), see CHEN Jian, *China's Road to the Korean War,* chap. 2 and 4; see also Shu Guang Zhang, *Deterrence and Strategic Culture: Chinese-American Confrontations, 1949–1958* (Ithaca, N.Y.: Cornell University Press, 1992), chap. 2.

12. Michael H. Hunt emphasizes that American foreign policy was shaped by an ideology based on a conception of national mission, on the racial classification of other countries, and on suspicion an even hostility toward social revolution (See Michael Hunt, *Ideology and U.S. Foreign Policy* [New Haven, Conn.: Yale University Press, 1987]). I find that Hunt's analysis offers an enlightening reference for understanding U.S. policy toward revolutionary China in the late 1940s and early 1950s.

13. Yang Kuisong, *Zhonggong yu mosike de guanxi, 1920–1960* [CCP's Relations with Moscow, 1920–1960] (Taipei: Dongda tushu, 1997), part 2, esp. pp. 462–64; Yang Yunruo and Yang Kuisong, *Gongchan guoji yu zhongguo geming* [The Comintern and the Chinese Revolution] (Shanghai: Shanghai People's Press, 1988), chap. 5; Liao Gailong, "The Rela-

tions between the Soviet Union and the Chinese Revolution," *Zhonggong dangshi yanjiu* [CCP History Studies], supplementary issue, 1991, 2–4.

14. Shi Zhe, *Zai lishi juren shenbian* [At the Side of Historical Giants: Shi Zhe's Memoirs] (Beijing: Zhongyang wenxian, 1991), 307–8.

15. For an extended discussion of why and how the Soviet Union offered (or failed to offer) support to the CCP during the early stage of the Chinese civil war, see CHEN Jian, "The Chinese Civil War and the Rise of the Cold War in East Asia," in CHEN Jian, *Mao's China and the Cold War* (Chapel Hill: The University of North Carolina Press, 2001), 17–37, esp. 29–32; see also Liao Gailong, "The Relations between the Soviet Union and the Chinese Revolution," *Zhonggong dangshi yanjiu*, supplementary issue on the relationship between the Soviet Union and the Chinese revolution, 1990, 2–6; Yang Kuisong, *Zhonggong yu mosike de guanxi*, 521–70; and Yang Kuisong, "The Soviet Factor and the CCP's Policy toward the United States in the 1940s," *Chinese Historians*, vol. 5, no.1 (spring 1992): 17–34.

16. For a discussion, see CHEN Jian, *China's Road to the Korean War*, 65–69; see also Yang Kuisong, *Zhonggong yu mosike de guanxi, 1920–1960,* Part II; Niu Jun, "The Origins of the Sino-Soviet Alliance," in Odd Arne Westad ed., *Brothers in Arms: The Rise and Fall of the Sino-Soviet Alliance, 1945–1963* (Washington, D.C. and Stanford, Calif.: Woodrow Wilson Center Press and Stanford University Press, 1999), 47–89, esp. 61–69.

17. See Shi, *Zai lishi juren shenbian*, 197–226. For an insightful study emphasizing that the common commitment to Communist ideology played a decisive role in keeping the Chinese and Soviet Communists together, see Michael M. Sheng, *Battling Western Imperialism: Mao, Stalin, and the United States* (Princeton, N.J.: Princeton University Press, 1998).

18. Andrei Ledovsky, "Mikoyan's Secret Mission to China in January and February 1949," *Far Eastern Affairs* (Moscow), no. 2 (1995), 72–94, esp. 75–77; Westad, ed., *Brothers in Arms*, 298–300; Shi Zhe, *Zai lishi juren shenbian*, 326–27.

19. See Shi Zhe (trans. by CHEN Jian), "With Mao and Stalin: The Reminiscences of a Chinese Interpreter," *Chinese Historians*, vol. 5, no. 1 (spring 1992): 45–56. For a Russian account of the visit, see Andrei Ledovsky, "Mikoyan's Secret Mission to China in January and February 1949." It is interesting and important to note that the Chinese and Russian accounts on this visit are highly compatible.

20. See S. Tikhvinsky, "The Zhou Enlai 'Demarche' and the CCP's Informal Negotiations with the Americans in June 1949," *Far Eastern Affairs* (Moscow, in Russian), no. 3, 1994.

21. For more detailed discussions of Liu's visit to the Soviet Union, see Shi Zhe (tran. CHEN Jian), "With Mao and Stalin: the Reminiscences of

Mao's Interpreter, Part II: Liu Shaoqi in Moscow," *Chinese Historians*, vol. 6, no. 1 (spring 1993): 67–90; Zhu Yuanshi, "Liu Shaoqi's Secret Visit to the Soviet Union in 1949," *Dangde wenxian* [Party History Documents], no. 3 (1991): 74–81; Jin Chongji et al., *Liu Shaoqi zhuan* [A Biography of Liu Shaoqi] (Beijing: Zhongyang wenxian, 1998), 646–54.

22. Shi Zhe, *Zai lishi juren shenbian*, 389. In the Russian minutes of this conversation, however, this statement was not included. (See "Conversation between Stalin and Mao, Moscow, 16 December 1949, CWIHP *Bulletin*, winter 1995/96, 5–7.) I believe that a possible answer to this discrepancy lies in the cultural differences between Chinese and Soviet interpreters: While for Mao this was a statement with crucial importance, the Russians, without being able to catch the CCP chairman's underlying meanings, treated it only as a part of insignificant "greetings." For a discussion, see CHEN Jian, "Comparing Russian and Chinese sources: A New Point of Departure for Cold War History," CWIHP *Bulletin*, nos. 6–7 (winter 1995/96), 21.

23. Telegram, Mao Zedong to Liu Shaoqi, 18 December 1950, in Zhang Shuguang and CHEN Jian, eds. *The Chinese Communist Foreign Policy and the Cold War in Asia, 1944–1950* (Chicago: Imprint Publications, 1995), 128–29.

24. Shi Zhe, *Zai lishi juren shenbian*, 437–39.

25. Telegrams, Mao Zedong to Liu Shaoqi, 2, 3, and 5 January 1950, in Zhang Shuguang and CHEN Jian eds., *The Chinese Communist Foreign Policy and the Cold War in Asia*, 131–34. For an enlightening analysis of why Stalin changed his attitude toward this issue, see Shen Zhihua, "Sino-Soviet Relations and the Origins of the Korean War: Stalin's Strategic Goals in the Far East," *Journal of Cold War Studies*, vol. 2, no. 2 (2000): 44–68.

26. For a detailed and informative discussion of how the Chinese and the Soviets bargained in the negotiations leading to the signing of the Sino-Soviet treaty, see Shen Zhihua, "Interest Conflicts in the Sino-Soviet Treaty Negotiations and Their Solution," *Lishi yanjiu* [Historical Research], no. 2 (2001): 39–55; see also Dieter Heinzig, *Die Sowjetunion und das kommunistische China 1945–1950: Der beschwerliche Weg zum Bündnis* (Nomos Verlagsgesellschaft, 1998), chap. 5.

27. *Zhonghua renmin gongheguo duiwai guanxi wenjianji, 1949–1950* [A Collection of Diplomatic Documents of the People's Republic of China] (Beijing: Shijie zhishi, 1954), 75–76.

28. Han Huanzhi and Tan Jinjiao, *Dangdai zhongguo jundui de junshi gongzuo* [Military Affairs of Contemporary Chinese Army] vol. 2, (Beijing: Zhongguo shehui kexue, 1989), 161; Wang Dinglie, *Dangdai zhongguo kongjun* (Contemporary Chinese Air Force, Beijing: Zhongguo shehui kexue, 1989), 78–79, 110.

29. Interviews with Shi Zhe, August 1992. Shi Zhe did not point out when Mao and Stalin had this discussion. But a recent revelation of a telegram Stalin sent to F. N. Shtykov (The Soviet ambassador to Pyongyang) indicates that Mao and Stalin discussed the Korean issue in late January or early February 1950. Stalin informed Shtykov: "During our talks with Mao Zedong, who is still in Moscow, we discussed the necessity and possibility to help North Korea to raise its military potential and defense capabilities." Telegram, Stalin to Shtykov, 2 February 1950, cited from Evgeniy P. Bajanov and Natalia Bajanova, "The Korean Conflict, 1950–1953: The Most Mysterious War of the 20th Century—Based on Secret Soviet Archives," (unpublished manuscript), 37.

30. Ciphered telegram, Stalin to Shtykov, 30 January 1950, CWIHP *Bulletin*, no. 5 (spring 1995), 9.

31. Yang Zhaoquan, *Zhongchao guanxi lunwenji* [Essays on Sino-Korean Relations] (Beijing: Shijie zhishi, 1988), 220–31, 392–428; and Bruce Cumings, *The Origins of the Korean War*, vol. 2 (Princeton, N.J.: Princeton University Press, 1990), 358–59, 363.

32. The CCP Central Committee's Orders of Maintaining Defensive in the South and Waging Offensive in the North, 19 September 1945, *Zhonggong zhongyang wenjian xuanji* [Selected Documents of the CCP Central Committee], vol. 13 (Beijing: Zhonggong zhongyang dangxiao, 1987 internal edition), 147–48; see also Ding Xuesong and others, "Recalling the Northeast Bureau's Special Office in North Korea During the War of Liberation in the Northeast," *Zhonggong dangshi ziliao* [CCP History Materials], no.17 (March 1986): 198.

33. Ding Xuesong, "Recalling the Northeast Bureau's Special Office in North Korea," 198–201.

34. For example, in the memoirs of Chai Chengwen, Chinese counsellor to North Korea in 1950, he mentions that when he was sent by Zhou Enlai to North Korea in July 1950, Zhou specifically emphasized that the North Korean Communists offered tremendous support to the Chinese Communist forces in the Northeast during China's civil war, so the CCP "would do our best to support the Korean comrades if they so asked." See Chai Chengwen and Zhao Yongtian, *Banmendian tanpan* [Panmunjom Negotiations] (Beijing: Jiefangjun, 1989), 40.

35. Telegram, Kovalev (Soviet general adviser to China) to Filippov (Stalin), 18 May 1949, AVP, Fond 45, Opis 1, Delo 331, Listy 59–61; Telegram, Shtykov (Soviet ambassador to North Korea) to Vyshinsky (Soviet Foreign Minister), 15 May 1949. These two reports, however, were different in describing how CCP leaders responded to Kim Il's request. Shtykov's report, apparently reflecting Pyongyang's perspective, stated that Mao not only supported the North Korean Communists' plan to attack the South, but also promised to offer military aid if necessary. Kovalev

stressed that Mao asked that the North "not to launch a military attack until a more favorable moment." In addition, Mao asked the North Koreans to wait until after the Chinese Communists had liberated Taiwan.

36. The number here follows my discussion with Chinese military researchers in May 1991, which, interestingly, is compatible with Cumings' account, which is based on studies of American intelligence reports. See his *The Origins of the Korean War*, vol. 2, 363.

37. Report, Nie Rongzhen to Liu Shaoqi and Zhu De, 20 January 1950, *Nie Rongzhen nianpu* [A Chronological Record of Nie Rongzhen] (Beijing: Renmin, 1999), 525; Nie Rongzhen, *Nie Rongzhen huiyilu* [Nie Rongzhen's memoirs] (Beijing: Jiefangjun, 1984), 732.

38. CHEN Jian, *China's Road to the Korean War*, 110–11.

39. See, for example, Kathryn Weathersby, "Korea, 1949–1950: To Attack, or Not to Attack? Stalin, Kim Il-Sung, and the Prelude to War," CWIHP *Bulletin*, no. 5 (spring 1995): 1, 2–9.

40. For a more detailed discussion, see Sergei Goncharov, John Lewis, and Xue Litai, *Uncertain Partners: Stalin, Mao and the Korean War* (Stanford, Calif.: Stanford University Press, 1993), chap. 5.

41. For a documentary account, see Kathryn Weathersby, "Korea, 1949–1950: To Attack or Not to Attack? Stalin, Kim Il-sung and the Prelude to War"; "The Soviet Role in the Early Phase of the Korean War: New Documentary Evidence," *Journal of American-East Asian Relations*, vol. 2, no. 4 (winter 1993): 441.

42. These accounts are based on my interviews with Shi Zhe in August 1992. Russian sources available now are generally compatible with these accounts. See telegram, Roshchin to Filippov, 13 May 1950; telegram, Filippov to Mao on 14 May 1950, in CWIHP *Bulletin*, no. 4 (fall 1994): 61.

43. Yu Song-chol, "My Testimony," *Foreign Broadcast Information Service*, 27 December 1990, 26.

44. Direct documentary evidence for Kim Il-sung's failure to inform Beijing of his schedule to attack the South is the unpublished part of Mao's draft telegram to Stalin in October 1950, in which the CCP chairman complained that Kim Il-sung had never told him that the North Korean Communist would begin the attack on 25 June 1950. Draft telegram, Mao Zedong to Stalin, 2 October 1950, CCP Central Archives. This part of the telegram is not included in any of the telegram's published versions.

45. For a more detailed discussion on how the outbreak of the Korean War presented a variety of challenges to Beijing, see CHEN Jian, *China's Road to the Korean War*, 126–30.

46. See, for example, Report, Zhou Enlai at the Central Military Commission's Enlarged Meeting, 26 August 1950, in *Zhou Enlai junshi wenxuan* [Selected Military Papers of Zhou Enlai] (Beijing: Renmin, 1997),

43–50, esp. 43–44; instruction, PRC General Information Agency, "On the Propaganda against the U.S. Imperialists' Open Interference with China's Internal Affairs," 29 June 1950, in Xinhua News Agency ed. *Xinhuashe wenjian ziliao huibian* [A Collection of Documentary Materials of the Xinhua News Agency] (Beijing: n.d.), vol. 2, 50.

47. Both Mao Zedong and Zhou Enlai emphasized this viewpoint at a CCP Politburo meeting in early August 1950. See *Junshi lishi* [Military History], no. 6 (1996), 4; Bo Yibo, *Ruogan zhongda juece* [Recollections of Several Important Decisions and Events] (Beijing: Zhonggong zhongyang dangxiao, 1992), 43.

48. Report, Zhou Enlai at the Central Military Commission's Enlarged Meeting, 26 August 1950, in *Zhou Enlai junshi wenxuan*, 44; see also Shen Zonghong et al., *Zhongguo renmin zhiyuanjun kangmei yuanchao zhanshi* [A History of the Chinese People's Volunteers' War to Resist America and Assist Korea] (Beijing: Junshi kexue, 1988), 7.

49. He Di, "The Last Campaign to Unify China: The CCP's Unmaterialized Plan to Liberate Taiwan, 1949–1950," *Chinese Historians*, vol. 5, no. 1 (spring 1992): 12–16; Xiao Jinguang, *Xiao Jinguang huiyilu* (Xiao Jinguang's Memoirs) (Beijing: Jiefangjun, 1990), vol. 2, 8, 26.

50. Letter, Mao Zedong to Nie Rongzhen, 7 July 1950, *Mao wengao*, vol. 1, 428; Han Huanzhi and Tai Jinqiao et al., *Dangdai zhongguo jundui de junshi gongzuo*, vol. 1, 449–50.

51. Telegram, Mao Zedong to Gao Gang, 18 August 1950, *Mao wengao*, vol. 1, 499; see also telegram, Mao Zedong to Gao Gang, 5 August 1950, ibid., 454.

52. General Chinese Association of Resisting America and Assisting Korea, comp., *Weida de kangmei yuanchao yundong* [The Great Movement to Resist America and Assist Korea] (Beijing: Renmin, 1954), 7–8; see also the various accounts in Fan Hanqing chief ed., *Zhiyuan kangmei yuanchao jishi* [A Factual Record of Supporting the Movement to Resist America and Assist Korea] (Beijing: Zhongguo wenshi, 2000).

53. See State Council and Supreme People's Court, "Instruction on Suppressing Reactionary Activities," issued on 23 July 1950, in CCP Central Institute of Historical Docuements, compilation, *Jianguo yilai zhongyao wenxian xuanbian* [A Selection of Important Documents since the Founding of the People's Republic] (Beijing: Zhongyang wenxian, 1992–1998), vol. 1, 358–60); and "Fifteen Telegrams and Documents on Supressing Reactionary Activities during the Early Stage of the People's Republic," and Zhang Min, "A Survey of the Struggle to Suppress Reactionaries in the Early Years of the PRC," *Dangde wenxian* [Party History Documents, Beijing], no. 2 (1988), 31–41.

54. See, for example, telegram, Stalin to Soviet ambassador in Beijing

(N. V. Roshchin) with message for Zhou Enlai, 5 July 1950, CWIHP *Bulletin*, nos. 6–7 (winter 1995–1996): 43.

55. See CHEN Jian, *China's Road to the Korea War*, 156; see also telegram, Filippov (Stalin) to Zhou Enlai, 27 August 1950, CWIHP *Bulletin*, no. 6–7 (winter 1995/96): 45.

56. Sun Baoshen, "Mao Zedong Had Predicted that the Americans Could Land at Inchon," *Junshi shilin* [Military History Circles, Beijing], no. 10 (1990), 13; Shi Zhe, *Zai lishi juren shenbian*, 492. Mao Zedong later complained to Stalin about Kim Il-sung's failure to listen to Beijing's advice on the possibility of American forces' landing operation at the Inchon-Seoul area. Telegram, Mao Zedong to Stalin, 2 October 1950 (unpublished manuscript), cited in Pang Xianzhi and Li Jie, *Mao Zedong yu kangmeiyuanchao* [Mao Zedong and Resisting America and Assisting Korea] (Beijing: Zhongyang wenxian, 2000), 12–13.

57. Chai Chengwen and Zhao Yongtian, *Banmendian tanpan* [The Panmunjom Negotiations] (Beijing: Jiefangjun wenyi, second edition, 1992), 77; transcript of Shen Zhihua's interview with Chai Chengwen, 12 September 2000.

58. Letter, Kim Il-sung and Pak Hon-yong to Mao Zedong, 1 October 1950. The text of the letter is published in Military History Institute at the Academy of Military Science, compilation, *Kangmei yuanchao zhanshi* [A History of the War to Resist America and Assist Korea] (Beijing: Junshi kexue, 2000), vol. 1, 148–49.

59. Telegram, Stalin to Mao Zedong and Zhou Enlai, 1 October 1950, CWIHP *Bulletin*, nos. 6–7 (winter 1995–1996): 114.

60. See CHEN Jian, *China's Road to the Korean War*, 171–75. In the book, however, I made a mistake: the meeting was held by members of the CCP Central Secretariat, not CCP Politburo Standing Committee. I am grateful to Ambassador Xue Mouhou for pointing out this mistake.

61. Telegram, Mao Zedong to Stalin, 2 October 1950, *Mao wengao*, vol. 1, 539–40. The text of the telegram published in this volume is an abridged version. In a research trip to Beijing in November 1998, with the assistance of the CCP Central Archives, I obtained a xerox copy of the telegram's original text in Mao's own handwriting.

62. The quotations in this paragraph, which are not included in the telegram's published text in *Jianguo yilai MaoZedong wengao*, are from the copy of Mao's original text in author's possession.

63. Since the Chinese Central Archives has provided me with a photocopy of the telegram's original text in Mao's own handwriting, there is no doubt that this is a genuine document, and that its contents reflected Mao's thinking. That this telegram is not found in Russian archives and that another version of Mao's message to Stalin does exist point to the possibility that although Mao had drafted the telegram, he may not have dis-

patched it. In actuality, the original of this telegram is different from many of Mao's other telegrams in format: while other telegrams usually (but not always) carry Mao's office staff's signature indicating the time the telegram was dispatched, this telegram does not. It is therefore possible that Mao drafted this telegram but never dispatched it to Stalin. This is likely the case because of top CCP leaders' difference of opinion and because Stalin had failed to clearly commit Soviet military support, and air cover in particular, to China. For a discussion, see Shen Zhihua, "The Discrepancy between the Russian and Chinese Versions of Mao's 2 October 1950 Message to Stalin on Chinese Entry into the Korean War: A Chinese Scholar's Reply," trans. by CHEN Jian, CWIHP *Bulletin*, nos. 8–9 (winter 1996–1997): 237–42.

64. For a detailed discussion of these meetings, see CHEN Jian, *China's Road to the Korean War*, chap. 5; see also Zhang Xi, "Peng Dehuai and China's Entry into the Korean War," trans. CHEN Jian, *Chinese Historians*, vol. 6, no. 1 (spring 1993): 8–16.

65. For a more detailed discussion, see CHEN Jian, *China's Road to the Korean War*, 181–86; for Russian documentation on the October 1950 Mao-Stalin exchanges, see Alexander Mansourov, "Stalin, Mao, Kim, and China's Decision to Enter the Korean War, 16 September–15 October 1950: New Evidence from Russian Archives" (article and documents), *CWIHP Bulletin* 6–7 (winter 1995–1996): 94–119 (Stalin's message to Mao quoted here on pages 116–17), and Roshchin's ciphered telegram no. 25348, 7 October 1950 (reporting on his talk with Mao on the evening of 6 October), Dmitrii Volkogonov papers, Library of Congress, Washington, D.C., located and translated by Vladislav M. Zubok, National Security Archive.

66. "Mao Zedong's Order to Establish the Chinese People's Volunteers," 8 October 1950; telegram, Mao Zedong to Kim Il-sung, October 8, 1950, *Mao wengao*, vol. 1, 543–44, 545.

67. This is the phrase Shi Zhe, Mao's and Zhou's Russian-language interpreter, used in describing how Mao was dealing with Stalin in October 1950 (author's interview with Shi Zhe, August 1992).

68. For a more detailed discussion based on Shi Zhe's recollections, the validity of which were checked against other Chinese sources, see CHEN Jian, *China's Road to the Korean War*, 197–200.

69. Telegram, Mao Zedong to Peng Dehuai and others, 12 October 1950, *Mao wengao*, vol. 1, 552.

70. For a more detailed discussion, see CHEN Jian, *China's Road to the Korean War*, 200–202.

71. Telegram, Mao Zedong to Zhou Enlai, 13 October 1950, *Mao Zedong wenji* [A Collection of Mao Zedong's Works] (Beijing: Renmin, 1999), vol. 6, 103–4. For a more comprehensive discussion of this key document, see CHEN Jian, *China's Road to the Korean War*, 202–3.

72. Telegram, Mao Zedong to Peng Dehuai and Gao Gang, 17 October 1950, *Mao wengao*, vol. 1, 567.

73. Telegram, Mao Zedong to Deng Hua, Hong Xuezhi, Han Xianchu, and Xie Fang, 18 October 1950, *Mao wengao*, vol. 1, 567–68.

74. When and how the Soviet Air Force entered operations in Korea has been a confusing question for scholars in recent years. While some scholars, basing their discussion on information provided by Russian recollections and documents, believe that this occurred as early as November 1950, others, following the insights gained from Chinese sources, argue that the Soviet Air Force began operations in Korea in January 1951. I believe that the key here is to make a distinction between operations for the purpose of defending China's Northeast and the transportation lines across the Chinese-Korean border, especially the bridge over the Yalu River, and operations designed for supporting Chinese-North Korean land forces fighting in Korean territory. While the former did happen as early as November 1950 (as an inevitable extension of defending the air space of China's Northeast), the latter did not occur until January 1951. See Tan Jinqiao et al., *Kangmei yuanchao zhanzheng* [The War to Resist America and Assist Korea] (Beijing: Zhongguo shehui kexue, 1990), 201.

75. Peng Dehuai, *Peng Dehuai zishu* [An Autobiography of Peng Dehuai] (Beijing: Renmin, 1981), 259; Shen Zonghong et al., *Zhongguo renmin zhiyuanjun kangmei yuanchao zhanshi,* 37–38.

76. Peng Dehuai, *Peng Dehuai zishu,* 259–60.

77. Jonathan D. Pollack, "The Korean War and Sino-American Relations," in Harry Harding and Yuan Ming eds., *Sino-American Relations, 1945–1955: A Joint Assessment of a Critical Decade* (Wilmington, Del.: Scholarly Resources, 1989), 224.

78. Telegram, Mao Zedong to Peng Dehuai, 21 December 1950, *Mao wengao*, vol. 1, 731–32.

79. Telegram, Peng Dehuai to Han Xianchu, Wu Ruilin, and Fang Fushan, 7 January 1951, in Wang Yan et al., *Peng Dehuai nianpu* [A Chronological Record of Peng Dehuai] (Beijing: Renmin, 1998), 465; see also Tan Jinqiao et al., *Kangmei yuanchao zhanzheng* [The War to Resist America and Assist Korea] (Beijing: Zhongguo shehui kexue, 1990), 100.

80. Telegram, Peng Dehuai to Mao Zedong, 27 January 1951, in *Peng Dehuai nianpu,* 469; telegram, Mao Zedong to Peng Dehuai, 28 January 1951, CCA. For a more detailed discussion of the exchanges between Mao and Peng, see CHEN Jian, "China's Changing Aims during the Korean War," in *The Journal of American-East Asian Relations*, vol. 1, no. 1 (spring 1992): 31–33.

81. Wang Yan et al., *Peng Dehuai nianpu,* 480–81; Wang Yan et al., *Peng Dehuai zhuan* [A Biography of Peng Dehuai] (Beijing: Dangdai zhongguo, 1993), 451–53.

82. Telegram, Mao Zedong to Stalin, 1 March 1951, *Mao wengao*, vol. 2, 151–53; for a more detailed discussion of Mao's changing attitude toward Chinese victory in Korea, see CHEN Jian, "China's Changing Aims during the Korean War," 34–36.

83. For a Chinese account of this offensive campaign, see Shen Zonghong et al., *Zhongguo renmin zhiyuanjun kangmei yuanchao zhanshi*, 94–109; see also Shu Guan Zhang, *Mao's Military Romanticism: China and the Korean War, 1950–1953* (Lawrence: University of Kansas Press, 1995), 144–52.

84. Telegram, Mao Zedong to Peng Dehuai, 26 May 1951, *Mao wengao*, vol. 2, 331–32. In this telegram, Mao acknowledged that it was impossible for the Chinese volunteers to annihilate a whole American military unit in a single campaign, and that "the American troops at the present time still strongly desire to fight and are self-confident." Mao also conveyed the telegram to Stalin, asking for the Soviet leader's opinions. Stalin replied that the Chinese/North Korean forces should be very cautious in planning a new offensive, and should fully understand that the U.S./UN forces were different from Jiang Jieshi's troops, who the PLA had defeated in the Chinese civil war. Ciphered telegram, Mao Zedong to Filippov [Stalin], 27 May 1951, and ciphered telegram, Filippov to Mao Zedong, 29 May 1951, in Chinese Military Science Academy, ed., *Guanyu chaoxian zhanzheng de eguo wenjian* [Russian Documents on the Korean War] (Beijing: Chinese Military Science Academy, 1998), 151–52.

85. For a more detailed discussion about the tortuous process of the Korean War armistice negotiations, see CHEN Jian, "China's Strategies to End the Korean War," in CHEN Jian, *Mao's China and the Cold War*, chap. 4.

86. The "Three Antis" movement was designed to oppose corrupt Communist cadres; the "Five-Antis" movement was aimed at the national bourgeoisie class "who should not be destroyed at this stage but who needed to be tightly controlled by the power of the people's state." For discussions, see Frederick C. Teiwes, "Establishment and Consolidation of the New Regime," in Roderick MacFarquhar and John K. Fairbank, eds., *The Cambridge History of China* (Cambridge: Cambridge University Press, 1987), vol. 14, 88–91.

Chapter 4

Korean Borderlands

Imaginary Frontiers of the Cold War

Lloyd C. Gardner

In February 1951, Secretary of State Dean Acheson responded to one of his critics, the father of a young marine serving in Korea. Acheson had many critics in those days. The marine's father complained about the pointlessness of the war. Throughout the Korean War he was reviled as the man who lost China—much later he would be held out as an example of American cold war inflexibility. And today he is seen as the prime architect of a foreign policy that ended in the collapse of the Soviet Union. In many respects Korea was "Mr. Acheson's War." At the end of the first week of hostilities, in early July 1950, President Harry S. Truman wrote Acheson a note congratulating him on his every step since word first arrived of the North Korean action: "Your handling of the situation since has been superb."[1]

The marine and his father did not agree—neither did vocal Republican critics. Criticism from the left had all but disappeared from the American political scene, however, silenced by the events of the cold war. Henry Wallace, who had waged a battle for Franklin D. Roosevelt's legacy in 1948, now stood four-square behind the administration's policies—which did little to save them from conservative attacks. Acheson always gave as good as he got in these exchanges—and usually better than he got—but the letter from the marine's father gave him an opportunity to do more than speak his

126

piece. He sympathized, he began, with the marine, who, like others of his generation, had expected to go on living their lives peacefully "in communities where they have breathed in with the air truth and tolerance of others' interests, generosity and good nature, hard work, honesty, and fairness."

But there were forces loose in the world—now focused in Korea—that did not want this way of life to continue:

> Distant and shadowy figures in the Kremlin, controlling millions of people far from them, are setting out to make impossible such lives . . . [young men like the marine] had every right and hope to have. . . .
>
> This agony of spirit, so understandable and right, makes it hard to believe that so monstrous an evil can exist in a world based upon infinite mercy and justice.
>
> But the fact is that it does exist. The fact is that it twists and tortures all our lives. And, I believe, to each of us in this case as in so many others, the great thing is not what happens to us but how we bear what happens to us.[2]

I believe I can make a pretty fair case for this letter as the key document for understanding not only the Korean War, but what came before and what has come after in the cold war. There is no explanation of why the battle must be joined in Korea in the letter; Korea's boundaries were not of great importance to Acheson. When the North Koreans crossed the 38th parallel, they moved from geography to world politics. President Truman declared to the nation that the North Korean aggression demonstrated that the Moscow-trained "Communists" had moved ideologically from subversion to open combat to achieve their ends. Russian experts in the State Department had their doubts about that, as did the Joint Chiefs of Staff. The top Russian expert, George F. Kennan, was excluded from the meetings where the initial decisions were taken to repulse the attack, a sign, he feared that stopping the North Koreans was not Acheson's only, or primary, concern.

Kennan believed that the Russian decision to "unleash a civil war" was closely connected to unilateral American policies in postwar Japan, now reaching a crucial stage where it appeared they would be excluded from a voice in the peace treaty with that country, in which, it was proposed, the United States would continue to have military bases.³ As the war progressed, Kennan was ending his work as chief of the policy planning staff—increasingly ignored by Acheson as something of a mystic, whose lengthy ruminations on the whole spectrum of foreign policy questions, provided the secretary with too few precise answers, and far too many ques- tions. It was something (actually more than something) of an irony that the author of the "X" article, which had introduced word "Containment" into the diplomat's lexicon, now felt himself cast aside as an unwanted Jeremiah—whose views on Korea clashed so completely with those held by men he had once hoped to instruct about the Soviet Union's expansionist outlook.⁴

Kennan had approved the initial decision to resist the North Korean action, even while questioning the major premise of Truman's public explanation that the war demonstrated a major shift, an escalation of Soviet ambitions, and a willingness to use armed force anywhere to achieve its supposed ends. When he de- clared himself against crossing the 38th parallel, the imaginary boundary between the "two Koreas," Kennan's apostasy was leaked "to a journalist as evidence of a dangerous waywardness of opin- ion on my part."⁵ The postwar division of Korea precisely at the 38th parallel was the work of a couple of army colonels, one of them, Dean Rusk, who would soon become famous for his deter- mination to "hold the line" against communism, not only in Korea but later in Vietnam. At the time, the colonels had no idea that they were establishing anything like a permanent boundary. At the time, also, Stalin had little reason to complain, calculating that while two-thirds of the Korean population lived below that line, the offer constituted a substantial buffer zone for his far eastern boundary. He may also have recalled, or been reminded, that Tokyo had once proposed that line as a division of spheres of influence, and the tsar's greediness had led to a disastrous war that brought on a pe- riod of political instability—the last thing the Russian dictator wanted. He may, indeed, have regarded the division as permanent.⁶

If that were so, nothing worked out according to plan. The Koreans established in power, Kim Il-sung in the North, and Syngman Rhee in the South, were both determined to abolish the dividing line. The emerging cold war raised the issue—much stressed by conservative critics of the Truman administration—that one could not have it black-and-white in Europe and shades of grey in Asia. And while the American military continued to believe that Korea was a liability strategically, especially in a time of demobilization of ground forces, there was a shift of attitudes taking place in the State Department—led by then Undersecretary of State Dean Acheson. During secret hearings on the Truman request for aid to Greece and Turkey, Acheson singled out Korea as a place where American power could also be an effective barrier to communist encroachment on the "Free World." Answering senators who feared the Truman approach meant extending the American defense perimeter to the entire world, the undersecretary tried to suggest that was not the case. Still, there were, he said, "other places where we can be effective. One of them is Korea, and I think that is another place where the line has been clearly drawn between the Russians and ourselves."[7]

The State Department developed plans for large-scale aid to Korea, plans that would total some $600 million—$200 million more than had been asked for Greece and Turkey. The British were quite surprised at the shift in American attitudes toward Korea—especially as it was not yet clear that negotiations to reunite the country had failed. In a memo of 26 March 1947, Asia specialist M. E. Dening wondered if the Americans "have thought this all out." What it suggested, he believed, was that the Truman administration believed the "challenge is of world-wide application."[8]

With Nationalist China deep in turmoil, American occupation policies in Japan floundering, and the crisis of decolonization threatening stability throughout the rest of Asia, policy makers had come to believe that Korea could not be left to its own fate—the stakes were too high. Korean borderlands thus became, imaginary or not, the place where issues of great moment for the world would play themselves out. Convincing Congress to commit $600 million to Korea proved too difficult in 1947, nevertheless, and soon Acheson was gone—at least temporarily—from government. He had long been convinced that the early New Deal intra-nationalist experimentations threatened basic institutions, especially if they set the precedent for postwar planning. It was especially irksome that Congress had responded to irresponsible calls to demobilize the army almost as soon as the war ended, ignoring the need for "steadiness and confidence which our forces gave and would have continued to give to millions all over a badly shattered and uncertain world."[9]

The major obstacle to America's assuming its rightful (and needful) role in the world was thus identified as the irresponsibility of public figures, whose behavior threatened not only as "the degradation of the democratic dogma, about which Brooks Adams warned, but the degradation of all mankind everywhere, paralyzing the very centers of moral action, until these oceans of cunning words wash through the minds of men like the sea through the empty portholes of a derelict."[10] It was hardly surprising that such sentiments would bring Acheson a bounteous portion of outraged wrath from those he called "the primitives;" but neither was it surprising, then, that he felt it necessary to practice Machiavelli's "Holy Pretense" to win over the confused to the side of righteousness. A George Kennan, scattering doubts where certainty should reign, had no place standing in the portals like the ancient mariner, handing out messages of foreboding and fear.[11]

It infuriated congressional leaders—especially Republicans—on the other hand, that Acheson, when he came back to government a second time as secretary of state in Truman's second term, seemed almost lackadaisical about aid to Nationalist China. No matter how many times, or in how many ways, he tried to explain that there was really nothing more the United States could do to save Chiang Kai-shek from the fate he had brought on himself by failing to do anything about corruption in his government, his listeners shook their heads in disbelief. In this mood, aid to Korea became a hard sell—as if, having given away the real prize, the administration wanted Congress to bid on a small piece of real estate filled with abandoned ruins from forty years of Japanese rule that no one really wanted anyway.

Undersecretary of State James Webb argued before the Senate Foreign Relations Committee in executive session that American policy in Korea was more than just holding the line, that the long-range objective was to provide a demonstration of the "value of a free republican form of government," and the "pull" would be "such as ultimately to unite the country." Senators were not persuaded, even so, that a united Korea was of great worth to the United States. But the thought of "losing" Korea in the wake of the Chinese Revolution put a different face on matters. Senator Henry Cabot Lodge put it thusly:

> I feel, too, that the significance of Korea is not so much within itself as the effect it would have on other parts of the Far East, and if we were to lose Korea under honorable conditions after

trying to do our best I would not feel it was a great tragedy, because *I do not think it is a very strategic part from the standpoint of the Russians that they haven't got already*, but I think for us just to toss it to the wolves would have a very demoralizing effect on China.

Senator Tom Connally:
  It was pointed out here the other day in somebody's testimony that Korea is the last thing we have in the Far East.
Senator Lodge:
  It isn't much good, but it's ours.
Senator Connally:
  Yes. We have got it, and if we should abandon it, it would look to the whole of Asia that we were washing our hands of it and letting it get away.[12]

What "letting it get away" meant had very little to do with Korea itself, Senator Lodge said. The boundaries of Korea ideologically, however, now extended to all of Asia—and, as matters developed, to all of the "free world." The economic boundaries of Korea had also to be designed to accommodate the economic recovery of Japan, that is to restore the prewar complementary nature of Japanese-Korean relations, while at the same time excising the "colonial" aspects of those exchanges. In September 1945, one of the first American officers in the occupation force walked into a Mitsui office in Tokyo, and was greeted by a man who pointed to a map on the wall that portrayed the infamous Greater East Asian Coprosperity Sphere Japan had ballyhooed as promising the end of Western dominance. "There it is," he said. "We tried. See what you can do with it!"[13]

By 1949 it hardly appeared that the United States was going to do much better than the failed Japanese attempt, despite its great wealth and still-usable reputation as an anti-colonial liberator. Secretary Acheson had made public his instructions to American diplomatic representatives that it was Washington's policy not to allow any more communist "victories," but how far would rhetoric go? And what should the rhetoric say, with or without military force to back it up? Perturbed by its limited options, the State Department struggled with a statement on the ferment boiling up in Asia. One of Acheson's aides, John Melby, criticized an early draft because of a sentence down in the last paragraph—where the author of the paper had casually summarized the American attitude saying that Asians "must realize their destiny in their own way." Melby's comment caught the fear of the moment, "Does this mean that if Asia elects to fulfill its destiny in cooperation with the Soviet Union and in a frame of mind hostile to the United States we are prepared to accept that?"[14]

At about the same time, Acheson briefly pondered what the prospects were for encouraging the idea that America's traditional Open Door policy could be offered to the new Chinese regime, providing for some room for maneuver. He could not believe that any Chinese government would settle for the sort of status imposed on Eastern Europe. But he was hedged in by "internal party politics," he cautioned British Foreign Secretary Ernest Bevin, and besides, it would not do to be seen as running after the communists. Let them come to us. Who knew what would happen? Something might emerge that would resemble a genuine coalition government. More likely, the Chinese Communists would have to find out for themselves "that the position of a satellite of Russia had little to recommend it." Meanwhile, he concluded, we should "be constantly on the look-out for the development of a Chinese version of Titoism."[15]

This was dangerous territory to enter. With the Communists in command in Beijing, the administration's critics were in full cry against any more "sell-outs." Korea was all but forgotten for the moment with the hullabaloo raised by documents leaked from the State Department in which Acheson had instructed American diplomats that U.S. policy was to "let the dust settle" and keep options open about future diplomatic relations with China proper, and supposed "leftist" influence on another policy decision to abandon Formosa as of no strategic value.[16]

Acheson pointed out that wartime agreements left no doubt that Formosa and Korea were to be taken from Japan, and the former returned to China. He made little headway with the argument. On 6 January 1950, President Truman stated that the United States would not extend military assistance to Chiang's minions on Formosa. Formosa was a question for the Chinese to settle themselves. And, as late as March 1950, Acheson was still defending that policy.

What we are concerned with in China are two great things.

The first one is that whoever runs China, even if the devil himself runs China, if he is an independent devil. That is infinitely better than if he is a stooge of Moscow. . . .

Now you find that the Communists are in control of China, and . . . you see that there are two . . . methods in which you can operate. One is to fight them. You can send over, directly or indirectly, airplanes, ships, soldiers, and go in and fight. The other one is to do everything you can to separate them from Moscow. . . .

I would put my money clearly on the second. I do not think we are going to or can put the amount of money, men, and materiel that would be necessary into a military overthrow of Communist China.[17]

Even as Acheson testified on the hope for a "Titoist" outcome in China, however, his aides were finishing work on a new all purpose directive, the famous NSC 68 document, which, more than the "X" article or any other pronouncement, globalized American foreign policy. The announcement that Russia had exploded an atomic "device" in September 1949 sent a severe shock wave through the nation. In part this was because American policy makers from Truman down to the lower echelons had boasted about the bomb's superiority over all previous weapons of war, even, in the president's statement after Hiroshima, going so far as to claim that the achievement could *only* have been made in America. In a curious twist, then, the shock wave from the Russian bomb was amplified many times over by American boasts from previous years!

Acheson had to worry also about a secondary aftershock from the Siberian blast. What would the consequences be in China—but also in other areas of what was soon to be called, with half-patronizing, half-fearful ethnocentrism, the third world? Recalling his feelings shortly after leaving office in 1953, Acheson explained what the early Russian success in apparently matching the United States really threatened: "We had the monopoly of the atomic bomb, we were riding on the top of the world, there was no problem so far as we were concerned; the Russians were on the under side of the circle, they were nowhere. . . . Now, suddenly, this business is dissolved. We haven't got the monopoly of the atomic bomb. This great thing that Churchill says . . . has policed the world has disappeared. It doesn't exist any more. What do you do?"[18]

What you do, Acheson answered himself, is write a doctrine. If you failed, "All the power of this rather primitive world is creating something which, in a very short time, is going to knock the daylights out of our world." The secretary was very fond of using the circle metaphor and variations such as perimeter and crescent to describe the outer boundaries of the American security system. Sometimes he mixed these. He also left confusing impressions of what he meant, of what was and was not included within the area. Japan was always placed at one end of the "semicircle" in Asia and India at the other. "There the great question is to find sources of raw materials for Japanese industry and to find markets."[19]

Acheson's most famous effort to describe the boundaries came on 12 January 1950, in a speech before the National Press Club. He had spent considerable time working on this speech, even though he later attempted to diminish the importance of his precise choice of words by pointing out that he spoke only from a few pages of notes. He knew exactly what he wanted to say. The postfacto camouflage served other purposes when criticism arose for leaving Korea outside in the cold war came back to haunt him. The purpose of the speech was threefold. First, he wished to draw a distinction between America's response to Asian yearnings for freedom, and what he described as Russian neo-colonialism in China—and threats elsewhere in Southeast Asia. Second, he wished to reassure areas outside those where American forces were stationed that while they would have to repel any initial attacks, they could feel certain they could rely upon "the commitments of the entire civilized world under the Charter of the United Nations." Extending these remarks, he made his third point: the United States could not "furnish loyalty of a people to its government." If that loyalty was there, however, along with will and determination, "American help can be effective and it can lead to an accomplishment which could otherwise not be achieved."[20]

Far from neglecting Korea, the speech spoke directly to American concerns about preserving American influence there and elsewhere. At the time Acheson spoke, American troops had been withdrawn—leaving behind what was thought to be an adequate defense system to protect South Korea from a North Korean attack. The greatest danger was thought to be from *inside* South Korea—from Syngman Rhee's inability to meet the demands of his people for more democracy, and, failing that, a foolhardy attempt to launch an invasion of the North in an effort to reunite Korea behind a bloody patriotism. Acheson was determined not to be dragged behind Rhee's rickety chariot—or, perhaps better put, to allow himself to be put in front of American tanks in a war that could involve Russia and China.

It is also useful to remember the setting of the 12 January speech. It was the American military that had declared on several occasions that Korea was not militarily significant, and especially not given the Truman directives that defense budgets should be kept as low as possible. As late as 1948, the Joint Chiefs of Staff had issued a warning that the United States should not become "so irrevocably involved in the Korean situation that an action taken by any faction in Korea *or by any other power in Korea* could be considered a casus belli for the United States."[21] The drafters of NSC 68 were working on the idea that there should be a vast new expenditure on defense, but even though a decision had been taken to build the "super," the hydrogen bomb, the urgency felt in State did not seem to be widespread in government, and certainly not on Capitol Hill—however loud the howling over the loss of China and supposed abandonment of Formosa. In a talk with British ambassador Sir Oliver Franks in late December 1949, Acheson had predicted that "the world across the Pacific Ocean would be the principal preoccupation of the State Department in 1950." The greatest danger, it appeared, would be a move south by China, into areas that already had large overseas Chinese populations. What made Acheson and his aides believe, contrary to some of the secretary's own statements about flexibility and possible accommodation, that Mao Zedong would go on the offensive? Acheson's answer was interesting. "The Communists would, by aggrandizement in the south, direct the gaze of the Chinese people from Manchuria." There was not much money available should the Chinese do as he predicted. "He had been scratching together what dollars he could, and believed he could lay hands on about 75 million."[22]

Those were the political boundaries inside the United States that Acheson confronted. While the nation caught up to his vision of the world as "a set of city blocks," he would continue managing the resources he had to best advantage. As historian Bruce Cumings contextualizes the 12 January speech, the secretary's purposes grew from that vision. "Acheson thought about his global city and its various blocks on a daily basis; he had visions, plans, and he knew how to keep a secret. Acheson rarely seemed to expect or care that those around him would understand; he enjoyed his private vision and the exercise of a hidden hand, secret power."[23]

All this does not mean, however, that the 12 January speech was an example of a carefully plotted seduction. Acheson did not have in mind maneuvering the North Koreans into firing the first shot. *If* Kim Il-sung's troops did march, however, Acheson had outlined what his likely response would be. He had also outlined, though in less clear detail, how the Rhee problem would be solved.

On 21 March 1950, Acheson met with Republican representative Christian Herter. Herter was alarmed by the false feeling of security among the American people. The secretary agreed that was the case, and that the people did not seem to realize that this was a global conflict. The situation had not deteriorated much, but certainly if, after the Chinese Revolution, the trend of the past six months continued, there would be more deterioration. What could be done, said Herter, to wake up the nation? Perhaps, he continued, we could break diplomatic relations with Moscow so as to create a situation of awareness. Acheson's reply is instructive:

> I replied that I do not believe it will be necessary to create such a situation, the chances are too good that the Russians will do so themselves.
>
> There was, for example, the proposed demonstration in Berlin, which might see as many as 300,000 German youths from the East attacking the populace of West Berlin. "That would certainly be a messy situation and a crisis." The Russians might try to order us out of Austria, he went on.
>
> Finally, I referred to the possibility of an overall attack on Formosa from the mainland of China where we understand air strips are being built, Soviet planes are being furnished, and Soviet crews are training Chinese crews.[24]

What makes Acheson's comment particularly interesting is that while he was giving Herter reason to believe that the Russians would move in a way to create "a messy situation and a crisis," his aides in the Department of State had completed a survey conducted on the question of whether and where the Soviets were likely to move with force. They made a survey of every point, "where we touched," Acheson told interviewers at the Truman Library. The conclusion was that they probably "would not." If it did happen, Korea was an unlikely place. "It might be in Yugoslavia, which really would be a tough one to handle."[25]

Trying to make a crisis out of an attack on Tito would be a tough one to handle, from almost every point of view. With NSC 68 drafted, the State Department was ready. The lead article in *Time* magazine for 1 May 1950, reported that the frequency of cold war "incidents" had intensified, most recently the shoot-down of a navy patrol bomber either near or over Latvia. "Lesser incidents than these, if anyone wanted war, could obviously provoke one," *Time* commented. "We must not forget," the magazine quoted an Acheson speech, "that it is we, the American people, who have been picked out as the principal target of the Soviet Communists."[26]

A close student of nineteenth-century imperial behavior might well notice parallels here with the rising tensions between the new superpowers, parallels also between the aggressive reconnaissance missions of the cold war and the gunboat diplomacy of that earlier era. Stung by charges that they had "lost" China—now carried to new heights at home by Senator Joseph McCarthy—the administration feared this new variant of "yellow journalism," feared that it would lose control of matters. And here was yet another parallel with the domestic turmoil inside the European nations as the Age of Imperialism reached its climax at the end of the century. To ease that danger, Republican "internationalist" John Foster Dulles was asked to undertake the task of writing a peace treaty with Japan. The purpose in having Dulles on board was to restore bipartisanship—all but destroyed in the quarrels over Far Eastern policy. If things were approaching a crisis, Dulles's presence in the front lines would be essential to national unity.

The Republican sought assurances that he had the full confidence of the administration, both from Acheson and Truman. In a conversation with the latter, Dulles tried to impress on Truman the need for "some early affirmative action . . . to restore the confidence of the American people that the Government had a capacity to deal with the Communist menace." Americans had lost confidence in their government "as a result of what had happened, particularly in the East."

It was this lack of confidence which I felt made it possible for men like McCarthy to make a deep impression upon the situation and to achieve prominence. *If we could really get going, the American people would fall in behind that leadership and attacks like McCarthy's would be forgotten.*

I said that I had various ideas which I was discussing with Secretary Acheson and that I hoped to be able to make some contribution along this line.[27]

Truman assured Dulles that he "quite agreed," and that "in talking with Secretary Acheson he had expressed much the same point of view." What they talked about—Acheson and Dulles—no doubt ranged over a good many areas of the world. But the Republican's assignment was to complete the drafting of a peace treaty with Japan. The mission called for considerable tact, given the still-fresh memories of Japanese aggression in World War II. Various areas had suffered differently, of course, and it would be his job to reassure the smaller countries that the Japanese had been "tamed." But that might be the easiest part of the assignment. He also had to convince America's cold war allies that a revitalized Japan would not become an economic menace; and he had to satisfy Congress that Tokyo would not become involved with "Red China" out of a *selfish* desire to get back its lost trade connections.

Korea was a key stop on the way to Japan. Rhee's anger at the United States for not being willing to countenance his strong desire to move north had to be assuaged in order to get cooperation for the proposed Japanese peace treaty. Lately, Rhee had sent emissaries to other Asian countries in search of a counterpart for the North Atlantic Treaty Organization (NATO). Washington was not ready for such a move, and certainly not one by Syngman Rhee, who was widely regarded throughout Asia as a warmongerer and a net liability for American policy—even by allies. Before he left on his tour of Asia, however, Dulles met with Ambassador John Chang Myun and told him that he had drafted a statement approved by Acheson that if Korea had to fight, it would not fight alone.[28]

There are several reasons why Acheson would approve such a statement, including most obviously, that he did not think that it in anyway differed from his 12 January speech. That more emphasis was placed on standing alongside the South Koreans in both Dulles's private conversations and his speech to the Seoul National Assembly did not indicate a policy reversal, but rather an acceleration of the "staging process" that economic historians sometimes speak about in describing the prerequirements for an innovative technique, mechanically or intellectually. Acheson expressed considerable amusement at photos of Dulles standing beside American and South Korean soldiers in the "trenches" near the 38th parallel, wearing his *de rigeur* Wall Street black homburg hat. But the symbolism was almost perfect, both as to the unity in American policy-making circles, and as contrast to a similarly "uniformed" Neville Chamberlain dressed as a City of London banker with bat-wing collar, drinking appeasement tea with Adoph Hitler at Berchesgarten.

The question of who started the Korean War has never really been the critical issue for historians. Joseph Stalin gave Kim Il-sung the green light, after the latter had impressed upon him the supposed weaknesses of the South Korean regime's hold on its people. Like the Americans who had overseen the creation of Syngman Rhee's government, the Russian dictator was deeply concerned about what might happen should Rhee succeed in any one of his various ploys to encourage Washington's support for a move north.

With the Japanese treaty about to be completed, moreover, there was the refitting of former Japanese air bases on Okinawa in order to make them ready for B-29s capable of carrying the atomic bomb. If we turn the Asian kaleidoscope to see how things might have appeared from Moscow's side of the world, a fertile field for carrying on the mission of world revolution becomes instead a dangerously unstable situation with the American right in an angry state over the "loss of China" and spoiling for an opportunity to give Mao a hard smack. America apparently was abandoning Korea to its fate, with two leaders ambitious to send one another to the guillotine and reunite their country; Chinese revolutionaries were bristling with hatred for the United States, most recently for aiding Chiang in his island redoubt, and were themselves spoiling for some sort of fight.

Stalin wanted reunification of Korea—but Kim Il-sung was not worth World War III. Almost as soon as the fighting began on 25 June, proposals were floated for reopening negotiations on Korean unification. On 6 July 1950, for example, Deputy Foreign Minister Andrei Gromyko had a serious discussion with the British ambassador and did not flinch at the latter's suggestion that not only an end to the fighting was required but also progress on negotiations leading to reunification. Stalin then reported this development to Mao. The British suggestion that the first step had to be a North

Korean withdrawal to the 38th parallel was "impertinent and unacceptable," he said. In the next paragraph, however, he gave notice that he would reply to the British that "the Korean question had become too complicated after the armed foreign intervention and that such a complex question can be resolved only by the Security Council with the participation of the USSR and China and with the summoning of representatives of Korea in order to hear their opinion." The message closed with a question about Chinese readiness to send divisions to the Korean border—and a promise to send jet fighter planes "for covering these troops."[29]

Stalin thus covered all his bets. When the British were told that Moscow desired a Security Council meeting with China present, it raised the political stakes very high. London had granted diplomatic recognition to the new government in Bejing—a position that would cause serious acrimony in transatlantic cable traffic for years to come. The British, in turn, were perturbed by Truman's seemingly deliberately provocative statements about Formosa that implied it should never go back to China so long as the Communist regime existed. Such an approach could hardly calm a tense situation made worse by the war in Korea. The McCarthyite infection of American politics had already reached a virulent stage, unfortunately, so that no matter what the State Department thinking might be, politically, Truman felt enough heat that he had to get out of the kitchen, without turning the gas burners off first. The upshot of the Gromyko-Kelly exchanges produced a flat Washington pronouncement that the only thing that needed settling in Korea was the presence of North Korean forces in the south and an end to the fighting. The Indian ambassador, Madame Pandit, who had also gotten involved in the pre-negotiations, was told that the seating of Communist China was an entirely separate matter that should not divert the world's attention from aggression in Korea. Assistant Secretary of State George McGhee noted that he "was aware that our position on this and other matters was being misinterpreted, but he feared that this was the price we had to pay for the role of world leadership which had been thrust upon us."[30]

Another official, Secretary of the Army Frank Pace, recalled later that the feeling was the Russians were "testing" us. "If we were going to stop this thrust, now was the time to do it. . . ." Asked if anyone in those early meetings at Blair House dissented from the decision to intervene, Pace replied a trifle ambiguously:

"Not really, no. The feeling was very unanimous there. People expressed it in different ways. Some were a little more complex. *I'm sure that a broader view of all the implications was made by Dean Acheson as Secretary of State,* but the President had the comfort of really a unanimous assessment that this was the thing to do."[31]

A more succinct summary of Acheson's thinking and key role, if understated here, probably does not exist. Russian "guilt" for the war's outbreak seems clear enough, as does Moscow's responsibility for resolving the last remaining issues concerning how a limited war extended Korea's borderlands to the entire world. Accepting the warm congratulations of the Norwegian ambassador for Washington's involvement—"This action will sweep away the skepticism"—the secretary of state replied, "This situation has pulled us together." He continued, "I observed that the present situation is completely different from the previous situation in which it had been urged that we intervene in Formosa."[32]

Less than a year later, after MacArthur's removal as commander of UN and American forces in Korea, a new skepticism about American policy had arisen. In Europe, the nation's allies were fearful that the Truman administration did not know where to stop; at home, the administration's critics feared that dark forces had prevented MacArthur from going far enough. During the hearings that followed the general's recall, the Chairman of the Joint Chiefs of Staff, General Omar Bradley, testified that MacArthur's plans for extending the conflict to strike at Chinese bases would be, in his famous statement, "The wrong war, at the wrong time, against the wrong enemy."

"Brad's" defense of limited war was hailed then, and now, as establishing a "code of conflict" for sophisticated waging of the cold war. Closely examined, however, his statement actually undermined the rationale for the Korean War as a defense against a Communist monolith, which, as Acheson had said in the final weeks before the North Korean invasion, "We must not forget that it is we, the American people, who have been picked out as the principal target of the Soviet Communists." The Bradley testimony came after MacArthur's ill-fated march to the Yalu brought the Chinese into the war. In its first months, after recovery from the initial attack, Korea was the "right war, at the right time, against the right enemy."

The "staging process" for Korea consisted of several steps: the Chinese Revolution, the Russian atomic bomb, the rise of McCarthyist criticism. All these were necessary to universalize Korea's borderlands. Acheson was fond of saying that "Korea saved us," when talking about the implementation of NSC 68. With Korea, and NSC 68 as formulae, the United States crossed another border—the arms race, whose momentum has outlived the cold war into the era of what some now call, the "unipolar moment." Korea also saw the beginnings of what has also been called the "Imperial Presidency." Acheson specifically rejected the idea that Truman should call for a declaration of war, in part because he was not yet sure in that first week that the nation was truly behind intervention, and, in part, because of his expectation that the cold war might entail future "police actions."

Truman's last book was a collection of essays on the presidents, edited posthumously by his daughter, entitled, *Where the Buck Stops*. Thomas Jefferson, he wrote, was "worth a lot of respectful attention." He devoted three chapters to Jefferson. Among Jefferson's greatest qualities was his ability to "stretch" the Constitution, as in the case of the Louisana Purchase. Despite the qualms of some of his opponents, Jefferson seized the moment to add that vast territory—and thereby ensure the future of the nation. "A lot of us had to stretch the Constitution at times," Truman added. And, in another essay, he stated: "Every good American president has been an expansionist to a certain extent."[33]

When Truman considered the question of presidential powers in terms of meeting the Korean situation, there was some talk of the need to consult Congress. It was resolved, in part, by calling the intervention a "police action," which also had the merit of implying that the North Koreans were lawbreakers or bandits. Indeed, even the thought of consulting Congress raised fears in Dean Acheson's mind that "you might have completely muddied up the situation."[34] This essay is not the place to go into the costs of the Korean War—for the Koreans, for whom it was an appalling catastrophe; for the Chinese, who suffered heavy casualties; and for the Americans, who also suffered and died in the war. Korea's legacy is practically incalculable as well in terms of the costs of the arms race, the international isolation of China, and for the impact on American political development. Korea did not provide, as some thought it would, an escape from McCarthyism's ill effects, but rather a narrowing of the "legitimate" areas of debate. And these were only some of the outcomes of the war for the Korean borderlands—imaginary frontiers of the cold war.[35]

Notes

1. Margaret Truman, *Harry S. Truman* (New York: William Morrow & Co., 1973), 471.
2. MacGeorge Bundy, *The Pattern of Responsibility* (Boston: Houghton, Mifflin Co., 1952), 298–99.
3. George F. Kennan, *Memoirs: 1925–1950* (Boston: Atlantic, Little Brown, 1967), 395.
4. Ibid., 34–35.
5. Ibid., 24.
6. William Stueck, *The Korean War: An International History* (Princeton, N.J.: Princeton University Press, 1995), 18–19.
7. Bruce Cumings, *The Origins of the Korean War,* 2 vols. (Princeton, N.J.: Princeton University Press, 1990), II, 48.
8. Ibid.
9. Dean Acheson, "Random Harvest: The Perverted Ingenuity of Propaganda," speech before the Harvard Clubs, Boston, 4 June 1946.
10. Ibid.
11. The dispute between the two did not end when Kennan left the State Department. Acheson was particularly incensed a decade later when Kennan, in a series of lectures on the BBC, called for the neutralization of Germany. If America pulled back there, he argued, where would it not abandon its "commitments"?
12. U.S. Senate, Foreign Relations Committee, *Hearings Held in Executive Session: Economic Assistance to China and Korea: 1949–1950,* Eighty-first Congress, first and second sess. (Washington, D.C.: GPO, 1974), 119, 180–81.
13. Bruce Cumings, "The Origins and Development of the Northeast Asian Political Economy: Industrial Sectors, Product Cycles and Political Consequences," *International Organization,* I (winter 1984): 1–40.
14. Memo, Melby to Butterworth, 12 September 1949, *John Melby Papers,* Harry S. Truman Library, Independence, Missouri.
15. Record of a meeting at the State Department, 13 September 1949, Public Record Office, London, England, FO 371, FE/49/1.
16. U.S. Senate, Foreign Relations Committee, *Hearings Held in Executive Session: Reviews of the World Situation: 1949–1950,* Eighty-first Congress, first and second sess. (Washington, D.C.: G.P.O., 1974), 164–66.

17. Ibid., 273.

18. Princeton "Seminar," 10 October 1953, Truman Library.

19. Senate Executive Hearings, *Reviews of the World Situation*, 152.

20. These points are developed further in Lloyd C. Gardner, *Approaching Vietnam: From World War II Through Dienbienphu* (New York: W.W. Norton & Co., 1988), 92–95.

21. Ibid., 96. Emphasis added.

22. Franks to Bevin, 17 December 1949, *The Personal Papers of Ernest Bevin*, PRO 800/462.

23. Cumings, *Origins*, II, 411.

24. "Conversation between the Secretary and Representative Herter," 21 March 1950, *The Papers of Dean Acheson*, Truman Library.

25. Interview, 18 February 1955, *Papers of Harry S. Truman: Post-Presidential Files*.

26. *Time*, 1 May 1950, 15–16.

27. Dulles to Acheson, 4 May 1950, encl. "Memorandum of Conversation with President Truman," 28 April 1950, *Acheson Papers*. Emphasis added.

28. Gardner, *Approaching Vietnam*, 9

29. See, Department of State, *Foreign Relations of the United States, 1950* (Washington, D.C.: G.P.O.: vd) VII, 312–13, and Stalin to Zhou, 13 July 1950, in Cold War International History Project, *Bulletin*, Issues 6–7, "The Cold War in Asia," 44.

30. *Foreign Relations, 1950*, VII, 418.

31. Oral History of Frank Pace, Truman Library, 70. Emphasis added.

32. Gardner, *Approaching Vietnam*, 98.

33. Margaret Truman, *When the Buck Stops* (New York: Warner Books, 1989), 236–37, 318.

34. See the discussion in Eric Alterman, *Who Speaks for America: Why Democracy Matters in Foreign Policy* (Ithaca, N.Y.: Cornell University Press, 1998).

35. I should like to thank Marilyn Young for providing inspiration for many of the arguments advanced in this paper.

Chapter 5

The Korean War

The Economic and Strategic Impact on Japan,
1950–53

MICHAEL SCHALLER

For all the talk of a forgotten war, Korea is well remembered, at least among scholars of war and diplomacy. Understandably, most of the remembering has focused on the war's impact on North and South Korea, the United States, the People's Republic of China (PRC), and Soviet-American relations. All nations involved in the fighting suffered terribly and took actions that prolonged the conflict.

Japan, however, proved an exception. For it, the Korean War proved an elixir that revitalized its economy, ended the American occupation, and shaped the peace and security treaties that continue to tether it to a Pacific Alliance with the United States. Japan emerged from the Korean carnage unscathed and, in a sense, reborn.

Several key American officials interpreted the North Korean attack of 25 June 1950 upon the Republic of Korea as directed ultimately against Japan. For example, as State Department consultant in charge of the Japanese peace treaty, John Foster Dulles, commented during the first months of fighting, the "communist offensive in Korea was probably aimed at getting control over Japan, for had Korea been conquered Japan would have fallen without an open struggle." The Korean attack made it "more important, rather than less important to" conclude a treaty. The "very fact" that communist aggression in Korea sought to "check positive and constructive action" in Japan proved the "importance to take such action." Dulles warned that if progress toward a peace treaty stalled "because of total preoccupation with the Korean war," the United States might "lose in Japan more than we can gain in Korea."[1]

Economic Impact of the Korean War on Japan

As of June 1950, despite two years of American reconstruction aid, Japanese industry lacked needed capital and export markets. The austerity program initiated in 1949 by Detroit banker Joseph Dodge, sent as "economic czar" to Tokyo by President Harry S. Truman's administration, curbed hyper inflation and halted deficit spending but triggered a severe recession. By June unemployment had reached 500,000, twice the level of a year before. Share prices fell sharply on Tokyo's stock exchange and small business failures increased dramatically. Although reconstruction aid had pushed the index of industrial production to over 80 percent of the prewar level, a credit crunch limited investment in new plants and equipment. More ominously, Japan exported less than half the textiles and manufactured goods it had before the war.[2]

The Toyota Motor Sales Company typified the problems in heavy industry. The company was squeezed between declining sales, unions resisting layoffs, and a credit crunch that prevented acquisition of badly needed technology. In June 1950, Toyota produced barely 300 trucks. President Kamiya Shotaro flew to the United States hoping to induce the Ford Motor Company to invest in Toyota. He arrived on 24 June, as news broke of the Korean attack.

At first, the fighting appeared to doom Toyota's prospects, because the Defense Department discouraged Ford from sending a management team to Japan, fearing it would divert resources. Despondent, Kamiya left Detroit with a sense of failure. The next month, however, Toyota received a military order for 1,000 trucks. Within a year it had sold 5,000 vehicles to U.S. forces and boosted monthly production to over 2,000 units. Workers annual wages doubled and the company paid its first dividend since 1945.

Years later, Kamiya described these orders as "Toyota's salvation." The company used profits from military sales and technology transfers to modernize its operations, reduce the power of organized labor, and begin passenger car production. Kamiya's happiness over Toyota's good fortune was tempered only slightly by a "sense of guilt that I was rejoicing over another country's war."

The outbreak of fighting in Korea accelerated the "Red purge" begun by the occupation authorities and the Japanese government months before. Previously, leftist activists had been fired from government agencies and industry, a process soon extended to nearly 10,000 workers in the private sector. Simultaneously, thousands of rightist politicians and businessmen who had been barred from public life were de-purged and permitted to resume positions of influence in government and the economy.

Many companies shared Toyota's good fortune. As jeeps and other vehicles used in Korea needed repair, they were often brought to Higashi Nippon Heavy Industries (later part of Mitsubishi Heavy Industries) near Tokyo. More than one hundred U.S. military and civilian technicians, using the latest imported machinery, supervised the Japanese workforce. Miyahara Toshio, production manager and later a director of Mitsubishi Motors Corporation, recalled, "everyone in the plant, from the foreman down, was given a chance to learn a mechanized, integrated process." Benefits from military procurement spread beyond heavy industry. Shortly after fighting began in Korea, the U.S. Army Procurement Office in Yokohama called in officials of firms that made bags for rice. "We need all the gunny sacks you have," he told them, "and we need them urgently for making combat sandbags. It doesn't even matter if they're used. Name your price and we'll pay for it." These companies eventually sold 200 million sacks to the U.S. Army at twice the usual price. This enabled the Nippon Matai Company to expand its force of sewing machine operators from 30 to 150. Adding new equipment and diversifying production, it eventually employed more than 1,000 people.[3]

War orders benefited the textile, construction, automotive, metal, communications, and chemical industries. At the peak of the Korean conflict, nearly 3,000 Japanese firms held war-related contracts while many others arranged with U.S. companies and the Defense Department to acquire new technology. During the first year of the Korean War, U.S. military procurements totaled $329 million, about 40 percent of the value of Japan's total exports in 1950. During 1952, procurement and other forms of military spending reached $800 million. The index of industrial production finally surpassed the pre–World War II level in October 1950, rose to 131 percent in May 1951, and kept climbing. During the three years of fighting in Korea, Japan earned nearly $2.5 billion from procurements, more than the value of American aid from 1945–1950. During the two years following the Korean armistice, Japan earned an additional $2 billion from military procurements. These orders initiated a twenty year period of nearly uninterrupted 10 percent annual growth in the Gross National Product (GNP).

Given the life breathed back into the Japanese economy and stock market by the fighting in Korea, it is no surprise that when Prime Minister Yoshida Shigeru learned of the North Korean attack, he reportedly exclaimed "it's the Grace of Heaven." Bank of Japan governor Ichimada Naoto called the procurement orders "divine aid." Speaking in the diet early in 1951, the tart-tongued Yoshida asserted that the "Korean War provided more stimulus for Japanese economic resurgence than did all the occupation efforts" under General Douglas MacArthur. Describing the situation he encountered in 1952, Ambassador Robert Murphy described the war as a "godsend" that enabled Japan to rebuild at "maximum speed." The procurement boom, he remarked, transformed Japan into "one huge supply depot, without which the Korean War could not have been fought."[4]

Japan also benefited greatly from the global production bottleneck generated by Korean War orders and Western re-armament in the early 1950s. For example, since 1945 Japanese shipyards had failed to win many foreign orders for large merchant vessels because they were both inefficient and faced occupation-imposed restrictions. The sudden increased demand for shipping gave Japanese facilities an edge that they had lacked for years. Similarly, to encourage Japanese production of needed supplies, the U.S. government encouraged American companies to sign licensing agreements with and transfer technology to Japanese manufacturers. This helped to rapidly modernize many obsolete plants.

The initial effort from 1948–1950 to promote Japanese export production presumed that China, Southeast Asia and, to a lesser degree, the United States, would furnish the raw materials and consumer markets Japan required. Because of anticipated resistance from American manufacturers and concerns about product quality, American economic planners doubted that Japan could substantially increase exports to the United States. China's entry into the Korean War and the subsequent American-imposed embargo on trade with Beijing left Tokyo more dependent on U.S. military orders, American consumers, and the promise of Southeast Asian development.

During the Korean War, American and Japanese officials initiated some of the regional economic projects that were proposed before June 1950 but were never funded. The U.S.-Japan Economic Cooperation program begun in May 1951 linked the procurement of military items in Japan with efforts to boost Japanese trade with Southeast Asian. This was designed to deflect Japanese trade from China while reducing the need for direct American aid to Tokyo.[5]

When Joseph Dodge returned to Tokyo in October 1950 after an absence of several months, the tight money policy he had instituted the previous year to balance the budget and rationalize industry had been rendered obsolete by the boom in war orders. He told business leaders in Yokohama that Japan had begun "receiving the benefit of a substantial and unexpected windfall of foreign exchange from direct procurement for the war in Korea." But, he cautioned, the orders would be only temporary (China had not yet entered the conflict) so they should not squander the windfall on consumption. Instead, dollar earnings should be invested in "essential capital improvements" for export expansion. He warned against any impulse to "ease up on the drive for industrial improvement, efficiency . . . and rationalization."

Dodge pressed government and industry to apply procurement profits to "achieve the long sought goal of economic self-support which is a fundamental requirement of political independence." Along these lines, he authorized the Japanese to use nearly ninety billion yen from U.S.-controlled counterpart funds (yen deposited in return for American aid) to upgrade transportation, power, shipping, and communications. This also provided credits for the purchase of critical foreign technology and for the Export-Import Bank of Japan, which promoted foreign sales.[6]

Dulles also saw Japan's economic stability as essential to the peace and security treaties. In October 1950 he told a group of current and former policy makers that unless Japan was "assured a satisfactory livelihood . . . without placing [it] in a position of dependence upon the communist-dominated mainland of Asia," any "peace treaty will be a failure." In January 1951 he told Congressional leaders that the "economic stability of Japan" was the key to its security. Because of Japan's "precarious economic situation," he alerted the legislators, they might have to appropriate substantial aid after the occupation ended.

Dulles worried greatly how Japan could cope with "the loss of the normal trading areas of China and Manchuria and the threatened loss of Southeast Asia with its ricebowl and other raw materials." Keeping Japan on the "side of the free world," Dulles told Charles Wilson, director of the Office of Defense Mobilization, depended on making sure "its industry can keep running and that it will receive sufficient quantities of the necessary raw materials." Without access to vital commodities, "it would be futile to expect the Japanese to keep away from Communism."[7]

During his February 1951 treaty negotiations in Tokyo (discussed below), Dulles grappled with economic questions in talks with General William Marquat, head of the occupation command's (or Supreme Commander for the Allied Powers [SCAP's]) Economic and Scientific Section (ESS). Among influential Americans, Dulles asserted, the "principal problem" in Asia was "how is Japan going to get along economically?" Would the United States have to carry Japan's trade deficits for an "indefinite period" or be compelled to "admit large quantities of Japanese goods to the United States?" With China off limits, Dulles and Marquat feared the consequences should "any one or all" of Japan's other "Asiatic markets pass out of the picture." Unless Japan "worked for us," they concluded—in an epigraph that captured American concern for the entire cold war—it "will work for the other side."

Both men doubted that Japan would ever sell many consumer products in the United States. For the short run, Japan's only real option was to "utilize unused industrial capacity . . . for the support of the United States mobilization effort" in Korea and elsewhere. If a country did not make "what the world wants, which today means war materials," Marquat opined, "it cannot get by." Even a modest investment might put enough idle plants to work to raise Japan's index of industrial production from the current 116 percent (of the pre–WWII level) to 200 percent.[8]

The ESS staff argued the case further in a detailed study, *Japan's Industrial Potential*, issued in three sections starting in February 1951. With sufficient raw materials, technology, tools, and financing, it contended, Japanese plants could easily supply military items to the United States and Southeast Asian nations during and presumably after the Korean War. Military orders would also promote "psychological" adjustment to cold war doctrines and insure that idle industry did not become a "means of ingress of subversive influence."[9]

Marquat's appeals found favor in the Pentagon. In March 1951, Secretary of Defense George C. Marshall instructed the armed services and the Munitions Board to make greater use of Japan for the "acquisition of supplies and equipment for use of U.S. forces, particularly in the Pacific area and in support of proposed U.S. military assistance programs in Southeast Asia." Marshall directed that industrial mobilization planning address post-Korea military requirements as well by placing what he called "educational orders in Japanese industry."[10]

In April, Marquat conferred in Washington with officials from several agencies. He admitted that the main reason Japan continued to experience a trade imbalance was the "preclusion of normal trade relations with China and Manchuria occasioned largely by the political influence of the United States." American restrictions denied Japan "those sources of cheap non-dollar primary raw materials" it would otherwise obtain from China. For now, American influence in Tokyo and the Korean War boom persuaded the Japanese to follow Washington's lead. But when the occupation and Korean War wound down, Marquat cautioned, the United States must have plans ready for Japan to participate in Western rearmament programs on a normal commercial basis. If not, pressure would build in Tokyo to "resume trade with Communist China which could well be attended by strong movements of local dissonant elements to achieve political reorientation with the communist orbit." Without new export options, China would become an irresistible temptation.[11]

On 17 May 1951, the ideas broached by Marquat and Dulles were incorporated in NSC 48/5, a wide ranging review of American objectives and courses of action in Asia approved by the president. The Truman administration concluded that the Soviet Union planned to gain control of East and Southeast Asia, and Japan, "primarily through . . . exploitation of the resources of Communist China." To prevent this, the United States would need to apply countervailing military, political, economic, and psychological power to depose the Chinese government or force a change in its policies. Washington must assist Japan to become "economically self-supporting and to produce goods and services important to the United States and to the economic stability of the non-communist area of Asia." Japan was expected to develop "appropriate military forces" and begin "the production of low cost military material in volume for use in Japan and in other non-communist countries of Asia."[12]

Upon his return to Tokyo on 10 May, Marquat spoke confidently of Washington's support for long-term "U.S.-Japan economic cooperation." After he conferred with General Matthew Ridgway, MacArthur's successor, the new occupation commander announced a "program for future United States-Japanese economic cooperation, including the use of Japan's industry to help build democratic might against the threat of communist aggression." It promised the "fullest economic cooperation and assistance, including United States government and private credits."

Although vague on long-range commitments and aid levels, the program promised "many orders on an individual basis starting soon." American officials agreed that Japan's industrial potential should be used "to a maximum extent to increase production of raw materials and also the industrial potentiality of Southeastern Asia." Japan would be encouraged to "supply Southeast Asia and other areas with capital and consumer goods not now available from normal sources in countries engaged in war production." American aid missions would promote the "development of programs linked to the overall United States-Japanese economic cooperation program."[13]

Charles Wilson, head of the Office of Defense Mobilization, followed this lead in July by organizing an inter-departmental committee on Far East Mobilization to seek means to "exploit the unused industrial capacity of Japan in the defense program of the free world." Wilson maintained that if "one-third to one-half" of Japan's idle industry was fully utilized, it could export "90 percent of the materials" that U.S. aid programs earmarked for Southeast Asia. This would ease strains on the American economy and ensure that "economic prosperity will come to the Pacific area." The Economic Cooperation Administration, which supervised non-military aid in Southeast Asia, established a Tokyo field office to encourage the "fullest utilization of the industrial capacity of Japan in the operation of the American aid program in Asia."[14]

At the committee's initial meeting on 1 August, chairman William Y. Elliott called for coordinated solutions to the "financial, material, shipping, and other problems of Japan and Southeast Asia." He stressed the links between the problem of "economic recovery and political defense in the Pacific."

In order to lower American aid costs, the committee recommended "developing Japan as an alternative source of certain critical items of equipment and supply" needed in Korea and by American allies. It endorsed the "mobilization of the complementary economic strength of Japan and Southeast Asia in order to strengthen the political situation in the entire area."[15]

During the summer of 1951, SCAP's Kenneth Morrow led a joint American-Japanese mission to Southeast Asia to "investigate prospects for increasing the flow of raw materials to Japan." It sought opportunities for "Japan to supply machinery, heavy equipment, consumer goods, and technical aid" in exchange for commodities. British diplomats in Tokyo reported that the mission hoped to acquire raw materials for industries "which would contribute to rearmament" and to the production of goods vital for the "maintenance of U.S. garrison troops and facilities." In public, however, the Americans were "anxious not to over emphasize the rearmament procurement side of these plans" as it "could easily be misinterpreted as a U.S. conspiracy to revive Japanese leadership of a Greater East-Asia Co-Prosperity Sphere with the added drive of U.S. backing."[16]

During the second half of 1951, the cooperation program led to a near doubling of procurement orders compared to the first six months of the year. By the end of 1951, the Defense Department began placing orders in Japan for ammunition to be used by the National Police Reserve. During 1952 the Munitions Board began buying military items in Japan destined for areas outside Korea.

The giant shadow cast by China's intervention in Korea affected all of Japan's economic prospects. In December 1950, MacArthur suspended Japan's small but growing trade with China. During 1951, a United Nations resolution imposing a trade embargo on China and North Korea, as well as the Battle Act, passed by Congress to prohibit aid to any country violating U.S. export controls, resulted in wider trade restrictions. United States authorities formulated a list of nearly 400 items that Japan could not sell to China, a more stringent ban than applied to Western sales to the Soviet Union. Shortly before the occupation ended, SCAP transferred enforcement power to the Japanese government. In the summer of 1952, Japan joined the American-sponsored Coordinating Committee for Export to Communist Areas (COCOM) and subsequently took a seat on COCOM's China Committee (CHINCOM).

In addition to these control measures, in September 1952 the United States pressed Japan to sign a secret bilateral accord that imposed limits on Japanese exports to China that went beyond even the COCOM/CHINCOM restrictions. Only the United States, South Korea, and Taiwan—which prohibited all trade with China—imposed tighter restrictions. These measures shrank Japan's 1952 trade with China to a mere 0.04 percent of total exports and 0.7 percent of imports—a dramatic change from 1941, when Japan drew 17 percent of its imports from and sold 27 percent of its exports to China. In 1941, Japan obtained 50 percent of its coal, 25 percent of its iron ore, and 75 percent of its soybean imports from China. Analyzing these numbers, a CIA study of May 1952 predicted that unless a substitute for China could be found quickly, Japan would be "tempted to seize opportunities for closer economic and political relations with the [communist] Bloc."[17]

In the final weeks of the occupation, Dodge and Marquat worked with their Japanese counterparts to formulate plans for continued economic cooperation while Yoshida requested a large development loan as a sort of "going away present." Dodge worried that Yoshida conceived of economic cooperation as a program in which "the United States will plan and blueprint the needs of Japan and then fit the economy of the United States into those needs—instead of the reverse."

To avoid this, he called for implementing mechanisms that linked the "expansion of Japan's industrial potential" to "the enlargement of her security forces." Dodge summarized his views in the following way:

There will be a substantial reliance on Japan in the post-treaty period for:

a. Production of goods and services important to the United States and the economic stability of non-Communist Asia
b. Cooperation with the United States in the development of the raw material resources of Asia
c. Production of low cost military material in volume for use in Japan and non-Communist Asia

d. Development of Japan's appropriate military forces as a defensive shield and to permit the redeployment of United States forces[18]

Suto Hideo, director general of Japan's Economic Stabilization Board, responded to Dodge on 12 February 1952. He proposed utilizing idle factories by "promoting and tightening" Japan's "economic cooperation with the United States, Southeast Asian countries, and other democratic countries in order to contribute to their defense production and economic development" while ensuring "imports necessary for Japan," raising living standards, and "strengthening progressively her self-defense power." Japan would contribute to the "rearmament plan of the United States [by] supplying military goods and strategic materials, by repairing and establishing defense industries with the technical and financial assistance from the United States" and thereby ensuring increased dollar earnings. Japanese officials remained wary of selling military equipment to countries other than the United States but were eager to cooperate "more actively with the economic development of Southeast Asia" to "increase the imports of goods and materials from this area."

In terms of military procurement, Japan desired long-term contracts to build and repair vehicles and aircraft, expand petro-chemical production, construct ships, manufacture uniforms and other textiles for American troops, boost steel and aluminum production, and increase electrical generation. Tokyo would assist Southeast Asia "mainly with technical skills and surplus machinery production capacity" and by providing fertilizer. By having the Mutual Security Program purchase goods and services in Japan bound for Southeast Asia, Japan could earn vital dollars.[19]

Marquat and Dodge appreciated these ideas but objected to Yoshida's reluctance to link American assistance to the expansion of Japan's armed forces. As Marquat told Dodge, under the prime minister's concept of economic cooperation, "Japan doesn't have to do anything—it's all up to Uncle Sam." Nevertheless, by the time the occupation ended in April 1952, nearly 3,000 Japanese firms held U.S. military contracts and about 42 percent of Japan's exports went to Southeast Asia, twice the level of 1935.[20]

The Security Treaty's administrative agreement, signed in February 1952, also promoted economic cooperation. It established a

"Joint United States-Japan Committee" on security and a joint economic council composed of embassy staff and Japanese officials to direct industrial mobilization plans. The economic council included a "procurement coordination subcommittee" with a staff of eleven Americans, including several SCAP/ESS veterans, financed by the Mutual Security Act.[21]

Japan's business community responded enthusiastically to the procurement program. In April 1951, the four largest business confederations declared, "above all else, organized business wanted the full mobilization of Japan's industrial power under a joint United States-Japan mutual defense program, which would provide the necessary financial resources."[22]

Following the September 1951 San Francisco peace conference, business groups established councils to work with government agencies in planning for post-occupation economic cooperation with the United States. The councils proposed procurement contracts that encouraged broad economic growth, rather than production of military end items. The powerful Federation of Economic Organizations (Keidanren) urged SCAP to return to former owners confiscated munitions facilities. During SCAP's final days of authority, Ridgway responded by transferring to the Japanese government control of nearly 1000 confiscated munitions plants and by permitting Japan to resume production of aircraft and weapons.

When the peace treaty came into effect, the Federation of Economic Organizations established an Economic Cooperation Council, whose sub-committees dealt with general policy, Asian development, and defense production. A prominent industrialist led each group, with Kiyoshi Goko, head of Mitsubishi Heavy Industries, in charge of the defense subcommittee. Big business worked closely with government organs such as the Ministry of International Trade and Industry (MITI) and the Supreme Economic Cooperation Conference, to shape procurement policies. The diet assisted large enterprises engaged in military production by relaxing the deconcentration laws during the summer of 1952.

Yoshida and MITI returned 859 of the 1,000 munitions plants released by SCAP to their former owners. The Japanese government confirmed its commitment to military mobilization in September 1952 by designating the weapons industry as a "national policy industry." This allowed MITI to select firms to participate in arms production and to offer them subsidies, tax breaks, access to hard currency, and other privileges.[23]

Apart from the infusion of American technology and capital, procurement orders hastened Japan's introduction to American management techniques—then considered the most progressive in the world. Even before the Korean War, SCAP invited business consultants to visit Japan. Several, like statistical quality control expert W. Edwards Deming, made useful suggestions on how to improve quality and increase efficiency. But, without ensured export markets, Japanese industry lacked the money and incentives to implement many of these recommendations. With Korean War orders for motor vehicles, munitions, and electronic equipment, they had both the motive and the capital to implement techniques that ensured improved productivity, quality, and efficiency. Japanese managers recognized that without such changes, they would be unable to hold onto export markets after the Korean War ended.

During 1950–1951, occupation authorities recruited consultants to teach concepts such as statistical quality control, continuous improvement in manufacturing, and worker training projects. Deming's particular interest in quality control found an avid audience when Japanese companies were required to produce advanced military equipment to exacting standards.

Numerous individuals and groups contributed to the managerial revolution. Among the most important was Training Within Industries, Inc.(TWI), a consulting group that specialized in innovative techniques for training managers, foremen, and workers in the use of new equipment and technologies. TWI techniques evolved during World War II to speed production and innovation within American munitions plants. During the Korean War, the army and air force expanded a TWI pilot program in Japan to enhance the training of managers, foremen, and skilled workers in methods such as quality control, continuous improvement, use of new machinery, and workers' quality circles. The consultants stressed recruitment of Japanese "trainers," who, by 1953, had introduced some one million fellow managers and workers to the program. In the following decades, graduates of the TWI course assumed key positions in companies such as Mitsubishi, Toyota, and Hitachi.[24]

State Department specialists continued to worry about Japan's "shallow economy," whose expansion remained dependent on military procurement. Although all forms of American military spending brought Japan $700 to $800 million per year from 1951 through 1953, the economic outlook remained murky. To be sure, humming factories had replaced idle plants. When calculated as exports, procurements boosted Japan's foreign sales to $1.5 billion by the end of 1951. But the war boom had not spilled over into civilian exports. Japan still had to import expensive raw materials, especially from the United States. Discounting procurements, Japan's trade deficit ranged from $600 million to $1 billion between 1951 and 1953. Two-thirds of the deficit resulted from imports from the United States.

While imports of American products into Japan surged to $700 million in 1951, civilian exports to the United States reached only $184 million, with military procurements masking the deficit. Meanwhile, European and American business interests frustrated Japanese plans to expand exports of items such as tuna, textiles, and sewing machines by implementing special quotas.[25]

State Department trade specialists considered Japan's long-run economic outlook as "seriously weak and vulnerable." They viewed with special concern the "strength of the natural economic affinity between Japan and Northern Asia," an attraction that was "probably greater and more fundamental than we like to recognize." Southeast Asia might partially compensate for trade with China but the region remained poor and underdeveloped, with limited purchasing power.

Many State Department planners concluded that Western governments should lower tariffs and accept more Japanese goods despite opposition from domestic producers. Even this would probably fall short of meeting Japan's needs. Washington would have to take "extraordinary measures," such as a special "system of Japanese trade controls . . . tailored to the economic relations between Japan and the [Chinese] mainland." A limited opening to China appeared the only way to "keep Japan completely on our side." Such trade might become "a lever of some utility in our efforts to bring changes within Communist China."[26]

State Department analysts criticized the refusal by Defense and Commerce officials to recognize the difference between strategic and non-strategic sales to China, even though they made the distinction in exports to the Soviet Union. When Japan joined COCOM, the multi-lateral agency regulating sales to communist countries, it would discover that Washington permitted the North Atlantic Treaty Organization (NATO) allies to sell to the Soviets many items Japan was forbidden to sell to China, and that these exceptions were made in order "to subsidize certain aspects of the European economy."[27]

Acting Secretary of the Army Karl R. Bendetsen saw only one solution to the dilemma. Southeast Asia could not help Japan in the short run and, he argued, a program "which relies to any substantial degree upon the protracted competitive introduction of Japanese products to the American market" would also fail. Japanese solvency, Bendetsen insisted, required not "artificial substitutes," but access to Northeast Asia. For Japan's sake, he called for action to remove the "political cancer" of communism, which made "China unacceptable as a trading partner of the free world."[28]

In August 1952, the National Security Council (NSC) assembled the disparate views of trade and security policy for President Truman's review and approval. The NSC recommended that Truman formally commit the United States to defend Japan, retain control of Okinawa, and promote economic growth. To prevent Japan from seeking an "accommodation" with China, the United States must enhance "Japan's ability to satisfy its economic needs through relations with the free world." In the "long run Japan's access to raw materials and markets for her exports" would make or break its cooperation with the United States and containment policy in Asia.

The NSC opposed a complete embargo on exports to China, but favored stringent "export controls" on Japan's trade with China. This required the United States to provide Japan with alternative trade outlets both in the West and in southeast Asia. Finally, to encourage its participation in the "defense of the free nations of the Pacific area," the NSC wanted Japan to "develop a balanced ten-division ground force" as well as air and naval strength.[29]

The secretary of defense and the Joint Chiefs of Staff endorsed this approach but also raised a warning flag. Because Japan's ability to rearm and its willingness to follow America's lead depended so heavily on securing access to what the Joint Chiefs of Staff called "her historic markets and the sources of food and raw materials in southeast Asia," United States "objectives with respect to Southeast Asia and United States objectives with respect to Japan" appeared "almost inseparable." The "loss of Southeast Asia to the Western World" would "almost inevitably force Japan into an accommodation with the Communist-controlled areas in Asia."[30](Of course, China, more than Southeast Asia, had been Japan's largest pre–World War II Asian trading partner. The Joint Chiefs either did not know this or, more likely, fudged the facts to justify greater military commitment to Southeast Asia.)

Unfortunately, the NSC observed, the American public remained largely indifferent to this struggle and it called for a propaganda campaign to "make clear to the American people the importance of Southeast Asia to the security of the United States so that they may be prepared for any" course of action.[31]

It fell to John Foster Dulles, nearing the end of his service to the Truman administration and anticipating higher office in the event of a Republican victory in the November 1952 election, to carry forth word of this policy. Addressing the prestigious French National Political Science Institute on 5 May, he described the wars in Korea and Indochina as common efforts to contain Chinese expansion. Although some Americans "misinterpreted" the Indochina war as "an effort by a colonial power to maintain its rule," Dulles praised the French for dispelling this myth by granting partial autonomy to the so-called Associated States of Vietnam, Laos, and Cambodia. He recalled his own effort to enhance their stature by inviting them to attend the 1951 peace conference on Japan. Americans now recognized that in Indochina an "alien despotism" fought "in the name of liberation, to impose a servitude, which would be a step toward further conquest."

But the most emphatic reason Dulles offered for holding the line against communism had little to do with extending freedom or preserving French glory. "Indochina," he declared, "is the key to Southeast Asia, upon the resources of which Japan is largely dependent." Its "loss to Communism would gravely endanger other areas and it is thus a matter of general concern."[32]

Impact of the Korean War on the Peace Treaty

For at least a year, conflict between the State and the Defense Departments over security arrangements for Japan had blocked progress toward a peace settlement. In effect, the State Department endorsed a security guarantee for Japan, but did not want to retain substantial bases or troops after the occupation ended. The Joint Chiefs of Staff were opposed to ending the occupation if it in any way limited the size, scope, and function of U.S. forces in Japan. On 23 June, MacArthur had tried to broker a compromise by proposing keeping only limited forces in Japan but granting the United States "unrestricted" base rights. The trick, as treaty negotiator Dulles saw it, was to get the military establishment to endorse "in a form as inoffensive as possible to the Japanese," an arrangement giving the United States "broad power . . . to place military forces wherever in Japan the United States may determine to be desirable."

Shortly after the fighting in Korea began, Dulles assured Secretary of Defense Louis Johnson that he now supported "the right to maintain in Japan as much force as we wanted, anywhere we wanted, for as long as we wanted." This, Johnson and the Joint Chiefs noted happily, provided a basis to "get together and go places." On 7 September, Acheson and Johnson agreed that once the "situation in Korea" stabilized, a settlement with Japan negotiated by the State Department should take effect. An accompanying bilateral security pact would give American forces virtually unrestricted rights in Japan. The United States would not be obliged to defend or retain its forces in Japan but could intervene to suppress riots or civil disorder if the Japanese government so requested. This memorandum, approved by the National Security Council the next day as NSC 60/1, endorsed Japan's "right to self-defense." On 8 July, MacArthur had already taken the first step toward rearmament by ordering Yoshida to create a 75,000-man National Police Reserve.[33]

In negotiating the terms of the peace and security treaties with Japan in late 1950 and early 1951, Dulles not only ignored the Soviets but paid little attention to the concerns of America's allies, especially the British Commonwealth nations. When the British complained that renewed Japanese dumping of cheap goods would threaten their position in Southeast Asia, the State Department responded with words familiar to American business leaders in subsequent decades. The British should "face the realities of the situation and be prepared to meet Japanese competition if Japan is to be kept oriented toward the West and free from Communist pressures."[34]

Dulles favored the idea of a multilateral Pacific defense alliance, but insisted that nothing slow the progress toward a peace settlement with Japan. Even after November 1950, when Chinese troops inflicted a humiliating defeat on American forces in North Korea, Dulles persisted. Unless Washington moved quickly, he argued, Japan would respond to events in Korea either by stiffening its peace terms or sliding toward neutrality. Already, security provisions he could previously have extracted from Japan "merely by suggesting them," now had "to be negotiated for and obtained as fully as possible." Truman agreed and on 10 January elevated Dulles to the rank of ambassador with full power to negotiate treaties with Japan, the Philippines, Australia, and New Zealand.[35]

Before Dulles returned to Tokyo at the end of January, *Newsweek* editor Harry Kern offered him some insights into Japanese thinking. The "protestations about the disarmament clauses of their constitution and their desire for perpetual peace" voiced by Yoshida were "made largely for bargaining purposes," Kern insisted. He worried, however, that the Japanese might "overstate their case" and somehow convince Dulles to allow them "disarmed neutrality." Kern saw "no harm in letting them have the fun of doing a little bargaining," so long as Dulles knew when to crack the whip.

Kern also reported that *Newsweek*'s correspondent in Tokyo, Compton Packenham, planned to follow up on "the suggestion conveyed . . . last summer from the Emperor" to bring Dulles together with Japanese businessmen and veteran politicians. Kern even undertook some lobbying, telling Dulles that James L. Kauffman, fellow member of the American Council on Japan and a lawyer representing Japanese firms, had a message from the Tokyo Shibaura Electric Company, the "General Electric of Japan." The company had "great interest in obtaining contracts from the United States for the production of electrical equipment useful in our war effort," Kern reported. Other Japanese wanted to speak to Dulles about making "use of some of their intelligence agents who formerly operated in China."[36]

Kern's advice found further expression in a feature run by *Newsweek* before the latter's departure for Japan. The magazine cover pictured a smiling, elegantly dressed Yoshida Shigeru standing in scholarly repose beside a bouquet of chrysanthemums. Titled "Yoshida: Late Enemy Into Latest Ally?", the article stressed the importance of assuring that in the coming "world showdown," Japan "cast its lot with the West, not the Communist East."

The special report, probably written with Dulles' assistance, outlined the likely terms of the peace and security treaties. It praised Japan's industrial prowess, the bravery and social cohesion of its people, and concluded that these traits made the former enemy the "most formidable nation in the Far East." Two dramatic maps sum-marized what the magazine called the key outstanding issues. One showed how American air and naval forces operating from this "northern anchor" could dominate much of China and Siberia. The second, superimposed on an outline of the Co-Prosperity Sphere, described Japan's critical need to "look to Southeast Asia" as a replacement for the coal, iron, soybeans, and other raw materials formerly imported from China. Because this new trade would de-velop slowly, Japan would remain dependent on American markets for some time. Also, *Newsweek* advised, the threat of communism "nearly everywhere . . . in Southeast Asia" required "something like a American-Japanese Alliance" to defend that region.[37]

Dulles made conciliatory remarks upon his arrival in Tokyo on 25 January 1951. "We look upon Japan as a party to be consulted," he declared, not as a vanquished nation to be "dictated to by the victors." In private he told his aides that the "principal question" to be answered was "do we get the right to station as many troops as we want where we want and for as long as we want or do we not?" Dulles spent the next two weeks seeking an answer.[38]

During a discussion with Yoshida on 29 January, Dulles learned that American military reversals in Korea had, as he feared, stiff-ened the prime minister's spine. Yoshida spoke of canceling occu-pation reforms liberalizing family and business laws and stressed Japan's need for additional American capital. Dulles found the prime minister's remarks about Japan's "long-standing necessity" to trade with China ("war is war" but "trade is trade"), along with his opinion that Japanese businessmen could serve as a "fifth column for democracy against the communists" especially vexing.

Yoshida seemed to be "throwing out bargaining hints," Dulles complained, but refused to discuss "broad principles." The approach struck him as "inane, naive, and unrealistic." Since America's allies demanded tighter economic controls on Japan, he told Yoshida not to press for concessions. Dulles wanted to know what kind of mili-tary contribution (he now thought in terms of a 300,000-man army) Japan could make to "the free world." Yoshida infuriated Dulles by insisting that the threat of "underground" militarism, economic weakness, and public opposition made any "precipitate rearma-ment" inadvisable. (To make sure the American took this seriously, Yoshida secretly encouraged anti-rearmament demonstrations dur-ing Dulles's visit.) Put off by this refusal to make "at least a token contribution" to collective security, Dulles left the meeting muttering about Yoshida's "puffball" performance.[39]

Yoshida turned to MacArthur for help. Knowing that the general opposed large-scale rearmament, he would tell Dulles that because Japan faced no credible invasion threat, it had no need for major ground forces. Instead, Washington should utilize Japan's "capacity for military production" and trained manpower on behalf of the "free world." Dulles promptly received from SCAP and Japanese sources a list of idle defense plants ready to start production.

On 31 January, Dulles and Yoshida reached partial agreement on several matters. Japan and the United States would cooperate as "equal partners" by allowing American forces remaining in Japan to defend it against attack. As its contribution to collective security, Japan would begin gradual rearmament. Technical details would be worked out at the staff level.[40]

Subsequent discussions revealed contrasting priorities. The Americans saw a peace treaty as a worthy goal, but considered a security pact the foundation of future relations. It must provide extensive base facilities, commit Japan to establishing at least a small army, and take effect as soon as the occupation ended. Japan could not meet these obligations simply by expanding its police force or boosting military production. Until Yoshida accepted his position, Dulles declined to discuss the terms of the peace treaty.

Unlike the Americans, most Japanese considered the restoration of national sovereignty a primary objective. To obtain it, they would swallow the bitter pill of a military pact, one preferably which made reference to the United Nations and had limited duration. Ideally, it would commit the United States to defend Japan without requiring extensive bases or large numbers of American soldiers. Nearly all Japanese opposed raising a large army or making the armed forces available for service abroad. Despite his warnings about latent militarism, Yoshida did not object to the principle of rearmament so much as its pace and direction. He insisted that economic recovery come first and that Japan's troops not become American surrogates charged with policing Asia.[41]

To placate Dulles, on 3 February the prime minister delivered an unsigned memorandum to the American delegation, in which he pledged to create a 50,000-man army separate from the National Police Reserve after the peace treaty took effect. This new force would coordinate its planning with U.S. authorities, while its modest size and flexible timetable made it unsuitable for early foreign deployment, say in Korea.[42]

Dulles accepted this proposal as a token of good faith and shortly after receiving it presented the Japanese with a six-page draft of a peace treaty imposing few controls and demanding no reparations. It specified Japan's right to self-defense and stipulated that the Ryukyu and Bonin islands be placed under American control in a sort of trusteeship. Yoshida described the terms as "magnanimous and fair."[43]

On 6 February Dulles handed the Japanese a reworked draft that called for a simple collective defense agreement that relegated all contentious details concerning bases and the status of American forces to an administrative agreement. This would be negotiated later and subject to approval by the Japanese cabinet rather than the diet. In effect, the diet would vote on the less controversial peace and security pacts before they faced the more intrusive administrative agreement.[44]

Negotiations culminated on 9 February when Yoshida and Dulles initialed five documents. These included a provisional description of the peace treaty, a draft collective self-defense agreement, a draft agreement permitting U.S./UN forces to utilize Japanese facilities in support of Korean operations, a draft status of the forces agreement, and an agreement regarding services and facilities Japan would provide to American forces.

The two parties agreed that Yoshida would "request" the United States to maintain "land, air, and sea forces in and about Japan" for use anywhere in the Far East. These forces were not required to defend Japan, could be withdrawn at any time, or used to suppress internal disturbances. Without setting specific targets, Japan pledged to assume "increasing responsibility for the defense of its homeland against direct and indirect aggression." The security treaty could be terminated only by mutual consent. Yoshida later claimed that Dulles informally agreed that rearmament would depend on the pace of economic recovery and future aid.[45]

Momentum for a treaty continued even after President Truman dismissed General MacArthur from his Korean and Japanese commands on 11 April 1951. In the wake of MacArthur's recall, Truman and Acheson sent Dulles back to Tokyo "to reassure Japanese leaders of our intentions." Before accepting Truman's request, he cleared the mission with Republican leaders. Senators Robert Taft,

H. Alexander Smith, Wiley, and Milliken told Dulles he should serve as Truman's emissary only if he could guarantee that the Chinese Communist government would not be a party to the peace settlement with Japan or be permitted to take control of Taiwan. Former Republican presidential candidate Thomas Dewey told Dulles he "was the only person who could perhaps salvage the situation in Japan." After securing his right flank, Dulles agreed to "help salvage something" so long as he was not set up as the "fall guy" in a democratic plan to "appease the communist aggressors or abandon the Asiatic off-shore island chain."[46]

In Tokyo, the American envoy reassured Yoshida that "U.S. policies toward Japan have firm bipartisan support and are unchanged." He listed points in the treaty draft that elicited opposition. The British wanted to mandate the return of Taiwan to China. The Philippines and some other nations demanded reparations from Japan and military controls. The Pentagon insisted on a more explicit right for American forces in Japan to fight in Korea. Dulles and Yoshida agreed to minor modifications, but the basic outline reached the previous February held. With Yoshida on board, Dulles set about calming America's restive allies.[47]

During the next several months, Dulles alternately cajoled and bullied the British Commonwealth nations and the Philippines into accepting American terms for making peace with Japan. To placate fears of revived Japanese militarism, he agreed to sign vague security treaties to Australia, New Zealand, and the Philippines. While rejecting British pressure to invite the Chinese Communist regime to attend the treaty signing ceremony, he promised to allow Japan to negotiate its own deal with Beijing following the restoration of sovereignty. In fact, after the treaty was signed in September 1951, Washington forced Prime Minister Yoshida to deal only with Taiwan.

The United States also placed many of the most controversial security provisions in a separate bilateral pact and an administrative agreement. At the insistence of the Joint Chiefs of Staff, U.S. forces stationed in post-occupation Japan would be free to carry out military operations both inside Japan and anywhere in the Far East, free to store nuclear weapons on Japanese soil, and, in many cases, made exempt from Japanese criminal law. Even Dulles privately condemned what he called the Pentagon's effort to revive the "unequal treaties" imposed by the West on China and Japan in the nineteenth century.

On 8 September, Japan and forty-eight other nations signed the treaty essentially as written by the United States. The Soviet Union, Poland, and Czechoslovakia refused. The treaty ended the occupation, restored sovereignty, and pledged Japan to negotiate reparations agreements with claimants. Tokyo's "residual sovereignty" over the Ryukyu Islands was confirmed, but it had to surrender administrative control to these and several other small islands to the United States. The treaty affirmed Japan's right of collective self-defense. Although barely noticed at the time, the treaty contained a preemption clause that barred U.S. nationals—such as former POWs—from suing Japan for wartime mistreatment and enslavement.

In a private ceremony that same day, Acheson, Dulles, two U.S. senators, and Yoshida Shigeru signed a Security Treaty along with a subsidiary agreement that authorized U.S. forces to use bases in Japan for Korean operations. A few days before, the United States reached defense pacts with the Philippines, Australia, and New Zealand.

On 16 January 1952, Dulles pressured Prime Minister Yoshida into releasing a public pledge to establish diplomatic ties with Taiwan, rather than the PRC. Three days later, the State Department sent the peace and security treaties to the Senate. In both public and executive testimony to the Foreign Relations Committee, Dulles and Secretary of State Dean Acheson emphasized that the United States required a friendly Japan as much as Japan needed American support. "Soviet leaders," Dulles declared "did not disguise the fact that they seek above all, to be able to exploit the industrial capabilities of Japan and Germany." If the Kremlin controlled these countries, "the stage would be set for a climactic struggle of doubtful outcome." The peace and security treaties with Japan, and the defense pacts signed with Australia, New Zealand, and the Philippines, would blunt Soviet penetration of the Pacific.

This argument carried the day, as Republicans joined the Democrats in support of the treaties. Save for William Jenner, a GOP ultra-conservative from Indiana who wanted to impose added restrictions on Japan, senators found little to criticize in either pact. On 20 March the senate approved the peace treaty by a vote of 66 to 10, and the security treaty by a margin of 58 to 9.[48] On 28 April 1952, the occupation formally ended, but 200,000 American troops remained in Japan and on Okinawa, as they would in large numbers for the next half century.

The Korean War and Japanese Rearmament

American participation in the Korean War coincided with the decision to rearm Japan. As occupation forces were deployed to the peninsula, MacArthur and the military chiefs in Washington decided that Japanese troops should partly fill the void. On 8 July 1950, MacArthur ordered Yoshida to create a National Police Reserve (NPR) of 75,000 men and to expand the existing Maritime Safety Force (MSF), a coast guard, from 8,000 to 10,000 men.

The NPR was organized and maintained separately from the existing police and placed under the direct control of the prime minister. Filling the ranks proved simple. However, MacArthur's refusal to employ former Imperial Army officers created a leadership gap. When General Ridgway replaced MacArthur in April 1951, he relaxed this prohibition. To maintain the fiction of the NPR's status, SCAP put an Annex of the Civil Affairs Section in charge of its training. Major General William Shepard explained the drill to American officers, including Colonel Frank Kowalski, who supervised Japanese recruits. Kowalski would be the:

> . . . only one in the camp who will know that you are organizing any infantry battalion. Others, of course, will suspect it. But only you will know. As far as the Japanese are concerned, and that applies to all Japanese, the governor, the police, and the NPR [recruits themselves]—you are organizing a police reserve. The Constitution of Japan prohibits an army. You will not call the men soldiers and you will not call the officers by any military ranks. The men are policemen and the officers will be superintendents. If you ever see a tank, it isn't a tank, it's a special vehicle. You can call a truck a truck.[49]

During 1952, the United States unilaterally devised plans to expand the police reserve to a 300,000-man force of ten ground divisions with air and naval capability. A military this large could help defend Japan, free American troops for other missions, and participate in joint operations. In lobbying congress for funds, General Ridgway argued that for "each dollar expended" the United States could "purchase more security through the creation of Japanese forces than can be purchased by similar expenditures in any other nation in the world, including the United States."[50]

During the summer of 1952, the army issued the "policemen" rifles, machine guns, mortars, bazookas, flame-throwers, artillery, and tanks. The navy provided the maritime force with eighteen patrol frigates and fifty landing craft. The Bureau of the Budget estimated that by the end of 1952 the value of equipment and training provided to Japan exceeded $1 billion.[51]

Yoshida deflected American pressure to rearm more extensively and deploy Japanese forces in Asia. Until his resignation in 1954, the prime minister did just enough to avoid a break with Washington on military issues. Although Yoshida raised NPR force levels to 110,000 in 1951, this represented only a third of what Washington demanded. Shortly before the occupation ended, Yoshida called for transforming the police reserve into "something along the lines of a Self-Defense Force." Japanese ground forces were located in thirty-seven bases, mostly near urban centers of domestic communist strength and organized into four army divisions. In Kowalski's words, it possessed "great potential for future development."[52]

During the Korean War, Japanese military personnel assisted American forces in several ways. Minesweepers of the MSF helped clear harbors along the Korean coast. The U.S./UN command secretly employed Japanese shipping and railroad experts with past service on the Korean peninsula. Much of the personnel and equipment bound for Korea passed through Japanese ports. Without the active and passive assistance of the Japanese government, laborers, business, and public, Ambassador Murphy asserted, "allied forces would have had difficulty remaining in Korea."[53]

On 6 December 1951, the tenth anniversary of Japan's attack on the United States, the Japanese press described a boom in base construction and military preparedness throughout the archipelago that followed the outbreak of the Korean War. With no hint of irony, the *Nippon Times* reported that new air, ground, and naval facilities for American and NPR forces would make Japan "Pearl Harbor proof" against a surprise communist attack.

Conclusion

The Korean War affected Japan in a variety of direct and indirect ways. On the eve of hostilities, American officials possessed a broad but diffuse vision of Japan's role as an ally. The Truman administration had reached a consensus in favor of ending the occupation and restoring industrial production. But civilian and military planners disagreed strongly over the type and extent of Japanese rearmament and the nature of its future military relationship with the United States. Even less certain was the question of how Japan could sustain economic growth given the Communist revolution in China, the upheavals within Southeast Asia, and expected resistance to finding a market for consumer goods in the United States.

The Korean War clarified these questions and propelled Japan along a new path. The peace and security treaties negotiated between Washington and Tokyo during 1951 tethered Japan to an American orbit. With its extensive network of American air, sea, and land bases, Japan served as the pivot of American military power during and long after the Korean War. The U.S. –China confrontation in Korea shredded Japanese hopes of rebuilding ties to the PRC and pushed it into a relationship with Taiwan. Meanwhile, U.S. military procurements, or "divine aid," surpassed the level of previous reconstruction assistance and sparked almost four decades of double-digit economic growth in Japan. Given the chronic instability in Southeast Asia and Communist control of China, the United States became the main destination of Japan's consumer exports. Convinced that export-driven growth held the key to keeping Japan loyal, the Truman and Dwight D. Eisenhower administrations encouraged high levels of Japanese exports. Washington's hope to divert some of this trade to Southeast Asia prompted a growing American obsession with holding the line against communism in Vietnam and along the so-called Great Crescent. As has been noted, the "ultimate" domino in the 1950s domino theory was Japan. Without the Korean War, the relationships forged among the United States, Japan, China, the Soviet Union, and the two Koreas would have been dramatically different.

Notes

1. Memorandum by Dulles, 6 July 1950, John Foster Dulles Papers, Princeton University; *Foreign Relations of the United States* (hereafter *FRUS*) 1950, VI, 1243–44; statement by Dulles in report to Council on Foreign Relations on "Japanese Peace Treaty Problems," 23 October 1950, box 48, Dulles papers.

2. For studies that link the politics and economics of the occupation,

see Michael Schaller, *The American Occupation of Japan: The Origin of the Cold War in Asia* (New York: Oxford University Press, 1985); Howard Schonberger, *Aftermath of War: Americans and the Remaking of Japan, 1945–52* (Kent, Ohio: Kent State University Press, 1989), 226; William Borden, *The Pacific Alliance: United States Foreign Economic Policy and Japanese Trade Recovery, 1947–1955* (Madison: University of Wisconsin Press, 1984), 98–102.

3. The impact of war orders on Japanese companies is recounted by the staff of *Asahi Shimbun* in the anthology, *Pacific Rivals: A Japanese View of the Japanese-American Relationship* (New York: John Weatherhill, Inc., 1972), 193–95; on Toyota management's use of war orders to restructure the company, see Fujita Kuniko, "Corporatism and the Corporate Welfare Program: The Impact of the Korean War on the Toyota Motor Corporation," in William F. Nimmo, ed., *The Occupation of Japan: The Impact of the Korean War* (Norfolk, Va.: MacArthur Memorial, 1990), 111–26.

4. "Divine aid" represented a play on the phrase kamikaze, the divine wind, or typhoon, which wrecked a Mongol invasion fleet centuries earlier. During World War II, the term referred to suicide pilots who attacked American ships in the final battles of the Pacific War. Yoshida's two remarks are cited in "draft history of Japanese rearmament," box 8, Frank Kowalski Papers, Library of Congress and Kozo Yamamura, *Economic Policy in Postwar Japan: Growth Versus Economic Democracy* (Berkeley: University of California Press, 1967), 53; economic data on the period 1951–53 is contained in Schonberger, *Aftermath of War*, 228–34; for comments on the Tokyo stock market, see William Diehl to Dodge, 20 July 1950, "Japan: Missions-Dodge," OASIA File, Department of the Treasury, FOIA; Robert Murphy, *Diplomat Among Warriors* (New York: Doubleday, 1964), 347. While noting the economic impact of the Korean War, Roger Dingman argues that it affected the pace, not the nature or direction, of Japan's recovery. See Roger Dingman, "The Dagger and the Gift: The Impact of the Korean War on Japan," *The Journal of American-East Asian Relations* (spring, 1993, vol. II, no. 1): 29–58.

5. Undersecretary of the Army Tracy Voorhees best articulated this idea. Before leaving office in May 1950 to work on mobilizing public opinion behind rearmament, Voorhees issued a call to "coordinate" containment and economic development programs by "modernizing" the Marshall Plan. He proposed using idle industrial capacity in Western Europe and Japan to contribute to the "production of defensive weapons." Dollars given to Germany and Japan could be targeted to resume weapons production. Money earned by the sale of weapons to other allies would then be used to "purchase our wheat, cotton, and tobacco," allowing each aid dollar to do the work of two. Henceforth, he predicted, the Japanese

should be expected to "earn their dollars by agreeing to provide most of the economic assistance required for Southeast Asia." By supplying low-cost military equipment to the region, Japan would assist containment, earn money, and require less American aid. See, Voorhees to NSC, 10 January 1950, in NSC 61 file, 27 January 1950, NSC Record Group, National Archives; Voorhees report of 27 May 1950, "A Proposal to Correlate Economic Aid to Europe with Military Defense," Cold War Coordination Staff memoranda, 39.32, box 62, Bureau of the Budget Records, RG 51, NA; Borden, *The Pacific Alliance*, 47–49. Similarly, Joseph Dodge described Japan as an economic and military "springboard" for American efforts to defend Southeast Asia. See, Halliday, *A Political History of Japanese Capitalism*, 197; Dodge testimony to ECA Advisory Committee on Fiscal and Monetary Problems, 28 April 1950, Joseph Dodge papers, Detroit Public Library.

6. Statement by Dodge in Yokohama, 7 October 1950, "Japan: Missions-Dodge," OASIA File, Department of Treasury Records, FOIA; Schonberger, *Aftermath of War*, 227; Borden, *Pacific Alliance*, 148.

7. Dulles remarks on "Japanese Peace Treaty Problems," 23 October 1950, box 48, John Foster Dulles papers, Princeton University; memorandum by Allison, 11–12 January 1951, *FRUS 1951*, VI, 790–92; memorandum by Allison, 18 January 1951, ibid., 804–5.

8. "Notes on Conversation between Dulles and Gen. Marquat," 5 February 1951, box 1, Japan Peace Treaty File, Lot 78D173, RG 59, NA. Kenneth Morrow, head of the ESS Program and Statistics Division, prepared a report detailing ways in which Japan could produce military equipment for American and friendly Asian forces. The report, which circulated in the Army, Treasury, and State Departments, called for expanding procurement orders beyond the Korean context to permit Japanese industry to provide military items to the "non-communist . . . countries in the Far East area, such as French Indochina, Thailand, Formosa, the Philippines, Malaya, and Burma." Japan was "particularly well suited" to "fulfill supply functions as a Zone of the Interior for the U.S. and the Western Powers in the Asiatic region." Enhanced military production, the ESS report predicted, would predispose Japan to accept rearmament and make its "armed participation" as a Cold War ally "more assured." See "Mobilization of Japanese Industrial Potential for U.S. Military Procurement," 7 February 1951, copy in W. W. Diehl to Arthur Stuart, 20 March 1951, box 13, OASIA File, Department of the Treasury, FOIA.

9. Borden, *Pacific Alliance*, 152–53; *Japan's Industrial Potential*, ESS reports of February 1951, October 1951, February 1952, ibid.

10. Marshall to Secretaries of the Army, Navy, Air Force and Chairman of the Munitions Board, 28 March 1951, box 317, CD092 Japan, Office of the Secretary of Defense, RG 330, NA.

11. Marquat to Department of the Army, 28 April 1951, box 13, OASIA File, Department of the Treasury, FOIA.

12. NSC 48/5, "United States Objectives, Policies and Courses of Action in Asia," 17 May 1951, *FRUS 1951*, VI, 33–63.

13. Statement by General Marquat, 10 May 1951, copy in Dodge Papers; Statement released by General Ridgway on 16 May 1951, *The New York Times*, 17 May 1951, and the *Washington Post*, 17 May 1951.

14. *Nippon Times*, 29 July 1951; Tokyo press release of 2 August 1951, "The First Step in Mr. Wilson's Plan," copies in Dodge Papers.

15. Summary of Interdepartmental Committee on Far East Mobilization, Meeting # 1, 24 August 1951, box 6799, Supreme Commander for the Allied Powers Records, RG 331, NA.

16. SCAP announcement of "SCAP-Japanese Mission to Visit Southeast Asia for Raw Materials Study," 4 July 1951, copy in Dodge Papers; British embassy in Tokyo to Foreign Office, dispatches of 6, 10 July 1951, FO 371/92642, PRO.

17. *FRUS 1952–54*, Vol. 14, 1295–1300, 1332–33; "The Probable Future Orientation of Japan," 22 May 1952, NIE-52, Truman Library; Yoko Yasuhara, "Japan, Communist China, and Export Controls in Asia, 1948–52," *Diplomatic History* (Vol. 10, no. 1, winter 1986): 75–89; John Dower, *Empire and Aftermath: Yoshida Shigeru and the Japanese Experience, 1878–1954* (Cambridge, Mass.: Harvard University Press, 1979), 410–14.

18. Joseph M. Dodge, "United States-Japan Economic Cooperation in the Post-Treaty Era," 1 February 1952, Box 1, "Office of Far East Operations-Japan Subject," RG 469; on this subject, see also Carl Burness (Mutual Security Agency) to Edwin G. Arnold, "Meeting on Japan," 6 February 1952, ibid.

19. Suto Hideo to General Marquat, 12 February 1952, "Establishment of a Viable Economy and Promotion of Economic Cooperation," copies in box 7, Japan-1951 Economic Cooperation, Dodge Papers and box 1, Office of Far East Operations, Japan Subject Files, RG 469.

20. Marquat to Dodge, cover letter attached to ibid; SCAP report on "Japanese Industrial Potential, February 1952, quoted in Schonberger, *Aftermath of War*, 233.

21. Borden, *Pacific Alliance*, 158.

22. Chitoshi Yanaga, *Big Business in Japanese Politics* (New Haven, Conn.: Yale University Press, 1968), 240.

23. Yanaga, *Big Business in Japanese Politics*, 248–56.

24. Alan G. Robinson, Dean M. Schroeder, and Nalini Dayanand, "The U.S. Training Within Industries Program and Their Role in the Development of the Japanese Management Style," unpublished paper in author's possession.

25. "Japan's economic problems and prospects," report of 15 May 1952, box 13, Japan, 1950–52, PSA Lot File, RG 59.

26. U.S. Post-Treaty Policy Toward Japan, 23 April 1952, box 13, PSA Lot File, RG 59; *FRUS 1952–54*, XIV, 1298–1300.

27. *FRUS 1952–52*, XIV, 1295–1300.

28. Bendetsen to Secretary of Defense, "NSC 125/1, United States Objectives and Courses of Action with Respect to Japan and Annex Thereto," 1 August 1952, box 317, CD 092 Japan, Office of Secretary of Defense, RG 330.

29. NSC 125/2 "United States Objectives and courses of Action with Respect to Japan," 7 August 1952, *FRUS 1952–54*, XIV, 1300–1308.

30. Omar Bradley to Secretary of Defense, 28 July 1952, *FRUS 1952–54*, XIV, 1289–90.

31. NSC 124/2, "United States Objectives and Courses of Action with Respect to Southeast Asia," 25 June 1952, President's Secretaries Files, Harry S. Truman Papers, Truman Library.

32. Address by Dulles on "Far Eastern Problems," 5 May 1952, Dulles papers.

33. For the record of State-Defense negotiations, see *FRUS 1950*, VI, 1259–1304.

34. For Dulles' contact with foreign states, see *FRUS 1950*, VI, 1332–54; John Allison, *Ambassador from the Prairie, or Allison Wonderland* (Boston: Houghton Mifflin, 1973), 151–52.

35. Dulles to Acheson, 4 January 1951, *FRUS, 1951*, VI, 781–83; Acheson to Marshall, 9 January 1951, 787–89.

36. Kern to Dulles, 15 January and 19 January 1951, box 53, Dulles papers.

37. "Yoshida: Late Enemy Into Latest Ally?" *Newsweek*, 22 January 1951 (vol. 37, no. 4): 32–35.

38. Memorandum by Feary, 26 January 1951, *FRUS 1951*, VI, 811–15.

39. Memorandum by Allison, 29 January 1951, *FRUS 1951*, VI, 827–30; diary entry of 29 January 1951, Sebald papers.

40. Yoshida at times used intermediaries to inform Americans of what he would accept, despite his public opposition to rearmament. See, for example, the message conveyed by Shirasu Jiro in memorandum by Feary, 25 January 1951, *FRUS, 1951*, VI, 810–11; memorandum by Allison, 29 January 1951, ibid., 827–30; undated memorandum by Yoshida, ibid., 833–34; Martin E. Weinstein, *Japan's Postwar Defense Policy* (New York: Columbia University Press, 1971), 81; Dower, *Empire and Aftermath*, 389–93; Igarashi Takeshi, "Peace-Making and Party Politics: the Formation of the Domestic Foreign Policy System in Postwar Japan," *Journal of Japanese Studies*, 11, 2 (summer 1985): 323–56; Richard Finn, *Winners in*

Peace: MacArthur, Yoshida and Postwar Japan (Berkeley: University of California Press, 1992), 276–77. Finn relies heavily on later accounts by Yoshida and his aides about their informal understandings with Dulles; on Yoshida's claim of a secret agreement with MacArthur, see his oral history in Dulles Oral History Project, Princeton University.

41. See, for example, Yoshida's undated memo handed to the Americans on 31 January 1951, *FRUS 1951*, VI, 833–34.

42. See editorial note regarding 3 February 1951 memorandum, *FRUS 1951*, VI, 849; Finn, *Winners in Peace*, 278.

43. Memorandum by Dulles Mission, 3 February 1951 (delivered on 5 February), *FRUS 1951*, VI, 849–55.

44. *FRUS 1951*, VI, 856–66.

45. Dulles to Acheson, 10 February 1951, *FRUS 1951*, VI, 874–80; Michael Yoshitsu, *Japan and the San Francisco Peace Settlement* (New York: Columbia University Press, 1983), 57–66; Finn, *Winners in Peace*, 281–83.

46. Memorandum on the Substance of Discussions at a Department of State-Joint Chiefs of Staff Meeting, 11 April 1951, *FRUS 1951*, VI, 969–71; memorandum by Dulles, 12 April 1951, ibid., 972–76; notes of conference between Smith and Dulles, 6 May 1951, box 103, H. Alexander Smith Papers, Princeton University.

47. Memorandum by Feary of Dulles Mission Staff Meeting, 17 April 1951, ibid., 979–82; memorandum by Feary of Dulles Mission Staff Meeting, 18 April 1951, 982–85; memorandum by Feary of conversation with Dulles and Japanese leaders, 18 April 1951, ibid., 985–89.

48. Dulles statement to Senate Foreign Relations Committee, 21 January 1952, box 61, Dulles papers; Report of the Committee on Foreign Relations, Eighty-second Congress, second session, *Japanese Peace Treaty and Other Treaties Relating to Security in the Pacific* (Washington, D.C., 1952); Senate Committee on Foreign Relations, *Hearings Before the Committee on Japanese Peace Treaty and Other Treaties Relating to Security in the Pacific, Jan. 21–25, 1952* (Washington, D.C., 1952).

49. Kowalski, later a member of Congress, published a memoir in Japanese about his role in organizing the NPR. That book, *Ninon Saigumbi* (Tokyo, 1969), was based on an English language manuscript entitled "The Rearmament of Japan." Kowalski's notes from the 1950s, which he used as the basis for his later book, are located in box 8, Frank Kowalski papers, Library of Congress.

50. Ridgway quoted in Melvyn Leffler, *A Preponderance of Power: National Seucurity, The Truman Administration, and the Cold War* (Stanford, Calif.: Stanford University Press) 466.

51. Collins to Ridgway, 17 December 1951, *FRUS 1951*, VI, 1141–43; Ridgway to Deptartment of the Army, 20 December 1951, ibid., 1451–

53; Lovett to Truman, 22 April 1952, *FRUS 1952–52*, XIV, 1243–44; memorandum of conversation by Young, ibid., 1309–10.

52. Notes in box 8, Frank Kowalski papers, Library of Congress; John Welfield, *An Empire in Eclipse: Japan in the Postwar American Alliance System* (Atlantic Highlands, N.J.: Athlone Press, 1988), 79.

53. The role of Japanese minesweepers in the Korean War is discussed in James E. Auer, *The Postwar Rearmament of Japanese Maritime Forces, 1945–71* (New York: Praeger, 1973), 53–68; Murphy, *Diplomat Among Warriors*, 348.

Conclusion

WILLIAM STUECK

In an earlier essay on Japan and the Korean War, Roger Dingman placed even greater emphasis than Schaller on ambiguity, but he also expanded the analysis by comparing the Korean War's impact with that of the Pacific war it followed.[1] Dingman's account provides a useful jumping off point for some concluding remarks, first, about the place of the Korean War in the international politics of the twentieth century and Korea's internal history, second, about ongoing debates among historians regarding the war, and, third, about areas beckoning further research and analysis.

Dingman points out that the Pacific war "transformed [the] . . . security environment" of Japan, leaving it with "a new friend, the United States; an old enemy, the Soviet Union; and Pacific Asian neighbors alienated, in varying degree, by their actions as colonial overlords or battlefield opponents." The defeat of Japan led to destruction of its navy and loss of outlying territories that provided a "forward defense of the home islands." Reforms of the U.S. occupation disarmed Japan, an imposition wholeheartedly accepted by most of the native population. Given the subsequent rise of cold war tensions, the Communist victory on mainland China, the Soviet explosion of an atomic bomb, and the establishment of the Sino-Soviet alliance, Japan's governing elites, along with their American counterparts, came to recognize "the essential security features of any peace settlement" prior to the outbreak of war in Korea. That is, U.S. forces would have to remain in Japan on a semi-permanent basis. Elites on both sides "also hinted at openness to Japanese rearmament."[2]

To be sure, hints of movement, even some movement itself, do not represent the firm establishment of a pattern. It is debatable how far the trend toward bipolarity would have gone in Asia with-

177

out the outbreak of war in Korea and the American and Chinese interventions there that followed. Arguably, the Taiwan issue would have been resolved quickly in favor of the communists and this development, combined with the absence of a Sino-American clash in Korea, would have left open the path to a far less confrontational relationship between Washington and Beijing.[3] Arguably, countervailing opinions in Japan would have remained sufficiently strong to prevent a decisive move toward a separate peace treaty with the United States and its allies and the creation of a durable military alliance with the United States.

On the other hand, in the spring of 1950 Beijing decided to assist its communist brethren in the struggle for Indochina, and Washington began providing aid to the French there.[4] It is possible that, absent the flareup in Korea, Indochina would have provided the necessary spark for continuing polarization on the Pacific rim.

The same argument can be made with regard to the European theater. World War II led to the destruction of German power, the further weakening of Great Britain and France, and the relative strengthening of the Soviet Union. These developments set the stage for growing Soviet-American tensions and a direct U.S. military presence in Europe. In both these areas, an upward trajectory was apparent prior to the outbreak of war in Korea. The North Atlantic Treaty Organization was already in place, as was a major U.S. program to assist in the rearming of Western Europe. There were public discussions of the need for augmented American military forces on continental Europe and private discussions within the Truman administration about West German rearmament.[5] The outbreak of war in Korea reinforced a preexisting trajectory, and Chinese intervention four months later solidified it still further. Yet, absent those developments in Asia, developments in Europe, such as new tensions over Berlin or Soviet military action against Yugoslavia, might have produced the same results.[6] Since Europe was the center of great power competition, they might also have led to a direct clash of Soviet-American forces, one that escalated into a full-scale war between the Western and communist blocs.

Another possible scenario is that, without a war in Korea, there would have been no Soviet provocation over the short term and that the absence of such would have prevented a substantial military buildup in the West. This, in turn, would have meant that by the mid-1950s the Soviets would have possessed both a substantial conventional military superiority in Europe as well as a capacity to do severe damage in a nuclear attack on the American homeland. This situation would have created a dangerous instability.

This exercise in hypotheticals points to the conclusion that, while World War II is an event of monumental importance because of the changes it actually brought about, the Korean War derives at least part of its significance from the developments it made less likely. That is, the deterrent value of the limited Western military action in response to the Korean War, both in Northeast Asia and in Europe, played a critical role in stabilizing Soviet-American competition.

Somewhat similar conclusions might be drawn regarding Korea's internal history. World War II made Korea's independence possible, as prior to Japan's defeat at the hands of the United States, Koreans showed no evidence of being able to overthrow their colonial masters. The inability of Koreans to contribute significantly to their liberation from Japan, combined with the military situation in Northeast Asia at the time of Japan's surrender, led to the division of the peninsula into Soviet and American occupation zones. World War II, in sum, transformed Korea's status and produced conditions leading to the conflict from 1950 to 1953 as we know it.

In structural terms, it remains unclear how different the peninsula would now be without the Korean War. As Millett points out, prior to the outbreak of the all-out conventional fighting in June 1950, a high level of violence existed in Korea, both within South Korea and between South Koreans and North Koreans. The North Korean attack of 25 June 1950, sought to end the country's division, which probably would have lasted indefinitely in its absence. Division lasted anyway due to U.S. and Chinese military intervention. Those interventions produced a long-term American military presence, as well as a formal defensive alliance between the United States and the ROK. Still, Korea's division was largely created out of the circumstances, internationally and among Koreans, of World War II and its immediate aftermath. By 1950 there was no chance for a peaceful unification. What the Korean War did, therefore, was to virtually eliminate the prospect for unification by force, a condition that exists to the present day.

The essays in this volume will not end debate on most of the issues addressed. The Korean War is too complex an event, its terrain too ideologically charged and the documentation on many of its parts too incomplete, to lend itself to scholarly consensus. For example, although scholars of a traditional bent, myself included, will concede to Gardner and other revisionists that the war produced some negative developments on the U.S. side, they will continue to dispute their weight in the overall equation, which they insist includes important forces for stabilization in international politics.

Other disagreements are sometimes too subtle to be neatly categorized into traditionalist and revisionist categories, and Gardner's integration of a variety of interpretive strains in his explanation of why the United States intervened to repulse the North Korean attack provides a useful case in point. For the sake of clarity, the basic issues surrounding U.S. intervention in June 1950 may be separated into two dichotomies, the strategic versus the symbolic and continuity versus discontinuity. The first involves the question of whether the intervention occurred largely because of Korea's importance for the military defense and/or the economic well-being of Japan, or to protect American credibility (or prestige) in the interests of both maintaining the confidence of allies and deterring enemies, in this case primarily the Soviet Union.

The significance to American leaders of Korea to Japan's military defense has not received emphasis from scholars in explaining U.S. intervention. The Joint Chiefs of Staff concluded in a key paper of September 1947 that Soviet control of Korea would be disadvantageous to the United States but could be neutralized through air power from Japan and Okinawa.[7] In the top-level meetings of late June 1950, Korea's importance to the military defense of Japan was mentioned only once, by Admiral Forrest Sherman, the chief of Naval Operations.[8] In an army paper at the time, to "make a profoundly favorable impression on the Japanese" was listed third among seven advantages of "successful" action to save Korea, yet no mention was made of the peninsula's importance to Japan's military defense.[9] In any event, President Truman and Secretary of State Acheson were the key decision makers during the crisis. Truman never emphasized Japan in explaining his reasons for intervention. Although Acheson stated in his memoirs that South Korea was "an area of great importance to the security of American-occupied Japan," he did not include the word "military" before the word "security;" his explanation in June 1950 was that Korea was "vital . . . as [a] symbol [of the] strength and determination of [the] west."[10]

Some scholars have argued that Korea's economic linkage to Japan and other areas of East Asia provides the primary explanation for U.S. intervention to save South Korea in June 1950. To revisionist Bruce Cumings, the most prominent proponent of this view, Acheson was the main architect of that intervention, and "the foundation" of the secretary of state's position " . . . was a world economy logic, captured by his metaphor of a 'great crescent' stretching from Japan through Southeast Asia and around to India."[11] Ronald L. McGlothlen, whose work does not fit comfortably into the revisionist school, views Acheson's concern more narrowly, as resting in Korea's traditional role as breadbasket for Japan.[12]

Ample evidence exists to demonstrate that Acheson and other leading planners possessed considerable sophistication in linking national economies together in the development of an overall plan for containing Soviet influence, and that they recognized Korea's potential significance to Japan's economic recovery. It remains doubtful that such calculations were central to the decision to send American troops back to the peninsula in June 1950. For one thing, neither at that time nor later did Acheson or other top officials emphasize the economic well-being of Japan as the primary reason for military intervention. For another, although State Department analysts going back to August 1947 sometimes mentioned Korea's economic linkage with Japan, reports on high level discussions of the U.S. stake in Korea emphasized the political/psychological ramifications of its loss in Japan, the region, and even the world. These ramifications derived from the involvement of the United States in Korea since 1945, its direct competition with the Soviet Union there, and, from late 1947 onward, the introduction of the Korean issue at the United Nations.[13] South Korea was not insignificant economically, but it was the belief of Truman and Acheson that North Korea, with Soviet support, was committing aggression and that the failure to respond effectively would seriously undermine American credibility in Northeast Asia and elsewhere that in late June 1950 weighed most heavily in the decision for large-scale military intervention.[14]

As the above discussion suggests, my view of that intervention stresses continuity with past U.S. thinking, at least in the State Department, and this position is consistent with Cumings's work as well as that of James I. Matray, the author of a leading monograph on U.S.-Korean relations from World War II to 1950.[15] Still,

Gardner's essay suggests that the timing of the North Korean attack was critical in the U.S. response and other scholars have argued explicitly that the American military intervention of June 1950 represented a reversal of past policy.[16] The evidence is ambiguous here, although all would agree that conditions both within the United States and abroad between the June 1949 withdrawal of American troops from Korea and their return a year later increased the prospects that the Americans would respond vigorously if North Korea attacked without direct Soviet or Chinese involvement and threatened to overwhelm the South.[17]

Debates involving U.S. policy are not likely to be resolved definitively through the release of new evidence, as a wealth of documentation is already available and, in any case, the evidence rarely leads all scholars in one direction. The best we can hope for is that the surfacing of more records from the Central Intelligence Agency (CIA) will clarify some points on who knew what about North Korea's plans and when.

In contrast, with the availability of records from the former Soviet Union and China still extraordinarily limited and records from North and South Korea even more so, prospects remain high that new releases will greatly advance our understanding on a variety of issues.[18] We know little, for example, about Stalin's thinking toward Korea prior to his March 1949 meetings with Kim Il-sung. A related issue that cries out for further illumination is the Soviet and North Korean role in South Korean unrest between the fall of 1945 and early 1950. Cumings suggests that it was minimal and the more balanced account of John Merrill concurs.[19] Millett, whose essay in this volume is too complex to place in the traditionalist or revisionist camp, implies otherwise, but his evidence is sketchy, as it is for the argument that North Korean infiltration was a major cause of ROK aggressiveness along the 38th parallel during the spring and summer of 1949. Weathersby's writings say little on the issue. Obviously more documentation is needed, including on the range of contacts between the North Koreans and South Korean politicians who opposed Rhee. Chinese Communist interaction with the North Koreans prior to June 1950 also remains largely a black hole. While we know that on occasion Mao was able to use North Korea as a secure base for some of his troops in the aftermath of World War II and that the North Koreans trained a large portion of the army that invaded the South in June 1950 in the Chinese civil war, the details of the Chinese-North Korean relationship remain uncertain. On the South Korean-American side, further study of land reform below the 38th parallel might give us new insight into the role of non-military actions by the U.S. occupation and the ROK government that undermined or furthered leftist agitation in the South. These are among the more obvious issues that are likely to keep researchers busy studying the origins of the Korean War for years to come.

As for the war itself, the issues for continuing debate and further research remain virtually boundless and encompass both sides. Decision making among the communist powers regarding North Korea's military operations during the summer of 1950 merits careful scrutiny, especially with regard to tactical decisions on the battlefield. North Korean forces came close to pushing the enemy off the peninsula during that period, and tactical choices, such as the delay in the march southward after the capture of Seoul in late June and the diversion of forces from the southeastern front around Pusan to the extreme southwest in July and August, were critical to failure; but we know little of how these choices were viewed from the Communist side.

Uncertainties remain over Mao's reasons for intervening in Korea in the fall of 1950. To Cumings, Mao's feeling of indebtedness to North Korea for its previous assistance in the Chinese civil war stands at the top of the hierarchy in explaining China's decision to enter the war.[20] Basing his account on evidence surfacing in China following publication of Cumings' main work, CHEN disagrees, although he does not deny the influence on Mao of North Korea's past support. CHEN's account summarizes and updates his 1995 book, which remains the most detailed examination of the background to China's intervention based on Chinese archival materials.[21] He acknowledges the importance of Mao's concern for the security of his northeastern border, which the old classic by Allen S. Whiting saw as the key factor in Beijing's intervention, but he broadens the analysis to emphasize the Chinese leader's revolutionary ideology in the context of domestic and international objectives.[22] CHEN also musters new evidence to argue that, whatever his hesitation, Mao was inclined toward intervention in Korea from August onward and hoped that Chinese forces could push the enemy entirely out of Korea, thus enabling Kim to achieve his initial aim in the June 1950 attack.[23]

Weathersby's coverage of the Soviet side reveals that as early as July Stalin encouraged Mao to prepare for possible intervention in Korea. At the same time, China and the Soviet Union made a limited effort until October to coordinate plans and then got bogged down on the issue of Soviet air support for Chinese troops. Whether or not Moscow had promised Beijing such support in July and reneged remains in question, but, to Weathersby, the firmness of Stalin on the matter in October serves to emphasize his continuing determination to avoid a direct Soviet-American clash over Korea.[24]

Once China was in the war and did well, however, Weathersby sees Stalin as generally pursuing a hard line on Korea. In the early months he supported Mao's offensives south of the 38th parallel and diplomatic positions clearly unacceptable to the United States. He also pressed his allies in Eastern Europe to follow the Soviet lead in building up their military strength. His continued restrictions on the participation of Soviet airmen in the Korean fighting indicate that he never abandoned his caution on initiating a direct confrontation with the United States, but even after he agreed to support the Chinese in their desire for armistice talks he counseled Mao to adopt a firm position in negotiations. Weathersby believes that during the year prior to his death Stalin represented the primary stumbling block to an armistice on the Communist side.

Although CHEN devotes little attention in his essay to the period of armistice talks, his other writings show a divergence with Weathersby over the centrality of Stalin's position in delaying an end to the fighting. Mao, CHEN argues, had his own reasons for rejecting the U.S. position on prisoners of war. These included his belief that China was in a strong position militarily in Korea— especially if it could garner additional Soviet assistance, which it did in the fall of 1952—and that a Chinese concession might convey weakness to the Americans and encourage their aggressiveness. He felt the Chinese should hold firm for a while longer, waiting to see the position adopted by the new president who would take office on 20 January 1953. The new president was likely to be Dwight D. Eisenhower, and he would probably attempt new ground operations in Korea, which the Chinese could repulse. With this show of strength, Beijing could alter its policy on POWs without appearing weak.

Whereas Weathersby views Stalin's death as a critical event in the move toward an armistice in July 1953, CHEN argues that an "inner logic" existed to the thought of Mao that was consistent with his Soviet ally's position all along. In other words, pressure by Stalin on Mao to continue the war was not necessary, as the two men were in fundamental agreement.[25] Nonetheless, the proximity of Stalin's death to the Chinese initiative to resume armistice talks less than a month later, after high level Sino-Soviet talks on the matter in Moscow, makes it difficult to ignore the impact of the change in Soviet leadership.

Still, less than two weeks before Stalin died the UN Command proposed an exchange of sick and wounded prisoners, which enabled the Chinese to couch their own overture five weeks later as a response to the other side's desire to negotiate. Over the next four months, the Chinese maneuvered carefully in coordinating moves at the bargaining table with action on the battlefield to avoid as much as possible any appearance of weakness. Even with the turmoil and uncertainty created in the Communist camp by Stalin's passing, Mao took care to make his key concession on POWs only after Chinese troops had made tactical gains in Korea.[26] In the end, the precise weight to be given Stalin's death in ending the war remains an area over which reasonable people may disagree.

The same may be said with regard to the Communist germ warfare propaganda campaign of 1952 in which the United States was accused of employing bacteriological weapons in Korea. Weathersby points to new documentation from the Soviet side indicating that the Chinese and North Koreans manufactured evidence for the campaign. On the other hand, CHEN uses documentation from China indicating that, in early 1952 at least, both Chinese commanders in the field and leaders in Beijing believed that the Americans *were* engaged in bacteriological warfare.[27] The weight of the evidence appearing to date indicates that the United States was innocent of the charges, although not all pertinent American records have been opened and documentation from China, Russia, and North Korea remains sparse. Moreover, the manufacturing of evidence by the Communists does not necessarily mean that all of those involved knew from the beginning that the general charges were false. The subject remains a promising one for additional investigation, as do most areas involving the Communist side and South Korea, where official records are available only on a highly selective basis.

On high policy, the above statement cannot be made with confidence in many cases involving the United States. The CIA, which in addition to gathering intelligence and reporting it to American leaders conducted covert operations in North Korea and China, remains unwilling to release most of its records, although on the eve of the national crisis that began on 11 September 2001 it was on the verge of an initiative on the matter.[28] Signal's intelligence records might provide new information both on the activities of the other side and on what U.S. decision makers knew and when they knew it. New evidence might shed light on the precise circumstances leading to General MacArthur's dismissal in April 1951 and the exact nature of the Eisenhower administration's alleged threat to use nuclear weapons against China in May 1953, but I am dubious that such evidence exists.

High-level policy aside, much remains to be learned about the interaction of the principles on both sides of the war, especially on the ground in Korea. Between the summer of 1950 and the summer of 1953, the Americans had between 100,000 and 300,000 armed personnel in South Korea; from late 1950 to the end of the war, the Chinese had between 200,000 and 1.3 million soldiers in the North. In the first case we have a number of journalistic accounts and memoirs that deal in some manner with the interaction of the visitors with their hosts, but no in-depth account by a historian.[29] We know that there was a good deal of condescension as well as some racism and brutality on the part of the Americans. Yet most South Koreans who lived through the war developed deep feelings of gratitude for the American role at the time and the military alliance generated by the war has lasted more than a half-century. These facts suggest that wartime interaction was complex, but that overall Koreans and Americans got along rather well. An in-depth study of that interaction would be welcome.

A study of Chinese-North Korean relations is also necessary. Shu Guang Zhang has offered some information and insight into the relationship in his history of China's role in the war.[30] He suggests that the interaction was sometimes tense, both at the high command level and lower down. Despite a continuing alliance relationship, Chinese forces left North Korea in 1958. The contrast with the continued stationing to the present day of nearly 40,000 U.S. military personnel in South Korea may relate more to the greater ease with which China could return to Korea in an emergency and to the Soviet presence nearby than to any difference in feelings between peoples derived from the wartime experience. Yet in the late 1950s Kim Il-sung purged the Chinese and Soviet factions within his own party, despite threats from Beijing and Moscow.[31] At the very least, the withdrawal of China's troops appears to be related to a power struggle at the top of the North Korean government. Much might be learned from new documentation on the issue.

This brief survey of ongoing disagreements among scholars and areas of sparse documentation suggests that finality's loss is vitality's gain. In analyzing a host of issues in the political and diplomatic spheres, the authors of this collection have evaluated and synthesized the large body of scholarship, much of it their own, that has emerged after more than a generation of labor in archival collections on the Western side and over a decade of exciting discoveries in Soviet and Chinese sources. The fact that many of the arguments presented in this book will be challenged reflects the relativity of much historical knowledge and the diversity of perspectives that is possible on a subject of such obvious importance. Future scholars will unearth new evidence and develop new insights, but they will not ignore the contributions presented herein.

Notes

1. Roger Dingman, "The Dagger and the Gift: The Impact of the Korean War on Japan," in William J. Williams, *A Revolutionary War: Korea and the Transformation of the Postwar World* (Chicago: Imprint Publications, 1993), 201–23.

2. Ibid., 203–5.

3. For the most persuasive treatment of U.S. policy toward Taiwan on the eve of the Korean War, see Robert Accinelli, *Crisis and Commitment: United States Policy toward Taiwan: 1950–1955* (Chapel Hill: University of North Carolina Press, 1996), 17–27.

4. On Chinese aid to the communists in Indochina, see Zhai Qiang, *China and the Vietnam Wars, 1950–1975* (Chapel Hill: University of North Carolina Press, 2000), 10–26.

5. On the Korean War's impact on NATO, see William Stueck, "The Korean War, NATO, and Rearmament," in Williams, *A Revolutionary War*, 171–84.

6. On the possibility of Soviet military action against Yugoslavia, see William Stueck, *The Korean War: An International History* (Princeton, N.J.: Princeton University Press, 1995), 351–53.

7. See U.S. State Department, *Foreign Relations of the United States,*

1947, vol. 6, *The Far East* (Washington, D.C.: Government Printing Office, 1972), 817–18. (Henceforth volumes in this series will be identified as *FRUS* with the year covered in the documents, the volume number, and the page numbers of the pertinent documents.)

8. Ibid., *1950*, 7.

9. Major General Charles L. Bolte to Secretary of the Army Frank Pace, 28 June 1950, 091 Korea (TS), Record Group 218, Military Branch, National Archives II, College Park, Md.

10. Dean Acheson, *Present at the Creation: My Years in the State Department* (New York: W. W. Norton, 1969), 248; Acheson to Alan Kirk (U.S. ambassador to the Soviet Union), 28 June 1950, Record Group 84, Diplomatic Branch, National Archives II, College Park, Md.

11. Cumings, *Origins*, 2: 49.

12. Ronald L. McGlothlen, *Controlling the Waves: Dean Acheson and U.S. Foreign Policy in Asia* (New York: Norton, 1993), chap. 3.

13. For more detailed coverage of this issue, see William Stueck, *The Road to Confrontation: American Policy towards China and Korea, 1947–1950* (Chapel Hill: University of North Carolina Press, 1981), 85–87, 98–99, 100, 105–6, and 156–59. For key documents, see *FRUS, 1947*, 6: 738, 820–21; *1948*, 6: 1139–41, 1163–69, 1337–40; *1949*, 7: 969–78, 1047–57.

14. I argue this point in greater detail in *Road to Confrontation*, 185–90. For a similar analysis that adds domestic political considerations to the equation, see Burton I. Kaufman, *The Korean War: Challenges in Crisis, Credibility, and Command* (New York: McGraw-Hill, 1986), 33–40. In his essay for this volume, Michael Schaller quotes John Foster Dulles, the chief U.S. negotiator of the Japanese peace treaty, as saying that "had Korea been conquered Japan would have fallen without an open struggle." (See Michael Schaller, "The Korean War: The Economic and Strategic Impact on Japan, 1950–53," 1.) Presumably, Dulles meant that Korea's fall would have had a devastating psychological impact on Japan.

15. James I. Matray, *The Reluctant Crusade: American Foreign Policy in Korea, 1941–1950* (Honolulu: University of Hawaii Press, 1985).

16. See Lewis McCarroll Purifoy, *Harry Truman's China Policy: McCarthyism and the Diplomacy of Hysteria, 1947–1951* (New York: Franklin Watts, 1976), 195; and John Edward Wiltz, "Encountering Korea: American Perceptions and Policies to 25 June 1950," in Williams, *A Revolutionary War*, 50–59.

17. For more detailed rebuttals to the "reversal of policy" argument, at least insofar as it relates to Acheson, see my *Road to Confrontation*, 289n67, and my *Korean War*, 30.

18. Actually, more records are available from the North than the South as a result of the capture of thousands of documents in Pyongyaug by the

United States in the fall of 1950. These records are available in Record Group 242 at National Archives II in College Park, Md. Charles K. Armstrong has exploited many of them in his *The North Korean Revolution, 1945–1950* (Ithaca, N.Y.: Cornell University Press, 2003).

19. Cumings, *Origins;* Merrill, *Korea.*

20. Cumings, *Origins,* 2: 740.

21. CHEN, *China's Road to the Korean War.*

22. Allen S. Whiting, *China Crosses the Yalu: The Decision to Enter the Korean War* (New York: Macmillan, 1960).

23. This view conflicts directly with the assertion by Cumings and Jon Halliday (*Korea: The Unknown War* [London, Viking, 1988], 144) that "China's goal was to push the USA and Rhee back into the South and settle for that."

24. The most detailed and dispassionate analysis of the issue of air support is in Xiaoming Zhang, *Red Wings over the Yalu: China, the Soviet Union, and the Air War in Korea, 1950-1953* (College Station, Texas: Texas A & M University Press, 2002). Zhang argues that there was vagueness in Soviet assurances regarding air support prior to October, which the Chinese may have considered more expansive than they actually were.

25. CHEN, *Mao's China,* 112–15.

26. See Stueck, *Korean War,* 325–30.

27. CHEN, *Mao's China,* 110.

28. Both Weathersby and I had been contacted during the summer of 2001 about consulting with the CIA on the matter. For works on CIA and other U.S. covert operations during the Korean War, see William M. Leary, *Perilous Missions: Civil Air Transport and CIA Covert Operations in Asia* (Tuscaloosa, Ala.: University of Alabama Press, 1984), chap. 8 and 9; Major General John K. Singlaub with Malcolm McConnell, *Hazardous Duty: An American Soldier in the Twentieth Century* (New York: Summit Books, 1991), chap. 5 and 6; William B. Breuer, *Shadow Warriors: The Covert War in Korea* (New York: John Wiley & Sons, 1996); Ben S. Malcolm, *White Tigers: My Secret War in North Korea* (Dulles, Va.: Brassey's, 1996); and Frank Holober, *Raiders of the China Coast: CIA Covert Operations during the Korean War* (Annapolis, Md.: Naval Institute Press, 1999).

29. For memoirs, see Ellis Briggs, Robert T. Oliver, *Syngman Rhee and American Involvement in Korea, 1942–1960* (Seoul: Panmun, 1978), chap. 13–19; General Mark W. Clark, *From the Danube to the Yalu* (New York: Harper & Row, 1954), esp. chap. 8–12; General Paik Sun Yup, *From Pusan to Panmunjom: Wartime Memoirs of the Republic of Korea's First Four-Star General* (Dulles, Va.: Brassey's, 1992). For an account by a British journalist critical of the Americans, see Reginald Thompson, *Cry Korea* (London: White Lion, 1951). For secondary accounts that touch on

the people-to-people relationship below the top levels, see Cumings, *Origins*, 2: chap. 19–21, and Cumings and Halliday, *Korea*.

30. See Zhang, *Mao's Military Romanticism*, 205–11.

31. See Andrei Lankow, *From Stalin to Kim Il Sung: The Formation of North Korea 1945–1960* (New Brunswick, N.J.: Rutgers University Press, 2002), 62, 102–3.

Contributors

LLOYD C. GARDNER is Charles and Mary Beard Professor Emeritus at Rutgers University, New Brunswick. Among his numerous books are *Vietnam: The Early Decisions* (1997) and *Pay Any Price: Lyndon Johnson and the Wars for Vietnam* (1995).

CHEN JIAN is C. K. Yen Professor of Chinese-American Relations at the University of Virginia. He is author of *Mao's Road to the Korean War* (1994) and *Mao's China and the Cold War* (2001).

ALLAN R. MILLETT is General Raymond E. Mason Jr. Professor of Military History at Ohio State University. He has authored several books and is coauthor of *For the Common Defense: A Military History of the United States of America* (rev. and expanded ed. 1994), coeditor of *Mao's Generals Remember Korea* (2001), and editor of *Their War for Korea: American, Asian, and European Combatants* (2001).

MICHAEL SCHALLER is Regents Professor of History at the University of Arizona. Among his books are *Altered States: The United States and Japan since the Occupation* (1997) and *The United States and China: Into the Twenty-first Century* (2002).

WILLIAM STUECK is Distinguished Research Professor of History at the University of Georgia. He is author of, among other books, *Rethinking the Korean War: A New Diplomatic and Strategic History* (2002) and *The Korean War: An International History* (1995).

KATHRYN WEATHERSBY is an independent scholar residing in Washington, D.C. She is a frequent contributor on matters involving the Soviet Union and North Korea to the *Bulletin*, published by the Cold War International History Project at the Woodrow Wilson Center for Scholars.

Index